EDUCATION FOR WHOM?

The Question of Equal Educational Opportunity

D0562071

LINDLEY J. STILES
Professor of Education for Interdisciplinary Studies
Northwestern University
Advisory Editor to Dodd, Mead & Company

EDUCATION FOR WHOM?

The Question of Equal Educational Opportunity

CHARLES A. TESCONI, Jr.

EMANUEL HURWITZ, Jr.

UNIVERSITY OF ILLINOIS AT CHICAGO CIRCLE

DODD, MEAD & COMPANY
New York   1974

To Our Children

Marc S. and Carla P. Tesconi
and
David L. Hurwitz

May yours be lives rich in opportunity.

ISBN 0-396-06904-5

Library of Congress Catalog Card Number: 73-15391

Printed in the United States of America

DESIGNED BY JEFFREY M. BARRIE

Contents

Preface

Herbert Spencer once asked, "What knowledge is of most worth?" Generally translated as "Education for What?," this query was a crucial one for educators long before Spencer wrote. It is just as crucial today. Indeed, it has served as the *raison d'être* for numerous professional and scholarly education societies and has been the impetus for innumerable national committees and White House conferences on education. Spencer's question rests on certain assumptions about the nature of knowledge. It implies a possible ranking of the relative value of certain kinds of knowledge. And it focuses on "the what"—the content—of education rather than on those who are to be educated.

Relatively recent events have forced a second question to the surface of educational concerns: *Who has greater access to, and opportunity to profit from, formal, public education?* "Education for Whom?," as it were, has come to supersede Spencer's question. This new query has led to several momentous court decisions; and, like Spencer's question, it sustains some scholarly societies, journals, and graduate student research. It was also the motivating question behind the Coleman study, the second largest social science research project in history. Of course, answers to "Education for Whom?" may overlap with answers to "Education for What?" But a people as pragmatic as Americans finds the latter inquiry too obtuse, too speculative, too close to the metaphysical. The former query is more compelling. The pragmatist knows that it speaks directly to his pocketbook. The moralist is painfully aware that any dawdling with respect to "Education for Whom?" may result in a nation of increasing inequalities or even a society rent asunder.

Our focus in this book shall be on "Education for Whom?" More specifically, we shall study the issue of *equality of educational opportunity*. No single educational problem divides the nation so deeply;

none is so pervasive in the current polemics over education. Today, almost 20 years after the most celebrated Supreme Court decision on equality of educational opportunity, *Brown* v. *Board of Education,* we find this issue still so controversial that it can make or break candidates for the highest political offices in the land. Moreover, the object of that Court's decision, segregation in the schools, is just as widespread now as it was in 1954. And as the dust begins to settle around the flurry of new policies and activities that decision engendered, we are beginning to see that segregation in the schools is only one element, albeit a major one, in the matter of equal educational opportunity.

So, then, equal educational opportunity is a crucial issue today. But it is not a new issue. It was a major ingredient in the drive calling for the establishment of the common school in the nineteenth century. Nevertheless, new research findings, the dramatic entrée of the federal government and the courts into local educational concerns, and, perhaps most important of all, a seemingly re-awakened collective American conscience have brought this issue into the spotlight again.

The drama surrounding equality of educational opportunity raises, however, some serious considerations about it as a subject for a book. The issue possesses or gives rise to numerous liabilities. "Wait for more data!," "Let the polemics subside!," "Wait for federal guidelines!," "See what the courts have to say!"—all these warnings cause any writer on education to ponder the value of a book on an issue so elusive as equality of educational opportunity. Yet the baffling need of academicians to get a handle on what is happening in education and, more importantly, the socially disastrous consequences which could follow from continued ignorance of this issue demand, if nothing else, at least a foray into this complex issue.

We admit openly that much of what is offered in *Education for Whom?* is subject to qualification. Yet, no one book, or two, or even a dozen—given the transient interpretations of equal educational opportunity—could reveal all the ramifications of this issue, much less put it to rest.

We are convinced that, in spite of these recognized hazards, equality of educational opportunity must be examined. We shall do our best to make some sense out of this major educational issue, to place it in meaningful perspective, and to arrive at a basic understanding of its nature and implications. Our claims about the value of this book are commensurate with these desires and, hence, relatively modest. We offer some basic research, concepts, ideas, and insights crucial to understanding this heady issue. We do not claim to provide any neat answers, nor do we offer assurance that the person who has critically reflected upon this issue will find himself less confused or less ambivalent about his or her thoughts on equal opportunity after reading this book. We do believe, however, that *Education for Whom?* serves seven major purposes: (1) It introduces the reader to the complexity of the equal educational opportunity issue. (2) It describes, illustrates, and analyzes the *major* elements in this issue. (3) It traces the various shifts in interpretations of the concept of equal educational opportunity. (4) It illuminates the major role played by the courts in determining the meaning of this concept. (5) It makes clear the emerging and increasingly favored interpretation of this concept among sociologists, economists, political scientists, and philosophers. (6) It reveals the way or ways in which academicians, jurists, politicians, and concerned citizens believe that equal educational opportunity can be achieved. (7) It identifies arenas in which particular interpretations of the equal educational opportunity concept might raise new educational issues.

In order to fulfill these seven purposes and to place this issue in historical, social, political, economic, philosophical, and legal perspective, we offer a framework for analyzing the concept of equal educational opportunity. The framework can help the reader to gain a better understanding of, and deeper involvement in, the issue.

In addition to those thinkers whose articles appear in Chapters 4 and 5, numerous scholars have contributed to the making and shaping of this book. We express particular thanks to our colleagues at the University of Illinois who listened to our ideas on equal educational opportunity and offered valuable criticism concerning not only our ideas but also the organization of this book. A special note of appreciation goes to our students, who willingly attacked educational issues through an analytical model which appears in refined form here. All these people, of course, are absolved of any responsibility for this book's shortcomings.

CHARLES A. TESCONI, JR.
EMANUEL HURWITZ, JR.

Chapter 1

Introduction:
Framework for Analysis

American public schools are microcosms of the society in which they operate. Given a certain time lag, they incorporate the values, trends, social conflicts, and inequalities—all the social and cultural proceedings of the society at large.

Certainly the school's long-established twin function as "transmitter" and "protector" of the culture implies a relationship between the schools and the values, tensions, and aspirations of the people who attend and support them. It is a relationship, or better yet a partnership, which has deeply entrenched roots in America. Our theocratic colonial ancestors, for example, established schools to ensure that their children learned to read and live by the Bible, the basal reader of the seventeenth century. Their eighteenth-century successors, caught up in the flush of a rapidly expanding country and a promising economy, saw to it that schools added the concerns of the material world to the spiritually oriented curriculum. They expected schools to teach their children to read, write, and cipher in order to prosper in this world as well as the next; material and spiritual success became the dual goals of schooling, and the former was taken as an indicator of the latter.

By the nineteenth century, Americans were in the midst of rapid industrialization. Consequently, they asked their public schools to educate the young in the secular subjects of mathematics, history, living languages, and science, and to offer training programs for occupational skills such as agriculture and the "mechanical arts." In the late nineteenth and early twentieth centuries, a people inundated with immigrants from southern and eastern Europe demanded that public schools serve as the Americanizing agent for the children of these newcomers. From the middle of the twentieth century to the present, the schools have been expected to reflect the dominant scientific world view of our increasingly technological society.

Public schools, then, have always been expected to swing with the times, to adjust to prevailing social desires and perceived social needs by offering scholastic programs which serve those desires and needs. But the school mirrors the larger society in other more subtle yet equally important ways. It echoes the mien, the cultural flavor and temper, of society. If, for example, that society is fervently anti-communist, the public school's implicit and explicit values, its formal and informal policies, and its scholastic program will all reflect this anti-communist orientation. If the larger society adheres to practices of sexism and racism, so too will the school. If the larger society believes that European immigrants carry cultural orientations and "old world" traditions which are out of place in, or possibly damaging to, American society, the schools will function in ways calculated to rid youngsters of any ethnic cultural "baggage"; even the unspoken values and policies of the school will suggest disdain for that baggage. If the larger society values competition, individualism, and nationalism, so too will the school.

The school as a social institution, then, is the dependent variable in the school-society relationship. We have the kind of schools we do because, for good or bad, these are the kinds of schools "society" wants. Nowhere, perhaps, is this relationship more vividly apparent today than in the area of equality and equal opportunity in education. Recent attempts to use the school as a vehicle for closing the gap between existing inequalities and our professed democratic interpretations of equal opportunity have come up short in the recognition that our public schools themselves contribute to and perpetuate that gap. Racial segregation, racism, ethnic strife, social class rivalry—all those social phenomena which manifest inequity are reflected in the schools. This recognition of the inequities existing in schools, coupled with a dramatic awakening of the collective American conscience concerning the widespread inequities in all aspects of our society, has made the principles of equality and equality of educational opportunity major issues today.

The principle of equal rights for all citizens is deeply embedded in the ethos of America. It is the foundation of our legal framework. And this principle has long been interpreted as including the right to equal educational opportunity. Nevertheless, this concept of equal educational opportunity, like the concept of equal rights itself, has a checkered past. It has been subject to numerous, often conflicting interpretations. Moreover, whatever the favored interpretation at a given time, attempts to translate it into specific applications have always led to additional discord.

Historically, equality of educational opportunity was interpreted as meaning that all persons were to have access to similar instructional resources in public schools, and the schools themselves were to be similar. When students failed, their failure was assumed to be a function of their own limitations, not something attributable to inadequacies of the schools or of society as such. On the other hand, it was thought that, should schools be found somehow to favor a particular race or social class, this favoritism could be eliminated merely by providing "equal" resources to the youngsters of all races and social class groups through inputs into the schools, integration of the schools, or the reshuffling of teachers, administrators, curricular offerings, and the like. In short, it was thought that equalizing "inputs" would overcome deficiencies reflected in such matters as race or class bias.

These kinds of remedies have been dramatically challenged in recent years. Equal inputs have not ensured equality of opportunity. Furthermore, the concept of equal opportunity in education has undergone some drastic changes in interpretations over the last few decades, especially since the *Brown* decision in 1954.

The changing interpretations of the concept of equality of educational opportunity, the inconstancy of meaning, and of resulting policies, lead to several questions in the minds of today's educators. What have the terms *equality* and *equality of educational opportunity* meant in the past? What do they mean now? What might they mean in the future? Whose obligation is it to provide equality of educational opportunity? Is it a valid and workable principle for American public education?

These represent the kind of questions to which this book is addressed. We do not pretend that the examination of educational opportunity offered here is a final answer to this very complex issue. We do believe, however, that the analysis presented offers a unique way of studying this issue (and other educational issues) and of involving the reader in the debate now raging over equal educational opportunity. This distinctive process is centered around a conceptual framework designed for systematic analysis of educational issues. The analytical framework, introduced in our earlier book,[1] is described below.

The Analytical Framework

Each of the four following chapters serves a particular function within a four-sided analytical framework. These functions, discussed briefly below, are *description, illustration, analysis,* and *projection.* We believe that the reader's encounter with the issue of equality of educational opportunity through each of these four dimensions will lead him to a deeper understanding of this matter than he would gain from conventional anthologies treating major educational issues.

1. *Description.* Description identifies the issue and the major actors and variables (for example, ideologies, philosophies, and social principles) involved in it—all the while avoiding, as much as possible, evaluation and justification. Even though objectivity is a rather stringent requirement when applied to a "hot" issue, it, nevertheless, is an important aspect of our description of equal educational opportunity.

2. *Illustration.* Once the issue has been described, an illustration of the ways in which it functions (affects people, institutions, processes) helps the examiner to lift it from the realm of the academic to the world of experience. Chapter 3, therefore, provides the reader with materials which give life to and illuminate the description. The illustrations are based upon U.S. court cases which have affected equality of educational opportunity through decisions on school segregation and school finance policies.

3. *Analysis.* Analysis separates an issue into its constituent parts in order to reveal their relation to one another and to the whole. Analysis deals with cause-and-effect relationships; it explains "why."

In Chapter 4 the reader will encounter the approaches and perspectives, the intellectual tools and patterns of inquiry, of those disciplines which comprise foundations of education and educational policy studies. History, philosophy, sociology, political science, jurisprudence, and economics all will be used to dissect the issues of educational opportunity. Not all the analyses offer purely one disci-

---

[1] Emanuel Hurwitz, Jr. and Charles Tesconi, Jr., *Challenges to Education* (New York: Dodd, Mead and Company, 1972).

plinary approach as opposed to another. Some reflect one approach; others combine several different disciplinary tools and perspectives.

4. *Projection.* By definition, issues are not closed. They speak to and follow from problems and conflicts which will continue to be open to question and doubt. Scholars often make predictions and offer prescriptions on particular controversial issues. They speculate about what the future may hold in light of the parameters of an issue at a given moment. Or they prescribe what should happen, what should be done, what kind of resolution should be reached regardless (or in spite) of present conditions.

Selections in Chapter 5, then, will focus on what some writers believe will or should happen regarding equal educational opportunity, and what implications this issue has for other matters. The projection selections, perhaps more than others, provide the student an opportunity to become intimately involved in the issues. Here he confronts conditions as they may exist when he will be a professional educator. Here, too, he confronts opinions, with all their biases and polemics laid bare.

Chapter 6 ties together the analytical framework provided in Chapters 2 through 5. It (1) summarizes the major points made earlier, (2) identifies areas which call for further research, and (3) suggests other areas in which this concept of equal opportunity is likely to call forth more reforms in educational philosophy, policy, and practice.

This book will, we trust, stimulate readers to think critically about, and perhaps even write about, the concept of equality of educational opportunity. Perhaps the reader will realize that some of his own perspectives, attitudes, and responses to this issue are shared by many people; and he may, in turn, wish to articulate a new perspective on equality of educational opportunity.

Chapter 2

A Sort of Equality:
A Description of the Educational
Opportunity Conflict

Democracy, according to Plato, "is a charming form of government, full of variety and disorder, and dispensing a sort of equality to equals and unequals alike." Plato's gibe follows from his opinion that egalitarian societies tend to blur distinctions and, hence, valid inequalities among people. Followers act like leaders, rulers like subjects, and "everything," he chided, "is just ready to burst with liberty." Plato was a master of irony; did he really see such a state as an incurable malady of egalitarian social orders? Or was he goading his audience to reflect upon dissimilarities among men which ought to be recognized, ministered to, and sustained in all kinds of social orders? Certainly our own history suggests that we have invested more in aspiring to "life, liberty, and the pursuit of happiness" than might be implied by the best-known catch phrase of the Declaration of Independence: *All men are created equal.* Do we understand what Thomas Jefferson meant when he penned this famous sentence? Is there confusion over the meaning of the word *equality* itself?

We know that when Jefferson wrote "All men are created equal," he meant equal before the law. Yet even this principle is vacuous until the respects in which men are equal or unequal are annotated— until criteria relevant to differential or equal treatment are presented and an order of priority among these criteria is specified. When, for example, is it just to act upon a criterion calling for differential rather than equal treatment? Certainly men may be equal or unequal in one respect, but not in any other. An equal right to apply for a job

6

does not imply an equal ability to execute the job; an equal chance for an education does not signify equal ability to gain from an education.[1]

Debates over the meaning of *all men are created equal* and *equality,* then, are not about whether people possess in equal measure the same talents, potentials, etc. They are about the criteria employed and the particular characteristics of persons that are singled out as the bases for judging equality. Egalitarianism does not strive to eliminate the distinctions among people. It is not a drive for "sameness" or homogeneity. It need not result in what Plato sarcastically prophesied as the elimination of reasonable distinctions between "better" and "worse." It does not suggest universal equality of endowments. Rather, egalitarianism strives to eradicate those norms calling for differential treatment of men which are arbitrary, purposeless, and unconscionable.[2]

Plato recognized, as we Americans are now discovering, that abolition of unconscionable distinctions is no easy task. Indeed, each man has his own criteria as to what is unreasonable and purposeless. Thus, the meaning of the term *equality* is only part of the problem. Specifying, justifying, and ordering criteria for differential or equal treatment pose numerous other difficulties. Furthermore, those who benefit from arbitrary distinctions are often quite loath to see them dissolve.

Nevertheless, during the last two decades we in the United States have been witnessing momentous attempts, from virtually all segments of society, to come to terms with what has indeed long been a "sort of equality." Most of these efforts have been aimed at narrowing the gap between our professed beliefs and the realities of pervasive inequalities. They have been reflected in a number of seemingly distinct developments: appeals from racial and ethnic minorities; the 1964 Civil Rights Act; poor people's campaigns; students clamoring for a greater voice in educational policy decisions; the rewriting of archaic state constitutions; the drive for equal rights for women; consumer protection demands; gay liberation; the 18-year-old vote; affirmation of the one-man, one-vote principle; the drive to preserve our natural resources; concern for the protection of the criminally accused; the push for "participatory" democracy; greater tolerance for

[1] Charles Frankel, *The Democratic Prospect* (Evanston: Harper Colophon Books, 1962), p. ix.
[2] *Ibid.,* p. 133.

a variety of emerging life styles; communities organizing in common concern for quality education, and so on.

Similar occurrences have taken place in the job market. Wage workers have begun to demand guaranteed incomes and other privileges salaried workers enjoy. Policemen, firemen, public school teachers, and other "public servants"—factory workers, miners, and even low-level "white collar" workers have all been striking over wages and working conditions. Rank and file union members have taken to task union leaders who put their own interests above those of the workers. Enlisted personnel in the armed services have protested their low status and have threatened to unionize.

These are only a few examples of the recent and intense concern with matters of equality. Some of these developments have not been expressed directly in terms of equality, but they all, in one way or another, reflect upon differential treatment of people. Moreover, each of these developments has focused attention on inequalities which pervade American society. Consider the matter of income and national wealth.

Income and Wealth

In the United States today, the poorest fifth of the population receives only about 4 percent of the nation's annual income; the next poorest fifth, only about 11 percent. About 40 percent of the U.S. population, then—or approximately 83 million people—receives only about 15 percent of the nation's income, while the richest 5 percent—about 11 million people—receives over 20 percent of the annual income.

These disparities are accentuated when one considers that only 1 percent (less than 3 million people) of the U.S. population controls more than one-third of the nation's assets. Among the almost 2 million corporations in this country, 0.1 percent—or approximately 2,000 corporations—controls 55 percent of the corporate assets; 1.1 percent—or 22,000—controls 82 percent. Conversely, 94 percent of the corporations own only 9 percent of the total assets.[3]

Another way of looking at inequalities in income and wealth is to consider the extent of economic poverty in the United States. The monetary definition of poverty set by the federal government

[3] Herbert J. Gans, "The New Egalitarianism," *Saturday Review,* May 6, 1972, p. 43.

has, during the past 4 years, hovered around $3,550 yearly income for a nonfarm family of four. Official government estimates indicate that close to 26 million people could thus be classified as impoverished. Michael Harrington, author of *The Other America,* considers this official estimate as much too conservative. Taking into account inflation, and what he regards as a governmental tendency to underestimate such matters, Harrington would add another 12 million Americans to the poverty rolls. Using the government's and Harrington's estimates as opposing extremes, it can safely be assumed that the number of persons falling below the poverty line numbers from 25 to 38 million (out of a total population of approximately 208 million), or from 12 to 18.2 percent.[4]

Nevertheless, monetary definitions of poverty can be misleading. They do not take into account different life styles. For some families of four an annual income of $4,000 does not signify poverty. On the other hand, a family of four living in a large city on $10,000 per year might feel impoverished.

Such definitions also do not reflect the often terrifying and dehumanizing conditions faced by those for whom poverty is a way of life. They do not reflect the difficulty the poor and "near poor" have in finding health care and other critical social services. Nor do they mention how many of them are hungry and/or undernourished. In 1968, the Citizens' Board of Inquiry into Hunger and Malnutrition in the United States reported that over 10 million Americans were suffering from hunger and another 20 million more were not adequately fed. The terminology in both instances (hunger and malnutrition) was based on medically defined measures. These figures mean, among other things, that many children never enjoy the nutrition necessary for normal physical and mental development. Malnutrition causes irrevocable physical retardation, including arrested brain development, in many children. For others, those who are among the 20 million poorly nourished, it means an excessive susceptibility to disease which, if not irreparably debilitating physically, can seriously handicap their educations.

Consider also that the poor pay a larger share of their income for

---

[4] Under guidelines published in 1973, the Labor Department defined the poverty level for a nonfarm family of four as $4,200. The poverty level for persons living on a farm is $1,800 for a single person and $3,575 for a family of four. A single person living in a nonfarm area is considered poor if his net income is less than $2,100 per year.

taxes than other groups. Moderate income groups do not fare much better. People earning between $8,000 and $10,000 per year pay only 4 percent less of their income than those making $25,000–$50,000.[5] Loopholes in the tax laws also enable businesses and persons "fortunate" enough either to know about the loopholes or be able to employ those who do, to escape paying taxes on a sizable portion, if not all, of their income.

Peter Henle, a Library of Congress labor specialist, has found that the share of wage and salary income going to people who are already well paid is slowly increasing, while the share for those more poorly paid is falling. Thus, some economic inequalities are increasing. He has estimated, for example, that between 1958 and 1970 the share of all job income that went to the top fifth of male wage earners rose from 38 percent to 40.5 percent. On the other hand, the bottom fifth's share dropped from 5 percent to 4.5 percent.[6]

Certain segments of our population—blacks, Latin Americans, Indians, women, the elderly—are more likely to live in poverty than others. Although these disparities are narrowing, the economic gap between white and black people, for example, is still immense. The number of black families existing below the poverty line has dropped dramatically since 1960, but the wages of black people still tend to run much lower than those of whites. In 1970, the black who completed 4 years of high school earned less than the white who finished only 8 years of elementary school. The black with 4 years of college had a median income of $7,754 while the white who had only 4 years of high school earned a median income of $8,154. Furthermore, underemployment, which means seasonal or part-time work, is much more common for blacks than for whites. Indeed, a black family has to have two or more workers to earn as much as a white family with one member at work.[7] Perhaps more importantly, these inequalities are also reflected in a higher rate of illness and lower life expectancy for nonwhites than for whites.

Economic irregularities of the sort discussed here are not limited to black–white or white–nonwhite categories. Many people existing below the poverty line are whites. Nevertheless, blacks and nonwhites generally suffer the most. So, too, with women. In 1968, for example,

[5] Gans, *op. cit.*, p. 44.
[6] *Time,* January 15, 1973, p. 69.
[7] *Time,* April 6, 1970, p. 94.

32 percent of families headed by a woman were below the poverty line. Of these, 25 percent were white. And in 1970, women earned 64 percent of the wages paid to similarly employed men.[8]

Age is another important category in economic stratification. Twenty million Americans are 65 or over. One of every four of these lives at or below the poverty line. More than 2 million subsist on Social Security. Those who fall near the poverty line also live a precarious existence, for their savings and fixed incomes are being rapidly devoured by the rising costs of goods and services.[9]

Young Americans also have more than their share of people living in poverty, as do the Southern states. In short, a person runs the risk of being poor if several of the following characteristics apply:

1. He (she) is nonwhite.
2. He belongs to a family with no wage earners.
3. He belongs to a family headed by a woman.
4. He belongs to a family with more than six children under 18.
5. He is between 14 and 25 or over 65.
6. He lives in a rural farm area.
7. He has fewer than 8 years of education.
8. He lives in the South.[10]

Political Inequalities

Economic inequalities deserve attention in any analysis of "equality" because they often are found, particularly in a capitalistic society, at the base of many persistent social ills. Indeed economic inequalities often contribute to the absence of democratic pluralism. Of course, wealth and political power do not always go hand in hand. Still, inequality among people is almost always accompanied by a great disparity in political power resulting from economic inequalities. Indeed, it was this feature which so influenced R. H. Tawney when he wrote his classic, *Equality,* first published in 1931. One of the distinguishing characteristics of his (English) society, Tawney wrote, "is the division between the majority who work for wages, but who do not own or direct, and the minority who own the material apparatus of indus-

8 *Time,* March 30, 1970, p. 38.
9 *Time,* August 3, 1970, p. 49.
10 "Everyone Is Discovering Poverty," *America: The International Teamster Magazine,* February, 1964, p. 16.

try and determine industrial organization and policy." [11] Tawney could
have added that owners and directors, as it were, also play a major
role in determining public policy. For their wealth brings them great
power not only in the social and industrial spheres, but also in shaping
public policy.

Herbert Gans offers this interesting observation about wealth and
political power in the United States:

> . . . since about 13 percent of the population is poor in terms of
> the official poverty line, an egalitarian political system would require
> that almost fifty congressmen and thirteen senators be representa-
> tives of the poor. This is not the case, however, even though big
> business, big labor, and even less numerous sectors of the population
> have their unofficial representatives in both houses of Congress.
> While Supreme Court action has finally brought about the one-man,
> one-vote principle in electing these representatives, the seniority
> system maintains the traditional pattern of inequality, and so a
> handful of congressmen and senators, many from rural districts,
> still hold much of the real power on Capitol Hill. Affluent individuals
> and well-organized interest groups in effect have more than one vote
> per man because they have far greater access to their elected repre-
> sentatives than the ordinary citizen and because they can afford to
> hire lobbyists who watch out for their interests and even help to
> write legislation.[12]

Moreover, these mutually reinforcing political and economic inequalities are not new to this country. From our very beginnings equality
has been pursued—and not adequately attained—in both realms. It is
true, of course, that the United States has never had the clear, well-
defined classes and historically enshrined aristocracy that have existed
in other parts of the globe. And it may be true that no society *so
pluralistic* as that of the United States has come close to matching its
record of egalitarianism, however tainted that record may be. Nevertheless, from its beginning the United States has been a society of unequals. In 1774, for example, among those few Philadelphians affluent
enough to pay taxes, 10 percent owned fully 89 percent of the taxable
property.[13]

The division of human beings into classes or strata, ranged in a

[11] R. H. Tawney, *Equality,* Third Edition (London: Allen and Unwin,
1938), p. 61.
[12] Gans, *op. cit.,* pp. 43–44.
[13] *Ibid.,* p. 44.

hierarchy of wealth, prestige, and power, is not uniquely American. It is a prominent and virtually universal feature of all societies. Indeed, stratification (that is, inequality) of this sort has always attracted the attention of social theorists. The classical Greek philosophers understood the interaction of the economic structure of a society and its political life. In modern times the way this interaction is conceived and portrayed results largely from the work of Marx and his followers. They, among others less prominent, have perceived that such inequalities are a function of certain social arrangements, man-made and capable of being eliminated. Man, they have taught us, is not condemned to defeatism regarding unjust social arrangements.

It is when people see particular inequalities as unjust *and* alterable that equality as an ideal becomes a potent force in thought and action. And those developments to which we referred earlier indicate that Americans today are acting to narrow the gap between their professed attachment to egalitarianism and the reality of widespread social inequalities.

Growing Impatience

What factors have led up to the growing impatience toward inequalities that Americans now feel? First, most Americans no longer need to be preoccupied with fulfilling basic needs. Today they are affluent enough to turn their attention to political, civic, and community affairs. They have the time and energy to improve the quality of community and national life. Moreover, relatively widespread affluence carries with it expectations of "what might be," and the willingness to try to realize those expectations. Ironically, then, affluence does not necessarily bring contentment. A taste of the "good life" carries with it a scent of a better life. Thus, sights become set on new horizons, and social inequities are seen as constituting barriers to the attainment of these new horizons.

The seeds of impatience, then, are found, in part, in our social system's success in satisfying the material needs of a majority of the population. Moreover, even the poorest man, encountering affluence through the media, becomes less satisfied with his poverty and less inclined to accept it as fate. The "have nots," too, develop visions of a better life; they want to strike out against those inequities which have contributed to their plight. Indeed, one contemporary social philosopher argues that the relative affluence of which we speak constitutes the base of what he perceives as a coming revolution. He writes, "The historical locus of the revolution is that stage of development where the satisfaction of basic needs creates needs which transcend the basic ones." [14]

Alongside the growing affluence is a growth in knowledge about the workings of the machinery of our social system, including its inequities. Today, nearly all Americans are aware of the attention which the media give to gross social inequities. The new social consciousness of Americans, then, results in large measure from their increased awareness—gained formally and informally, in schools and from the media—of social inequalities in their society.

Population growth and the expansion of governmental bureaucracy have also caused increasing frustration and impatience with the quality of American life. The seemingly ever-present lag between the perceptions of needs and a political decision to see those needs met has brought the public's frustration to a head. Furthermore, the disruptions and uncertainties accompanying urban renewal and other large-scale social reconstruction projects have enraged people living in urban neighborhoods. The bold, but unrealized, promises of the 1960's, such as Lyndon Johnson's courageous "We Shall Overcome" speech to Congress, have only turned frustration into seething anger.

Ultimately, all these forces have contributed to the impatience of Americans so that today, perhaps more than ever before, they are demanding that both business and government help them to realize a more equitable society. Inevitably, in making these demands, they are focusing their attention on the public school. Indeed, turning to the schools in times of crisis is not a new phenomenon. Whether looking to the school as the culprit or their most useful tool, Americans always have believed that the school was more open and responsive to demands for change than perhaps any other social institution. In looking to the school today, however, people have discovered that our public schools are a major part of, if not a major contributor to, the problems of social inequality.

Unfortunately, problems of meaning associated with the term *equality* are even more complex when examined in the context of schooling and education. Here the issue becomes that of *equality of educational opportunity*. And, as we shall see, this abstraction is open

[14] Herbert Marcuse, *Counterrevolution and Revolt* (Boston: Beacon Press, 1972), p. 14.

to various interpretations, all of which hinge upon definitions of *educational* and *opportunity* as well as *equality*.

Equality of Educational Opportunity

Since its inception, the public school has been thought to be the major instrument through which equality and, more specifically, equality of opportunity would be ensured. Indeed, one of the most persuasive arguments for the establishment of the public school was that such schooling would open a gateway to opportunity that would otherwise be closed to many youngsters, and that education would eliminate or dwarf the social inequities which plagued other nations. In his annual report on education in 1848, Horace Mann claimed that free public education is "beyond all other devices of human origins the greatest equalizer of the conditions of man—the balance wheel of the social machinery." [15] But if public education is to be the vehicle for *equality of opportunity in society at large,* there must be *equality of educational opportunity.* This fact has long been recognized and affirmed in principle. It is embedded deep in both American law and the American ethic. It has been espoused repeatedly by advocates of educational practices ranging from busing and federal aid to education to pleas for state aid to parochial schools. The successful arguments for free textbooks, state equalization funds, and certification of teachers have all been based on this concept. Even those who defend segregation of the races in the public schools profess attachment to this principle by citing the "separate but equal" prescript enunciated in 1896 by the U.S. Supreme Court in *Plessy* v. *Ferguson.*[16] Yet our attempts to live out the concept of equality of educational opportunity have been like walking through quicksand. Our faltering is not merely a function of disagreements over the nature of education, who should be rewarded by it, and so forth. For although equal educational opportunity may be crucial to equal opportunity itself, the former, at least in part, is also a function of the latter. There is an interdependent, mutually supportive relationship between these two ideals.

What does *equality of educational opportunity* mean? What do we imply when we assert that the opportunity of student John Doe to

---

[15] "Annual Report on Education—1848," *Life and Works of Horace Mann,* Volume III (Boston: Walker, Fuller and Co., 1865–1868), pp. 666–69.

[16] W. O. Stanley, et al., *Social Foundations of Education* (New York: The Dryden Press, 1956), p. 227.

get an education is equal to that of student Jane Smith? Some people argue that since the amount and kind of education a person acquires are functions of his inherent ability to learn, and since this ability varies among persons, educational opportunity ought to be a function of, to be determined by, the ability or capacity to profit from education.

This argument is essentially valid. People do vary in their capacity to benefit from formal education, and most thinkers agree that an educational system should reward its clients unequally in ways corresponding to the unequal distribution of capacities. But this observation is misleading. How do people come by their capacities? In part, and maybe in large measure, individual capabilities are functions of one's environment, and the principle of equality of educational opportunity is based upon this reality. In short, equality of educational opportunity refers not to inherent capacities, but to the environmental influences that shape and condition the growth and development of the individual. The concept does not denote equality of intellectual and physical capacity of all men in all places. Instead, it rests on assumptions relating to the origins of inequalities. It assumes that social inequalities stand in the way of educational opportunity and, thus, constitute barriers to general equality of opportunity. The key word, then, is *opportunity,* the opportunity to get an education of whatever amount and kind one's capacities make possible. It is *opportunity* that must be equalized.[17]

But what does it mean to *equalize* the *opportunity* to get an education? Does it mean, for example, mitigating or balancing in some way the fortunes or misfortunes of birth? We know that those who are born into the more affluent communities in this country have a far better chance of receiving a good education than do those who are born among the poor and near poor. Even the founders of the public school recognized this situation. One of the major reasons for establishing public schools was to improve the position of the poor by providing them the same access to man's fund of knowledge as the rich enjoyed. It was thought that merely bringing the wealthy and the poor together in the same schoolhouse would by itself serve an equalizing function. Yet, this has not proven to be enough. The wealthy, not so wealthy, and the poor seldom go to the same school. Moreover, some communities are better able to support public schools than others. Differences in financial capabilities of this sort exist not only between various regions of the country, but even between bordering school

---

[17] *Ibid.,* p. 228.

districts. In Illinois, for example, some elementary school districts spend three times as much per pupil as others. Per pupil expenditures in Illinois vary from $390 in some districts to $1,100 in others. In California the range of variation is from $402 to $918. In New York State the range is from $633 to $1,193. (See columns 1 and 3 in Table 1.) Nationally, spending levels in suburban schools average almost 30 percent above those in city schools. Table 1, compiled by the Education Commission of the States and published in March of 1972, reveals these wide-ranging disparities.

If facilities, well-trained teachers, adequate instructional materials, varied course offerings, length of school year—all those things that money provides for education—are important variables in the quality of education, then the opportunity to get an education is clearly related to the geographic region and economic class in which a person finds himself.

This persisting geographical unevenness in the quality of education accounts for the traditional and still widely shared view that equality of educational opportunity can be attained only when there exists roughly equal opportunity for all people in the population to compete for the benefits of the educational system by attending schools which are similar in terms of their "inputs." It is a minimum condition of this "input" view that every child have access to a school, at the public level at least, with curricula, facilities, staff, and management, which are comparable to those in all other schools. If there are children for whom no school exists, then those children do not have equal educational opportunity. Moreover, if the schools available to some youngsters provide significantly less adequate facilities, curricula, or staff than other public schools, then these youngsters do not have equal educational opportunity. The traditional "input" notion of equality of educational opportunity thus consists of two major elements. First, anyone who wishes schooling should have access to a school. Second, and most significant, all schools should have approximately equal resource inputs in terms of materials, teachers, curricula, and the like.

This input view has long prevailed in the United States. In fact, for many decades the courts and some school districts used it to justify segregation of the races in public schools. Segregation was permissible under the Supreme Court's dictum, coming out of the *Plessy* v. *Ferguson* case, that "separate but equal" schools were constitutional. This view prevailed until 1954 when the Supreme Court decided that another variable, racial mix, was a crucial ingredient in

TABLE 1 Disparities in the Distribution of Educational Resources

State	District Minimum per Pupil Expenditure	District Maximum per Pupil Expenditure	Per Pupil Expenditure at the 90th Percentile	Total Expenditure to Raise to the 90th Percentile (Millions)	ASSESSED VALUATION PER PUPIL			Ratio Maximum to Minimum
					Minimum	Maximum	Average	
Alabama	$294	$ 580	$ 473	$ 40.2	$ 1,961	$ 8,817	$ 4,662	4.5-1
Alaska	480	1,810	1,254	10.2	18,427	72,629	36,486	3.9-1
Arizona	410	2,900	991	88.1	2,984	66,385	14,561	22.2-1
Arkansas	294	1,005	512	37.1	3,682	39,338	22,725	10.7-1
California	402	3,187	918	731.2	8,416	206,804	52,271	24.6-1
Colorado	444	2,801	853	65.0	1,853	21,192	8,166	11.4-1
Connecticut	499	1,311	1,002	126.8	11,483	62,295	21,281	5.7-1
Delaware	633	1,081	1,081	32.3	10,239	56,072	21,349	5.5-1
Florida	582	1,036	824	117.2	6,962	64,568	22,877	9.3-1
Georgia	364	735	706	162.6	10,224	47,564	23,588	4.7-1
Hawaii (1 school district)	489	489	...	...	...	...	...	...
Idaho	483	3,172	904	33.6	3,234	9,544	4,858	3.0-1
Illinois	390	2,295	1,129	401.6	5,034	101,183	19,196	20.1-1
Indiana	373	961	729	112.9	3,116	54,147	9,338	17.4-1
Iowa	591	1,166	912	85.4	17,596	91,080	36,521	5.2-1
Kansas	489	1,572	798	69.6	195	35,661	10,364	182.8-1
Kentucky	344	885	576	57.1	6,514	56,060	24,253	8.6-1
Louisiana	499	922	730	53.6	2,089	28,113	5,335	13.5-1
Maine	215	1,966	660	23.1	4,115	45,909	22,643	11.2-1
Maryland	634	1,036	1,037	175.2	11,361	31,249	19,101	2.8-1
Massachusetts	454	4,243	963	236.0	7,772	80,452	28,189	10.4-1

Michigan	409	1,275	888	326.6	2,085	62,649	14,880	30.0-1
Minnesota	373	1,492	777	107.2	10,940	56,599	28,920	5.2-1
Mississippi	321	825	541	40.6	1,491	7,748	3,936	5.2-1
Missouri	213	1,929	808	107.1	1,508	44,706	8,783	29.6-1
Montana	467	8,515	1,358	62.5	3,915	9,268	5,117	3.1-1
Nebraska	274	3,417	786	48.3	2,664	50,726	26,221	19.0-1
Nevada	746	1,678	929	8.1	5,141	20,526	13,728	4.0-1
New Hampshire	280	1,356	739	16.9	20,409	91,679	34,022	4.5-1
New Jersey	484	2,876	1,009	285.6	11,387	119,422	363,000	10.5-1
New Mexico	477	1,183	645	25.3	5,898	126,320	35,203	21.4-1
New York	633	7,241	1,193	537.7	1,320	111,150	25,770	84.2-1
North Carolina	467	732	675	84.9	13,026	41,139	23,050	3.2-1
North Dakota	327	1,842	776	17.7	2,815	4,724	3,676	1.7-1
Ohio	412	1,684	881	471.8	4,165	44,468	13,892	10.7-1
Oklahoma	309	2,565	662	55.4	2,050	45,957	22,711	22.4-1
Oregon	431	4,491	914	54.6	17,739	94,668	36,748	5.3-1
Pennsylvania	535	4,230	1,102	456.8	5,716	60,077	17,141	10.5-1
Rhode Island	531	1,206	1,045	45.3	15,270	33,110	21,428	2.2-1
South Carolina	397	610	562	28.2	8,293	72,758	22,936	8.8-1
South Dakota	175	6,012	750	20.1	3,843	37,274	24,802	9.7-1
Tennessee	315	774	629	88.9	9,552	90,874	28,303	9.5-1
Texas	197	11,096	668	263.4	1,581	71,311	17,213	45.1-1
Utah	533	1,514	630	13.1	12,863	110,012	29,081	8.6-1
Vermont	357	1,517	905	21.4	13,891	46,386	25,839	3.3-1
Virginia	441	1,159	776	130.8	10,245	69,537	24,119	6.8-1
Washington	433	3,993	981	107.2	6,789	84,678	32,394	12.5-1
West Virginia	502	721	706	30.8	7,453	27,048	14,517	3.6-1
Wisconsin	408	1,391	849	89.3	1,481	115,440	29,347	77.9-1
Wyoming	617	14,554	1,146	27.1	4,542	27,774	11,582	6.1-1

SOURCE: Compiled by the Department of Research and Information Services, Education Commission of the States.

the traditional input interpretation of equal educational opportunity.

In any case, the "input" interpretation suggests that whether or not persons successfully secure the benefits of education is a function of their choice and "native" abilities. Equal opportunity will have been provided even though some may not or, given their "natural" abilities, cannot take advantage of such opportunities. Thus, the fact that certain social groups may not benefit equally from the system has nothing to do with the system so long as the inputs are distributed equally.

This input view of equal educational opportunity has led to the establishment of state equalization funds for the support of local schools, various programs of federal aid to education, and the consolidation of school districts so as to offer a wider base for educational resources. These programs continue. In May of 1972, for example, the National Education Finance Project recommended that school consolidation continue until the present 18,000 or so districts are reduced to 2,500. In spite of such efforts, however, wide variations obviously remain in the financial support communities can give to schools. Indeed, recent court decisions in California (*Serrano* v. *Priest,* 1971), Texas (*Rodriguez* v. *San Antonio Independent School District,* 1971), Minnesota (*Van Dusartz* v. *Hatfield,* 1971), and New Jersey (*Robinson* v. *Cahill,* 1972) have declared the basic tax structure for financing public schools unconstitutional.

These court decisions grew out of suits brought on behalf of students from districts which, because of low property values, were not capable of providing the same financial support to their schools as were bordering, more affluent districts. The local property tax, long the backbone of public school financing in all states except Hawaii, has become, according to these court decisions, an instrument of economic exploitation of the poor and less advantaged. It has led to a situation wherein a child's educational opportunities are clearly related not only to his family's income, but also to the economic value of the real property in the school district in which he lives.

The courts in California, Texas, and Minnesota relied upon the Equal Protection Clause of the Fourteenth Amendment. Adopted in 1868, this amendment enfranchised blacks by providing simply that "No state . . . deny to any person within its jurisdiction the equal protection of the laws." As interpreted by the courts, "equal protection of the laws" means the protection of equal laws. The laws, then, must *treat* all people equally. Because black and white schools segregated by law constituted unequal treatment, the Supreme Court in

1954 declared unconstitutional state laws requiring school segregation. The Equal Protection Clause, then, prevents states from arbitrarily treating people differently under the laws. Thus, the law may not allow white children different access to public schools than black children; nor, according to these more recent state court decisions, may it through taxes allow some school districts to spend far more per pupil than other districts.

In the *Rodriguez* case, however, the United States Supreme Court recently handed down a landmark 5–4 decision in which it found that education is not among the rights afforded explicit protection under the Fourteenth Amendment. In effect, the Supreme Court decision overrules not only the Texas decision, but the California and Minnesota ones as well. However, the final disposition of these cases remains an open question which will be discussed along with the unique New Jersey case in Chapter 3.

In any case, the court decisions make clear that the complexities associated with equality of educational opportunity are not based merely in the school system. They are born of social, political, and economic phenomena which, however unrelated to education they may seem, nevertheless play havoc with the chances of all youngsters to receive an equal education. They are functions, at least in part, of unequal opportunities in general. Clearly, the matter of equal educational opportunity is not likely to be settled by merely desegregating the schools, nor by restructuring their financial support system. The issue is much too complex.

Let us suppose, for example, that financial support of schools was equalized by state, local, and federal aid in some way; and as a consequence, the schools of all communities were deemed to offer equal curricula, facilities, and staff. Let us go further. Suppose that *all* resources imaginable were equally shared by all public schools. Could it then be claimed that equal educational opportunity had been attained? According to the input view it would be completely established, for any one child would have access to as "financially good" and "resourcefully good" a school as any other child. Neither the lack of wealth and social class standing of the youngster, nor the financial poverty of the geographic location in which he finds himself would affect *his chance to attend* an "equal opportunity" school.[18]

Yet opportunities would still be unequal. Many children would

[18] *Ibid.,* p. 229.

remain disadvantaged by the financial poverty and limited educational background of their families. Children raised in an environment in which the abilities, talents, and skills fostered are not those which the school uses to measure success will not have an equal opportunity to compete for the school's rewards with those whose environment more closely matches the culture of the school. Thus, if we extend the equal treatment premise of the input view beyond tangible, measurable inputs (property tax, scope and range of the curriculum, age of building, etc.) to the child's background, and regard the opportunities provided by that background prior to schooling as "inputs" which the child brings to school, we run into new—and major—difficulties in providing equality of educational opportunity.

This variable, socioeconomic background, turned up as the most crucial in an extensive study of equality of educational opportunity The Civil Rights Act of 1964 mandated the Commissioner of Education to assess the "lack of equality of educational opportunity among racial and other groups in the United States." This study, carried out with government financing under the direction of Johns Hopkins sociologist James Coleman, was and remains the only nationwide survey of education and race. The study, published in 1966 and now commonly called "The Coleman Report," has come under heavy criticism. Nevertheless, its findings have been corroborated by research on individual school systems.

Coleman and his colleagues expected to discover gross inequities in the quality of schools attended by youngsters from dominant and minority groups. They assumed that inequalities in the age of school buildings, instructional facilities, class size, teacher background, and so forth would account for differences in academic achievement among dominant and minority group students. This assumption underlies current federal aid programs, as well as the recent court decisions to which we have referred. Indeed, the major thrust of educational policy in this country has always been at equalizing inputs, to provide the resources necessary to bring below average and average schools up to the level of the best.

Coleman did find the inequalities he had predicted. But much to his surprise, he found that differences in the quality of schools, when measured by these input criteria, were not very closely related to differences in student achievement. Coleman and his associates did not find a strong, positive correlation between low student achievement and inadequate educational "inputs." On the contrary, their massive survey showed that neither black, nor white, Mexican-American, Puerto Rican, Indian-American, or Oriental children from a given socioeconomic class did significantly better in schools with high financial inputs.

Coleman did find that the achievement scores of black children were higher for those who attended racially mixed classes than for those who attended all black or predominantly black schools. This in itself was not a new finding, but Coleman added that: *improvements in educational achievement among blacks from poor backgrounds was owing to the fact that they picked up, somehow, conventional middle-class academic skills* by mixing with *middle-class* whites. In short, Coleman found that social class mix, not merely racial mix, was the most important variable affecting academic achievement of all youngsters, regardless of race. Hence, a white child from a low socioeconomic class background improved academically when studying with children from a mixture of social classes. The crucial mix is yet an open question, but Coleman's research suggests that improvement in achievement is less likely when poor children make up more than 60 percent of a school's enrollment. In any case, the crucial point, according to James Coleman, is that *schools have little influence on a youngster's achievement that is independent of his social, economic, and cultural background*.

Coleman's study is by no means the final answer on the relation of social class background to educational achievement. Although numerous studies have since corroborated Coleman's findings, and though his is the largest study of its kind, much research must yet be done to test his findings. Nevertheless, his study does raise serious questions about the traditional "input" approach to equality of educational opportunity. Indeed, using academic achievement as the major ingredient in defining equality of educational opportunity, Coleman found that, as measured by standardized tests of mathematical and verbal performance, formal instructional inputs, including the "quality" of teaching, make relatively little difference compared to the social and economic composition of fellow students. In this sense the Coleman study has turned our attention from a simple definition of inputs to the consequences of schooling, given various kinds of inputs including the socioeconomic class background of students.

Coleman's study has given added impetus to efforts to overcome inequities in educational opportunity. It provides new justification for busing in a time when the forced transportation of youngsters to achieve racial balance in our schools is one of the most controversial issues in American life.

Until recently, judicial rulings that schools must integrate were largely limited to the South, where Jim Crow laws still meant dual school systems. Now courts are declaring that segregation in the North must also be dismantled, at least where the school board has contributed to keeping schools segregated. The forced busing produced by these court orders has provoked an explosive outburst of discord and hate that has shaken domestic politics as well as the public school.

The busing issue is an odd one. Without busing many American children might never have access to formal education at all. Nearly 40 percent of the nation's elementary school children take a bus to school; and if consolidation of school districts continues, this percentage is likely to increase rapidly no matter what happens to the issue of busing. Yet millions of parents—white and black alike—are angry over court edicts to bus their children in order to achieve racial balance in schools.

Some of the anti-busing sentiment is clearly motivated by irrationality, ignorance, and racism. Other objections stem from parents' fears that busing will either bring the problems of the ghetto to their schools or take their children into the midst of the ghetto. In short, some white parents fear that their children will be exposed to what blacks have long put up with: the conditions that have turned many large city schools into testing grounds for survival. Furthermore, whites who have moved to a suburb because of the good schools there are angry over court decisions which insist that some of their children will have to go to school elsewhere.

By 1972 the issue of busing had become so controversial that it propelled Alabama's Governor George Wallace into the political spotlight, and even moved President Nixon to say that he strongly opposes "busing of children for the sake of busing."

While the social results of busing may be uncertain, Coleman's study shows that the academic ones are not. Indeed, it suggests that busing children to different schools might be extended so as to achieve an appropriate, educationally sound, *social class mix* of youngsters in our schools.

Social class background apparently influences educational achievement throughout the world. In preparation for the 1971 International Conference on Education,[19] the International Bureau of Education prepared a document called "The Social Background of Students and their Chance of Success at School," based on replies to a questionnaire sent out to UNESCO's member states. After analyzing these replies, the report concluded "that in practice . . . social background [of students] has a very real effect on access to education, academic success and the choice of an occupation." Here are some excerpts from that report:

[*From Belgium:*] It is self-evident in Belgium as elsewhere that the children of well-to-do families start appreciably ahead of the rest.

[*From Hungary:*] The social background still influences the school career of the pupils to a great extent.

[*From the United Kingdom:*] The literature suggests that children from higher social categories do better at school. The nature of the problem is thus partly one of enrichment of the education of children from disadvantaged homes, partly one of removing financial or other barriers to their continued education.

[*From the Netherlands:*] The falling behind of the lower classes, which finds its origin in the phase preceding infant age, is most obvious in the highest phase of education; university education . . . We can speak of complete democratization of education when the social classes are equally represented in education as in the total population.

[*From the United States:*] There are areas of rural poverty in the country where . . . teachers and facilities are often sub-standard and tax resources for improvement are virtually non-existent. The educational and occupational aspirations of students in these areas are negatively affected by their low socio-economic status, and in some cases by geographic isolation.

Clearly, equal access or opportunity to education, as well as the capacity to profit from an education, is related to socioeconomic background. Consider that in merely attending school a youngster must have books to study, materials with which to work, appropriate clothes to wear both to school and for physical education and extracurricular activities and all the other materials that a good school requires. The cost of these items can become prohibitive,

[19] Thirty-third International Conference on Education, September 15–23, 1971, at the Geneva Headquarters of the International Bureau of Education.

especially for parents who do not have even a few dollars to spare. As a result, their children cannot purchase the materials basic to schooling even in its narrowest sense. Some school systems have developed ways of making these materials available to economically disadvantaged children at no cost or for a small rental fee. But parents and children on the receiving end of such practices often are demeaned by them and refuse to accept such aid. Furthermore, these procedures do not cover all the materials needed, and for some parents even a small rental fee is too costly.

What if all such materials were provided free to everyone and all indirect costs of educating one's children were eliminated? Coleman's study suggests that even this would not be enough. How about the youngster whose poverty has led to malnutrition or physical defects? He or she cannot profit from the school as much as a child who has had adequate medical care and proper food. How about the youngster whose home is too crowded for him to study there? who cannot get a peaceful night of sleep? who must hold down a part-time job which leaves him or her little time for study and sleep? All these factors, and many others, contribute to a person's opportunity to receive and profit from education.

The thrust of the Coleman Report, then, is that if equality of educational opportunity is to be measured by those factors that most affect learning, the focus should not be primarily on school inputs, but rather on the equalization of human resources—what children take to school. It suggests that educators should assess equal educational opportunity by the *outputs* of schooling rather than its *inputs*.

Let us suppose, for example, that two schools are equal or comparable in staff competencies, facilities, instructional materials, curricula offerings—in short, in their inputs. In terms of the traditional input notion, children attending these schools would be provided with equality of educational opportunity. Suppose, however, that youngsters coming out of these schools do so with glaring disparities in achievement, and those from the lower socioeconomic classes are disproportionately represented among these low achievers. Generally speaking, we do not worry very much about different individuals coming out of the schools with different abilities, talents, honors, rewards, and the like. On the contrary, we expect schools to sort out their students in just this way. On the other hand, if certain social groups taken as aggregates achieve far more than other social groups, then we have a problem. And, of course, this is exactly what Coleman found. Students from lower socioeconomic classes, regardless of race, achieve in terms of traditional school measures at a rate significantly lower than their age and grade peers from higher classes. Furthermore, the disparities in achievement increased the longer children stayed in school. More specifically, poor achievers from a low social class background often achieve at an increasingly poor rate as they progress through school. They *regress* as they move up the lock-step grade ladder. Who can argue that no inequality exists here?

Coleman's study leads us, on one hand, to conclude that disparities in achievement result from the cultural and social baggage the youngsters take to school with them. But that such disparities become more pronounced the longer youngsters remain in school suggests that the school somehow contributes to them. It may even be that intangible differences in "inputs" account for these disparities. No doubt this is often the case, even though Coleman might consider them fairly insignificant. As Thomas Green noted, however, these qualifiers are irrelevant to our focus on *achievement* in assessing equality of educational opportunity. Green put it this way:

> The point is to see that even in the absence of such differences of input, the range and distribution of *results* are relevant in determining when unacceptable inequalities of educational opportunity exist. The point is conceptual. As a matter of *a priori* fact, the concept of equal educational opportunity is not confined to equal provisions of schooling for each child. We do, in fact, extend the concept to include some consideration of equal results.[20]

When Coleman and others contend that equal educational opportunity should be defined, at least in part, in terms of output, they mean that equal educational opportunity will be achieved when "(1) the range of the distribution of . . . [achievement] and (2) the distribution within that range is approximately the same for each relevant social group within the student population." [21] In more simple terms, equal educational opportunity is achieved when individual disparities in achievement are as wide or close within one social group as they are in another. Green notes that three important points need to be made about this conception:

---

[20] Thomas F. Green, "Equal Educational Opportunity: The Durable Injustice," *Philosophy of Education 1971: Proceedings of the Twenty-Seventh Annual Meeting of the Philosophy of Education Society,* April, 1971, p. 128.
[21] *Ibid.,* p. 130.

First, it does not mean that everyone must reach the same level of achievement. It means only that the *range* of achievement and the distribution *within* that range should be about the same for each social group. Secondly . . . equal opportunity in this . . . [outcome] sense is compatible with and may even require unequal opportunity in the resource [input] sense . . . Third, it seems too much to claim that equal benefit [achievement] is what we *mean* by equal educational opportunity; but it is not too much to say that its attainment would be a sufficient condition for the claim to have achieved equal educational opportunity. For under these conditions, the disadvantaged of society would no longer be *educationally* disadvantaged. We would have reached a point at which neither social class, income, race, nor sex would be a barrier to educational achievement. Thus even though . . . [this] view does not capture all that we *mean* by equal educational opportunity, still it seems to set forth sufficient conditions for its attainment.[22]

There are still other aspects of equality of educational opportunity that must be considered. For example, in many school systems grades are given on the basis of achievement *in relation to ability*. The gifted student may have to achieve an average of 95 to receive an A grade, whereas the below average student may need only an average of 70 to receive such a grade. Does differential grading based on measures of ability (which, by the way, have often proved to be culturally biased) reflect the principle of equality of opportunity? How about ability grouping? Is a youngster provided equal educational opportunity if on the basis of his low scores on some standardized test he is not grouped with average or above average students? Do such procedures condemn a child to a continuously mediocre learning environment? Do the testing procedures constitute due process? Is a youngster provided equal educational opportunity if, through school ability grouping procedures, his formal education takes place within the confines of a relatively homogeneous group of students? How about the lower-tracked youth whose teachers grow to expect (from standardized test scores, academic records, etc.) him or her to perform poorly?

Consider another aspect of this issue. We know that different socioeconomic groups instill their children with different aspirations, motivations, and talents. Given such conditions, what type of educational program constitutes equality of educational opportunity? Should

[22] *Ibid.*

the school offer a common curriculum for all children? Surely no one program would meet the needs and interests of all students. Indeed, Americans have long recognized that equality of educational opportunity does not imply equal educational treatment, that is, a common curriculum. But how much diversity in school programs is desirable as well as economically feasible? All citizens need certain skills, attitudes, values, and knowledge; and the school is expected to instill a certain "common culture." Moreover, the amount and range of variety in educational programs is directly affected by the value placed upon those talents and skills which are deemed desirable by the larger society. After all, the school is expected to value and reward those skills. Reflect upon the following argument: [23]

> Certain positions in any society are fundamentally and functionally more important than others, and require special skills for their performance.
>
> Any society has only a limited number of individuals who possess the talents which can be trained into the skills appropriate to these positions.
>
> In order to attract the persons who have the requisite talents for these positions to undergo the training and sacrifices attached to reaching them, the positions must carry an inducement value in the form of differential access to the goods, prestige, powers, and the like in society.
>
> Differential access to these kinds of rewards has as a consequence institutionalized social inequality.
>
> Social inequality, therefore, is inevitable and functionally crucial to the continuance of any society.

This observation does not argue for what should be. It calls attention to what *is*. And it has at least two major implications with regard to equality of educational opportunity.

First, the apparent functional necessity of social inequality, that is, stratification, suggests that the school is limited in the amount to which it can cater to individual needs as a way of providing equality of educational opportunity. It is limited, as the dependent variable in the school-society relationship, because it must invest most of its efforts in those programs and curricula which serve the functionally

[23] Based upon a thesis presented by sociologists Kingsley Davis and Wilbert Moore in "Some Principles of Stratification," *The American Sociological Review*, Vol. 10, No. 2 (August, 1945), pp. 242–249. This thesis has been the source of much debate among social science theorists.

important positions. Furthermore, the argument implies that the school must direct itself to that range of talent in its clientele which can be matched to the prerequisites of these positions.

Second, and in a broader, yet more complicating sense, the argument suggests that since social inequality is necessarily built into every society, schools will not only serve but mirror that *functionally* important social inequality. This argument complicates the issue for one simple reason: unequal educational opportunity is directly related, as we have observed repeatedly, to the social and economic inequalities which exist in the larger society. Functionally crucial social stratification may perpetuate these inequalities.

In every society, no one really knows all the talent present in the population. But the more rigidly stratified a society is, the less chance it has for discovering new talents among its members. Social stratification limits the chances available to discover, recruit, and train functionally important talent. Furthermore, the unequal distribution of rewards in one generation tends to result in the unequal distribution of hopes and motivation in the succeeding generation. Also, there is always a tendency among those in privileged and functionally important positions to restrict access to these positions. The recruitment and training of physicians illustrates this phenomenon.[24] For example, whether or not an applicant has a relative who is a physician is used by many medical schools as a criterion for admitting students.

Clearly, then, all of us suffer to some extent from social inequalities and the consequent inequalities in educational opportunity. The systematic deprivation of equal educational opportunity that has been passed on by each generation has deprived all of us of the tangible social and economic benefits which can be realized when all are afforded equal opportunities. But here is the rub. Few can agree on what constitutes equality of educational opportunity. To arrive at a generalizable, workable definition of this term would constitute a major social and educational breakthrough. Perhaps the collective American conscience, which seems so concerned with equality and equal opportunity today, is a hopeful sign in this regard. Even if a workable definition of *equal educational opportunity* could be developed, however, and even if it attracted the support of virtually every citizen, we still could not be sure of its import on *equal oppor-*

[24] Melvin M. Turnin, "Some Principles of Stratification: A Critical Analysis," *The American Sociological Review,* Vol. 18 (August, 1953), pp. 387–393.

tunity in the larger society. Indeed, the recent research of Christopher Jencks and his associates suggests that schools do not contribute significantly to equality among adults.[25] In their study, Jencks and his associates conclude that: (1) Although economic poverty is largely a subjective concept, it cannot be eliminated unless people's incomes are prevented from falling too far below the national average. (2) Equalizing *opportunity* in the economic realm will not do very much to equalize results. Reforms must be directed at reducing the distance between those who have "made it" economically and socially and those who have "failed." (3) Making schools more equal will not help very much. Differences among schools have little effect on equality and inequality among adults.

Thus, though Jencks would contend that school reform, including financial reform, helps improve the lives of children, he would argue, nevertheless, that it cannot contribute very much to equality in society at large. In order to attain economic equality in society at large, Jencks believes that we will have to begin by changing our economic institutions—not by changing our schools.

Jencks' study challenges long-cherished beliefs about the place of the school in American society. It emphasizes, among other things, that the burden of achieving *equality of educational opportunity* cannot be borne by the educational system alone. It depends upon not only what we do in the schools, but also what we do elsewhere in the economy, in the polity, and in the society at large.

Jencks' hypothesis is supported by reviewing some of the aspects of this issue which we have discussed. We have noted that equality of educational opportunity involves consideration of, at the very least:

1. Native capacities to profit from schooling
2. Environmental circumstances which shape growth and development
3. The financial ability of communities to support their schools
4. Interpretations of the Equal Protection Clause of the Fourteenth Amendment
5. Racial mix in the schools
6. The socioeconomic background of the student
7. Social class mix in the classroom
8. Achievement in relation to ability

[25] Christopher Jencks *et al., Inequality: A Reassessment of the Effect of Family and Schooling in America* (New York: Basic Books, 1972).

9. Tracking and ability grouping
10. Teacher expectations
11. Diversity of educational programs
12. Functional social stratification

In the chapters that follow, these variables and others will be illustrated and analyzed. They provide the basis for speculation over what is, or should be, the future of equality of educational opportunity. In considering the issue on which this book focuses—*what is equality of educational opportunity and how can it be achieved*—remember, then, that its boundaries extend far beyond the school. It is an abstraction which both influences and is influenced by American social, political, and economic life. The following questions, which should be kept in mind as the issue is discussed in the following chapters, illustrate the complexity and far-reaching consequences of the concept of equality of educational opportunity.

1. In what sense is the meaning of equal *educational* opportunity dependent upon equal opportunity in society at large?
2. To what extent are talented children from lower socioeconomic classes precluded from receiving a quality public education?
3. To what extent are able youngsters from racial and ethnic minorities precluded from receiving a quality public education?
4. To what extent are girls and young women precluded from receiving a quality public education?
5. Do racially segregated schools constitute a denial of equality of educational opportunity?
6. Are schools which are homogeneous in terms of the social class mix of their students a denial in fact or in principle of equality of educational opportunity?
7. Does equality of educational opportunity mean that exposure to a given curriculum provides *opportunity?*
8. Does equality of educational opportunity mean that school programs should be established in accordance with whatever a child needs?
9. Does equality of educational opportunity mean that each child should have the same amount of money spent on him through public funds?

10. Does equality of educational opportunity mean the elimination of all indirect costs of elementary and secondary education?
11. How much equalization is necessary before we have equality of educational opportunity?
12. What must be equalized?
13. Does the concept of equality of educational opportunity contradict or conflict with other social principles?
14. Is the property tax obsolete as a means of financing our public schools?
15. What fraction of the total cost of operating the public schools should be borne by the federal government? by the state?
16. What principles should govern the distribution of federal funds to the schools?
17. Is busing an appropriate vehicle for bringing about some measure of equality of educational opportunity?
18. How can the learning gap be closed for economically disadvantaged children?
19. What role, if any, do teacher expectations play in the matter of equal educational opportunity?
20. Is ability grouping an infringement upon equal opportunity?
21. Is education a human right?
22. Is education merely a privilege?

These are just a few of the questions that can and should be asked about equality of educational opportunity. Perhaps a concerted, broad-based national effort to answer these questions would result in a dramatic challenge to Plato's description of "a sort of equality."

Chapter 3

Desegregation and School Finance: Two Illustrations of the Struggle for Equality

Within just a little over a year, two dramatic illustrations of the struggle for equality of educational opportunity have emerged in the United States. One is a new chapter in the desegregation of schools, and the other is a fundamental challenge to the long-established structure of school financing. Both these developments have implications and ramifications which may eventually affect every American family.

Since the struggle for equal educational opportunity is so well characterized in the recent desegregation and school finance controversies, they will be used here as illustrations of the overall issue. No effort will be made in this chapter to analyze the two controversies. Instead, the significance of each will be illustrated as the various positions are outlined and their influence on society as a whole is revealed.

The School Desegregation Controversy

No discussion of the concept of equal educational opportunity would be complete without a review of the celebrated Supreme Court decision known as *Brown* v. *Board of Education of Topeka, Kansas*.[1] On May 17, 1954, amidst an atmosphere charged with emotion, the

---

[1] *Brown* v. *Board of Education of Topeka, Kansas,* United States Supreme Court, 347 U.S. 483, 1954.

Supreme Court ruled that state-imposed segregation was no longer legal. The country soon became divided angrily along many lines. Segregationists and states' rightists formed one alliance, while civil-rights advocates and liberals formed another.

At the time of the *Brown* decision, about 40 million Americans lived below the Mason-Dixon line and about 10 percent of these were black. Because they were black, they were subjected to special laws, most of which were written during Civil War days. The cumulative effect of these laws was to deprive black citizens of the free choice which was readily available to white people. In the middle of the twentieth century, blacks of the South did not have the right to select the neighborhood in which they lived. Neither did they have the legal right to sit in any seat in a public bus. Blacks were forbidden to share public facilities with whites. Above all, they had to be educated in separate, all-black schools. Twenty-one states and the District of Columbia, at the time of the *Brown* decision, had laws which either compelled or permitted the separation of whites and blacks in educational institutions. In 17 of these 21 states, constitutional provisions, state statutes, and local ordinances made segregated schools a requirement. In the remaining 4 states the maintenance of segregated schools was legally optional.[2]

Until the *Brown* decision, the legal notion of equal educational opportunity did not require desegregation. In fact, the 1896 Supreme Court case of *Plessy* v. *Ferguson* upheld the right of the states to provide "separate but equal" facilities for white and black passengers on trains.[3] This ruling was extended later to cover separate but equal school facilities as well. By 1954, however, times had changed and, in the words of the Supreme Court, "today, education is perhaps the most important function of state and local governments." The Court ruled, as a result, that "separate" educational facilities could not be "equal."

Almost all the voluminous arguments presented on behalf of the plaintiffs in the *Brown* case were designed to show that segregation in education is, itself, a form of inequality. The twelve variables listed toward the end of Chapter 2 are but a few of the many areas of conflict still being examined today. The question now, though, is not

---

[2] Albert P. Blaustein and Clarence C. Ferguson, *Desegregation and the Law* (New Brunswick, N.J.: Rutgers University Press, 1957), p. 6.

[3] *Plessy* v. *Ferguson,* United States Supreme Court, 163 U.S. 537, 1896.

merely whether per pupil expenditures, physical facilities, curricular offerings, courses of study, and qualifications of teachers are equal. The contemporary controversy evolves, essentially, around whether reasonable, economical means for ensuring equality in these categories *can* be found. As we will see in the subsequent discussion of the *Swann* case, however, segregationists and states' rightists still capitalize upon school desegregation cases in their efforts to obstruct school integration.

During the more than half a century between the *Plessy* and *Brown* cases, the United States turned from isolationism to become the strongest power in the world. Industrialization, farming, and all forms of economic and political life grew spectacularly. There was an explosion of knowledge in all conceivable areas. In short, the era of *Plessy* had little in common with the post-World War II–Korean War era of the *Brown* decision. Based upon its cognizance of this social change, the Supreme Court in 1954 overthrew the *Plessy* "separate but equal" ruling for a new doctrine more attuned to the times. Through the *Brown* decision, they ruled that the Fourteenth Amendment to the Constitution with its Equal Protection Clause could be reinterpreted according to the spirit of the present. In 1896, *equal protection* meant "separate but equal" facilities. By 1954, *equal protection* was interpreted as nothing less than the same facilities for all. Why the reversal of the *Plessy* doctrine? Simply, the Court decided that in the late 1800s public education was not yet a serious American value, especially in the South where virtually no blacks attended school. The half-dozen or so significant cases handed down between 1896 and 1954 which led to the reversal of the *Plessy* decision illustrate the changes in interpretation of the Fourteenth Amendment as applied by the Supreme Court up to that time. (See the detailed discussion of these cases on pages 107–124.) Since 1954, as will be seen in the discussion of the *Swann* case, the Equal Protection Clause has been extended to ensure integrated schools in the South regardless of economic burden or physical inconvenience to the residents of the school district.

The changing interpretation of the Equal Protection Clause over many decades illustrates the status of only one of the variables implicit in the struggle for equality of educational opportunity. Others, such as (1) racial and social class mix within the schools, (2) diversity of educational programs, (3) native capacity to profit from schooling, and (4) achievement in relation to ability can also be traced to the

Brown case. In fact, one crucial variable, the influence of environmental circumstances upon child growth and development (sometimes referred to as the effect of segregation on children), was the crux of the social science argument in the Brandeis brief in the *Brown* decision. This statement, presented to the Court by 32 psychologists, sociologists, and anthropologists headed by Professor Kenneth Clark, argues that racial segregation in the schools, whether tangible facilities are equal or not, provides a psychological handicap to the pursuit of curricular objectives.[4] A child's school environment plays a major psychological role in his opportunity to learn. The arguments used in the Brandeis brief illustrate and clarify the principles of equal educational opportunity underlying the Court's thinking in 1954. The social scientists stress both the effects of segregation and the consequences of desegregation in showing why "separate" cannot be "equal." Some of the salient points of this brief, summarized below, indicate the highly sophisticated evidence brought before the Court to show how segregation denies black children equal opportunity in school.

The authors of the brief first presented research studying how racial prejudice influences the development of a healthy personality. They drew heavily from the report of the Mid-century White House Conference on Children and Youth, which states that segregation damages the personality of all children whether they be from a minority or majority group.

> . . . As minority group children learn the inferior status to which they are assigned—as they observe the fact that they are almost always segregated and kept apart from others who are treated with more respect by the society as a whole—they often react with feelings of inferiority and a sense of personal humiliation. Many of them become confused about their own personal worth. . . . This conflict and confusion leads to self hatred and rejection of their own group.
>
> Not every child, of course, reacts with the same pattern of behavior. The particular pattern depends upon many interrelated factors, among which are: the stability and quality of his family relations; the social and economic class to which he belongs; the cultural and educational background of his parents; . . . personal characteristics, intelligence, special talents, and personality pattern.

[4] Appendix to Appellants' briefs in *Brown* v. *Board of Education of Topeka, Kansas. Minnesota Law Review*, Vol. 37, 1953, pp. 427–439.

Some children . . . may react by overt aggression and hostility directed toward their own group or members of the dominant groups. Anti-social and delinquent behavior may often be interpreted as reactions to these racial frustrations. These reactions are self destructive in that the larger society not only punishes those who commit them, but often interprets such aggressive and anti-social behavior as justification for continuing prejudice and segregation.

. . . Segregation imposes upon individuals a distorted sense of social reality. Segregation leads to a blockage in the communication and interaction between two groups. Such blockages tend to increase mutual suspicion, distrust, and hostility. Segregation not only perpetuates rigid stereotypes and reinforces negative attitudes toward members of the other group, but also leads to the development of a social climate within which violent outbreaks of racial tensions are likely to occur.[5]

After Clark and his colleagues outlined the above-mentioned effects of segregation, they turned to the question of whether segregation, as only one feature of the complex social setting, is actually the cause of these effects.

To answer this question, it is necessary to bring to bear the general fund of psychological and sociological knowledge concerning the role of various environmental influences in producing feelings of inferiority, confusions in personal roles, various types of basic personality structures. . . .

On the basis of the general fund of knowledge, it seems likely that feelings of inferiority and doubts about personal worth are attributable to living in an underprivileged environment only insofar as the latter is itself perceived as an indicator of low social status and as a symbol of inferiority. . . . While there are many other factors that serve as reminders of the differences in social status, there can be little doubt that the fact of enforced segregation is a major factor.

This seems to be true for the following reasons among others: (1) because enforced segregation results from the decision of the majority group without the consent of the segregated and is commonly so perceived; and (2) because historically segregation patterns in the United States were developed on the assumption of the inferiority of the segregated.

In addition . . . the child who, for example, is compelled to attend a segregated school may be able to cope with ordinary

[5] *Ibid.*

expressions of prejudice by regarding the prejudiced person as evil or misguided; but he cannot readily cope with symbols of authority, the full force of the authority of the State—the school or the school board, in this instance—in the same manner. . . .[6]

Following the Supreme Court decision in *Brown* v. *Board of Education,* it became apparent that most school boards in the South did not intend to desegregate "with all deliberate speed." The courts were forced, therefore, to turn to such considerations as proper racial mix in the schools, the financial responsibilities of communities to support desegregated schools, diversity of educational programs, and the like.

In *Griffin* v. *Prince Edward County (Virginia) School Board,* the Supreme Court confronted the question of financial responsibility.[7] Prince Edward County had closed all its public schools to avoid integration and was making tuition payments to private schools set up for the white students. The Court ordered the county to reopen its schools and to cease making the tuition payments.

In *Greene* v. *New Kent County (Virginia)* the Court specified that school boards are obligated not only to develop desegregation plans but also to propose plans which promise to be workable.[8] Here racial mix and similar variables important to equal educational opportunity were considered. Questions of integrating school staffs according to mathematical ratios arose in Alabama in *U.S.* v. *Montgomery County Board of Education.*[9] The Court ruled that a federal judge can order integration of the staff if the circumstances so demand.

As the Supreme Court began to deal with the many questions of implementation associated with the *Brown* school desegregation order, one question was predictable: how would the Court rule on forced busing of children out of their neighborhoods for the sole purpose of integration? On April 20, 1971, the atmosphere was again charged with emotion as the Supreme Court announced that it had unanimously upheld the busing of students as a legitimate tool for desegregation. It also approved various techniques for rezoning school

[6] *Ibid.*
[7] *Griffin* v. *Prince Edward County School Board,* United States Supreme Court, 377 U.S. 218, 1964.
[8] *Green* v. *New Kent County,* United States Supreme Court, 391 U.S. 430, 1968.
[9] *United States* v. *Montgomery County Board of Education,* United States Supreme Court, 395 U.S. 225, 1969.

attendance areas as a means of bringing an abrupt end to the dual school systems of the South. Some 17 years after it had shown that where there is segregation, there is no equality, the Supreme Court ordered massive busing to integrate the Charlotte-Mecklenburg County, North Carolina school system.[10] The nation was waiting for a decision on this highly explosive question. When it came, reaction was quick and emotional. From the *Times-Dispatch* in Richmond, Virginia came these angry words:

> Following a grotesque logic, the Court arrived at the unanimous conclusion that there is, in effect, a dual standard on school integration in this country. While busing may be required in the South, it may not be required in the North.
>
> Neighborhood schools are acceptable . . . in the North but they are to be forbidden in the South. Serenity in Boston, said the Court, and chaos in Richmond. . . . A five-year-old in New Haven may walk to his neighborhood school, while a five-year-old in Richmond will ride across town to a strange school in a strange and remote neighborhood.
>
> It is an appallingly harsh decision, sickening to all who had hoped the Supreme Court would restore a measure of reason to the school desegregation policies now emanating from federal district courts.[11]

The Houston Chronicle had this to say:

> The decision written by Chief Justice Burger for a unanimous Court goes right down the line in upholding cross-town busing and the pairing, clustering or grouping of schools for the purpose of eliminating remaining vestiges of dual educational facilities for whites and blacks. . . .
>
> The Court has spoken. This is the law—until some future Court or constitutional amendment changes it. We fear it is going to hasten the white exodus from our central cities to the suburbs—a process already under way.[12]

Still another emotional outburst came from *The Dallas Morning News*:

> The Supreme Court's decision on busing to break up the pattern of neighborhood schools was a masterpiece of compound contradic-

[10] *Swann* v. *Charlotte-Mecklenburg Board of Education,* United States Supreme Court, 91 S. Ct., 1967, 1971.
[11] Editorial, *Times-Dispatch* (Richmond, Va.), April 22, 1971.
[12] Editorial, *The Houston Chronicle* (Houston, Texas), April 21, 1971.

tions. In telling the lower federal courts they could push ahead with plans to set up their own preferred racial proportions in each school, the Court adopted a position that has been opposed by the President, by the Congress—in several laws—and by the great majority of the American people.

Busing children back and forth across school districts solely for the purpose of establishing racial proportions is a concept that is popular with theoreticians but with almost no one else.[13]

The tone expressed in the above comments was predominant in much of the urban South following the Charlotte-Mecklenburg decision. Another point of view, however, was well expressed by the Little Rock, Arkansas, *Gazette:*

Across the South, there has been much pious condemnation of busing to integrate schools, in total disregard of all the years in which we in the South bused pupils of both races in every direction to keep them apart.

The sanctimony has been as hypocritical as the true motivation—resentment of integration—has been apparent.

In any event the Court has ruled in a fashion that [no one] can misinterpret. . . . Everywhere in the South, the effort to save the dual system is now doomed. School boards may no longer argue that they are waiting for the decision on Charlotte-Mecklenburg. To the contrary, they have their decision from Charlotte-Mecklenburg and let them fashion their policies accordingly.[14]

The above quotations are but a very small sampling. No single concept in all the arguments surrounding school integration has created so much fear and anger as busing. The notion of taking children out of their own neighborhoods to help integrate a school elsewhere outrages many parents. One need only recall the mob attacks on school buses carrying black children to previously all-white schools to remind himself of the intensity of emotion. The mob violence in Lamar, South Carolina, and Pontiac, Michigan, in the early 1970s exemplified the explosiveness of the issue in both the North and South.

Busing itself, however, is not the real issue. The underlying question is whether the Constitution requires students of individual public schools in multischool districts to be mixed racially in proportions equivalent to the composition of the entire district's student

---

[13] Editorial, *The Dallas Morning News* (Dallas, Texas), April 22, 1971.
[14] Editorial, *Gazette* (Little Rock, Ark.), April 21, 1971.

population. Herein lies a basic question of equal educational opportunity. At a time when so many segments of society are seeking equal treatment under the laws, the Supreme Court has applied the Equal Protection Clause to public school education with dramatic force. Its action has helped the lower courts to deal with many abuses of the 1954 *Brown* order to desegregate.

In *Swann* v. *Charlotte-Mecklenburg Board of Education,* the Court decided that mandatory racial mixing of school children is constitutional. The decision even mentioned a number of permissible methods for achieving such mixing.

> . . . One of the principal tools employed by school planners and by courts to break up the dual school system has been a frank—and sometimes drastic—gerrymandering of school districts and attendance zones. An additional step was pairing, "clustering" or "grouping" of schools with attendance assignments made deliberately to accomplish the transfer of white students to formerly all-Negro schools. More often than not, these zones . . . are not contiguous; indeed, they may be on opposite ends of the city. As an interim corrective measure, this cannot be said to be beyond the broad remedial powers of a court.[15]

The Court's firm stand regarding corrective measures was consistent with the thrust of every school decision since *Brown,* that is, that state-enforced separation of races is discrimination that violates the Equal Protection Clause of the Fourteenth Amendment. The remedy for such discrimination has been to dismantle dual school systems, and this is what was accomplished by the *Swann* case.

The Supreme Court provided in *Swann* an excellent illustration of one meaning of equal educational opportunity. The Court's decision considered many of the variables, including school environment, racial and class mix, and curricular diversity, which play such a crucial role in the quest for equal opportunity in the schools.

The Swann Case and the Desegregation Controversy

Until 1971, the forty-third largest school district in the country operated its schools with a dual system that separated black and white children. This deliberate enforcement of local governmental segregation policy conflicted sharply with the *Brown* decree, and it was not

---

[15] *Swann* v. *Charlotte-Mecklenburg Board of Education,* op. cit.

surprising when Charlotte-Mecklenburg was ordered by the Supreme Court to obey the law. This case has become a landmark decision because it provided an opportunity for the Supreme Court to define in more precise terms the scope and duty of school authorities and district courts in implementing the *Brown* decision. Prior to the *Swann* decision, the Supreme Court had not dealt with the intricate details of desegregation. Between the two decisions, school authorities and courts had used largely a process of "trial and error" in implementing the *Brown* decree. The *Swann* decision gave them detailed criteria with which to proceed.

The Charlotte-Mecklenburg school district covers 550 square miles of beautiful North Carolina countryside. The system serves approximately 85,000 pupils in over 100 schools. About 71 percent of those pupils are white; 29 percent, or approximately 25,000, are black. Of the 25,000 black students, 21,000 attended schools within the city of Charlotte. The important statistic is this: of the 21,000 black children attending school in Charlotte, two-thirds, or 14,000, attended 21 schools which were either totally black or more than 99 percent black.[16] Needless to say, this situation, with its obvious racial imbalance, fell short of meeting the conditions for a unitary school system under the law. In 1969 Mr. Swann filed suit against the schools, and the two-year federal court battle began. The United States District Court for the Western District of North Carolina heard lengthy testimony and held the school system guilty of discriminatory actions resulting from deliberate decisions to locate new schools in black residential areas—thereby failing to use the power of the board of education to desegregate the schools. In early 1969, the District Court ordered the school board to develop a plan for desegregation. When the board tried to stall by offering inadequate and unworkable desegregation plans, the court appointed Professor John Finger of the University of Rhode Island, an authority on educational administration, to prepare a scheme. By February, 1970, both the board and Dr. Finger had presented their plans.

A comparison of the "board plan" and the "Finger plan" suggests the sensitive issues faced by the district court. The board plan called for the closing of seven all-black schools and a restructuring of attendance zones to achieve greater racial balance. But the board rejected techniques such as the pairing of all-white and all-black

[16] *Swann* v. *Charlotte-Mecklenburg Board of Education,* op. cit., p. 1271.

schools as part of its desegregation effort. Using a scheme of pie-wedge shaped attendance zones extending into the suburbs, the board developed a desegregation plan producing a student body 17 to 36 percent black in nine of its ten high schools. The tenth school, however, was to be left only 2 percent black. A similar plan was offered for the junior high schools, only here the scheme would have left one school almost totally black. The elementary school scheme did even less toward achieving desegregation. Using gerrymandered zones, the board plan placed half the black children in nine schools that were to be 86 to 100 percent black while half the white students were to go to schools 86 to 100 percent white. It was clear that the board plan would not satisfy the courts. The Finger plan, which in effect modified the board plan, was eventually adopted by the court.

The first objective of the Finger plan was to desegregate all schools. The one high school left almost all white by the board plan, therefore, had to be integrated by busing black students to it. For the junior high schools, the Finger plan employed the concept of "satellite zones," geographical areas which fed into the school but were not contiguous with the main attendance zone surrounding the school. To ensure desegregation of all elementary schools, Dr. Finger proposed a combination of rezoning, school pairing, and grouping techniques with the result that all student bodies would range from 9 to 30 percent black, a figure very roughly approximating the 71 to 29 percent white-black ratio of children in the schools. It was essentially the Finger plan that was ordered into operation by the District Court and upheld by the Supreme Court.

Chapter 4 will analyze the legal arguments underlying the *Swann* case, including judicial intervention and the application of the Equal Protection Clause. In this chapter, our emphasis remains on illustrating the myriad facets of equal educational opportunity as seen through developments in desegregation in recent years. With some of the specifics of the *Swann* decision in mind, let us turn to how that case has helped clarify the law regarding student assignment in school districts.

As mentioned earlier, the most far-reaching aspect of the *Swann* decision was the Supreme Court's support of busing children to desegregate the schools. The remedy ordered by the Court, that is, the Finger plan, involved substantial amounts of busing. The Court reminded the Charlotte-Mecklenburg school board that "bus transportation has been an integral part of the public education system for years, and was perhaps the single most important factor in the transition from the one-room schoolhouse to the consolidated school." [17] Furthermore, the Court implied that the concept of neighborhood schools, long cherished in urban communities, must be abandoned if, as in this case, it did not guarantee racially mixed schools for children in predominantly minority neighborhoods. The board apparently tried to hide behind the historically reputable, neighborhood school in its persistent effort to avoid dismantling its system of dual schools. If one reads between the lines of the *Swann* decision, it is possible to sense that the Court expected the neighborhood school to decline as a vital educational institution. In the North as well as the South, neighborhood urban schools are no longer melting pots of larger society where children of different ethnic backgrounds can submerge their subcultural identities while becoming "Americanized." Thus, the desire to maintain the neighborhood, which has always been the principal argument against busing, seems to be losing its standing.

The *Swann* decision also has helped discourage one-race schools in systems which had historically maintained a segregated system. The court observed that the Charlotte metropolitan area was like many others where minority groups are often found concentrated in one part of the city. In areas such as this, certain schools may remain all of one race until new schools can be provided or neighborhood patterns change. The Court did warn, however, that "schools all or predominantly of one race in a district of mixed population will require close scrutiny to determine that school assignments are not part of state-enforced segregation." [18] Thus, even though the Court did not outlaw one-race schools, it did create conditions which make such schools in formerly dual districts almost impossible to maintain. This ruling, combined with the Court's support of busing, probably foreshadows the end of *de facto* segregation in the largest cities of the North as well as South.

A final major question arose in the *Swann* case: to what extent must racial balance be achieved in a biracial school system? On this point, the Court was quite emphatic in ensuring lower courts the right to order racial balancing in a school district. It even went so far as to

[17] *Swann* v. *Charlotte-Mecklenburg Board of Education*, op. cit., p. 1282.
[18] *Swann* v. *Charlotte-Mecklenburg Board of Education*, op. cit., p. 1281.

allow the mathematical 71 to 29 percent, white-black ratio to stand. Chief Justice Burger spoke directly to the Charlotte-Mecklenburg Board of Education when he wrote for the Court:

> The constant theme and thrust of every holding since *Brown* is that state-enforced separation of races in public schools is discrimination that violates the Equal Protection Clause. The remedy commanded was to dismantle dual school systems.
>
> Our objective in dealing with the issue presented in this case is to see that school authorities exclude no pupil of racial minority from any school, directly or indirectly on account of race. . . .
>
> As the voluminous record in this case shows, the predicate for the District Court's use of the 71–29% ratio was two-fold . . . second, its finding that the school board had totally defaulted in its acknowledged duty to come forward with an acceptable [desegregation] plan of its own, not withstanding the patient efforts of the District Judge who, on at least three occasions, urged the board to submit plans. . . . It was because of this total failure of the school board that the District Judge was obliged to turn to other qualified sources, and Dr. Finger was designated to assist the District Court to do what the board should have done.
>
> We see, therefore, that the use made of mathematical ratios was no more than a starting point in the process of shaping a remedy. From that starting point, the District Court proceeded to frame a decree that was within its discretionary powers. . . . Awareness of the racial composition of the whole school system is likely to be a useful starting point in shaping a remedy to correct past constitutional violations. In sum, the very limited use made of mathematical ratios was within the equitable remedial discretion of the District Court.[19]

What were the reasons offered by the Court in its support of a fixed ratio as "equitable remedial discretion" on the part of lower courts? There were at least three reasons, all of which reveal the Court's dissatisfaction with the slowness of desegregation. First, Charlotte-Mecklenburg had been operating a "dual system" in violation of the *Brown* decision long enough, in the judgment of the Court. The fixed ratio was, therefore, necessary to ensure action on the part of the board.

The second reason the Court decided to impose an iron hand on the Charlotte-Mecklenburg school authorities was that they had failed

---

[19] *Swann* v. *Charlotte-Mecklenburg Board of Education*, op. cit., p. 1280.

to make an effort "in good faith" to submit an acceptable alternative plan to the district court. The attitude of the Supreme Court on this point is apparent in the above remarks about the "patient efforts of the District Judge" and the total failure of the school board to do its job prior to the hiring of Dr. Finger. Thus, out of desperation the Court ordered the establishment of a black-white ratio which provides a standard by which to measure the amount of desegregation attained by the board. In effect, the *Swann* decision declares that there is a limit to the time that a school board can engage in dilatory tactics to avoid compliance with a court order to desegregate.

Finally, the Court employed the fixed ratio to force the board to act because, while it did force the board to act quickly, it also remained flexible and constituted only a "starting point" for remedial action. The Court was trying to leave the door open for lower courts to apply a similar remedy at their discretion, depending on the local circumstances.

Again in *Swann*, as in *Brown*, the Supreme Court has asserted its desire to see racial balance in all schools now suffering from state-imposed segregation. The Court does not intend to relax its position on this matter regardless of increasing pressure from the President and Congress to do so.

The President, Congress, and the Struggle for Educational Equality

In recent years, the controversy over school desegregation has engulfed not only the judiciary but also the executive and legislative branches of government. The determination on the part of the Supreme Court to guarantee implementation of the *Brown* decree and, thereby, to ensure equal protection of the laws to all, regardless of race, is just one aspect of contemporary school desegregation doctrine. Since 1970, both the President and Congress have tried to influence desegregation principles. With both the increasing public debate initiated in Congress and the difficult political predicament faced by the President—who is responsible for enforcing Supreme Court decisions—the meaning of equality of educational opportunity has become even more cloudy. The political ramifications of present-day desegregation doctrine, however, are becoming clearer. In fact, the political implications dramatize the importance of that doctrine in a society determined to achieve equality in all realms of human activity.

President Nixon made it clear as early as March, 1970, that he would not risk losing Southern support by taking a strong stand in favor of increased school desegregation. In fact, while the Supreme Court was considering whether to hear the *Swann* case, the President tried subtly to influence the Court's decision by praising the ideal of the neighborhood school and attacking the use of busing. He was, in effect, suggesting a slowdown of integration, and his words were widely applauded by Southerners still seeking to delay desegregation. When the Court decided to hear the *Swann* case, the President immediately ordered the Justice Department to enter the deliberations on behalf of the Charlotte-Mecklenburg school board. The argument presented by the Nixon Administration was that the desegregation plan was not constitutionally required and that massive cross-town busing, redrawing of school districts, and a 71 to 29 percent white-black ratio were all impractical and would lead to chaos and the exodus of the remaining whites from the city of Charlotte. The Justice Department contended further that excessive busing was being demanded and that children had the right to attend their own neighborhood school.

The intrusion of the President into this case was more political than legal. A stance against strong federal enforcement of desegregation is popular in both the North and South, and President Nixon has tried to capitalize on this sentiment. Some Court watchers waited anxiously for the *Swann* decision because it was the first major school desegregation case since the appointment of Chief Justice Warren Burger. Since it now appears that the Supreme Court intends to continue its liberal approach to school desegregation issues, the President is torn as to whether to adopt a more active role in upholding justice in keeping with *Swann* and other desegregation principles. With racial friction still dividing the nation, however, the President's stance seems to be to enforce the law minimally in the South. His reaction to the Court's ruling was low-keyed, even bland. Following the landmark *Swann* decision, President Nixon merely authorized his press secretary to observe that administration officials "will continue to carry out their statutory responsibilities regarding enforcement of this Supreme Court decision." As one columnist noted, that statement does not have the ring of strong presidential leadership on one of the nation's most agonizing and enduring domestic crises.

The role of the President in the days before and after the *Swann* decision illustrates the wide discrepancy among national leaders and even the branches of government regarding the most effective way to bring about equal educational opportunity. It also serves as a reminder that the struggle for educational equality cannot be separated from the overall political milieu.

While President Nixon was remaining quiet over the latest episode in school desegregation litigation, the Congress was engrossed in one of its most intense debates. Calls for anti-busing legislation, a Constitutional amendment to ban busing, and demands for widespread debate were triggered by both Southern and Northern Congressmen. The cause of the congressional upheaval, oddly enough, was the Supreme Court's inaction, not its action in the *Swann* decision. The Court angered the South by not attempting to decide whether the federal judiciary should require school boards to submit plans to reverse the rapid rise in *de facto* segregated schools in Northern cities. The *Swann* ruling did not apply to situations where voluntary neighborhood patterns created racial imbalance in schools or even where other official agencies, such as planning boards and housing authorities, helped create or sustain segregated neighborhoods. The failure to deal with *de facto* segregation caused many Southerners to question the double racial standard seemingly being practiced. The Court ordered tough action against the urban South but no action at all against large Northern cities.

Some Southerners felt that the Court was more interested in punishing them than in eradicating segregation. They noted that school segregation in the North was more extensive than in the South. In 1971, in the Northern states roughly 58 percent of black school children were attending schools that were 80 to 100 percent black; in the South only 39 percent of black children fell into that category. Only 28 percent of Northern black pupils go to schools where there is a white majority, compared with 40 percent of Southern blacks.[20] Figures like this caused several Congressmen to try to force the North to "practice what it preaches."

The Senate spent the entire week following the *Swann* decision debating the difference between Northern and Southern segregation. As a result, liberal Abraham Ribicoff of Connecticut and conservative John Stennis of Mississippi co-sponsored a controversial bill designed to require nationwide desegregation of all metropolitan areas. The proposal was to require city and suburban schools to disregard their

[20] "Busing: The Court Rules," *Newsweek*, May 3, 1971, p. 27.

boundaries in order to achieve a minimum racial balance within a 12-year period. Each school in the region would be required to enroll black students at a rate of one-half the percentage of black students residing within the given area. This program, which was an amendment to a Nixon-Administration Southern desegregation bill, provoked bitter debate. Not only did Southern Senators attack their Northern colleagues, but the debate found liberals arguing with fellow liberals. Most notable was a charge by Senator Ribicoff aimed at liberals in general and Senator Jacob Javits of New York in particular. Ribicoff noted the hypocrisy of many Congressmen who prefer not to confront their liberal white constituents with a desegregation dilemma, especially when "these people have moved to the suburbs for the sole purpose of avoiding having their children attend schools with blacks." While his bill was being defeated, Ribicoff warned that without such a measure the country will move closer to apartheid, with the cities black and the suburbs mainly white.

As of this writing, the struggle for equal educational opportunity continues to influence political and educational decision making. In the presidential primaries of 1972, for example, school desegregation played a crucial role. Governor George Wallace, the Democratic Party winner in the State of Florida, outspokenly opposed busing. He also considered himself to be a proponent of equal educational opportunity. This seeming paradox, that there can be equality of educational opportunity without desegregation, was ascribed to by 80 percent of the Florida voters. When asked if they were against busing, 80 percent said "yes," while approximately the same percentage voted affirmatively on a resolution calling for equal educational opportunity practices.

In an effort to clarify the concept of equal opportunity in education, the Supreme Court will soon attack the difficult problem of *de facto* segregation in large Northern cities. These forthcoming decisions will bring new meaning to the concept of equality because they will affect not only schools but the entire political and economic life of the North.

The School Finance Controversy

Today's judicial system provides us with another dramatic illustration of the continuing struggle for equality in education: the recent challenge to long-established patterns of school finance in the United

States. The similarities between the desegregation and finance issues are striking. First, both challenge deep-seated and well-accepted traditions. In the case of desegregation, we have seen how federal law was changed so as to eliminate state-imposed segregation. Now previously unquestioned state school finance structures are being attacked because of the inequalities they create for certain segments of our society.

A second similarity between the desegregation and school finance controversies is that both have been challenged in the courts by means of the Equal Protection Clause of the Fourteenth Amendment. Finally, both focus on the same basic variables, the same aspects of equality of educational opportunity. For example, in the desegregation illustration, the variable of educational equality was found to be related to racial mix, environmental circumstances, and the like. Similarly, the quest for both quality and equality in education has played a major role in the rapidly emerging school finance controversy.

Until the early 1970s, school finance was a topic practically unheard of and certainly not at all understood by the layman. Now, however, because of a number of recent court decisions declaring typical state school finance structures unconstitutional, there has been an upsurge of interest in educational finance. Previously, neither the average citizen nor the typical school administrator or legislator was conversant in the language of density factors, state sharing ratios, teacher units, foundation programs, and the other technical terms used in deriving formulas ostensibly designed to guarantee equal educational opportunity. Today citizens are becoming familiar with the terms. Newspapers regularly feature such stories as "State Court Questions the School Tax," "Governors Urged to Equalize School Cost," and "The Property Tax Found to be Cause of Unequal Education." What is the background of the "traditional" system being questioned, and why does it cause unequal education?

Historically, American education has been supported in a number of ways. The notion of supporting schools at public expense evolved slowly and sometimes painfully. The first American schools were private ones supported by tuition, endowments, and voluntary contributions. There were no precedents for public schools, and the early settlers did not readily recognize the need for them. There was, however, early recognition that education was a state function. The people were well aware that the federal Constitution did not mention education and that the Tenth Amendment provided that "The powers not delegated to the United States by the Constitution; nor prohibited by it to the States, are reserved to the State respectively, or to the people." Thus, silence about education in the Constitution, coupled with the Tenth Amendment, placed the burden of public education on the states. Even though education was recognized as a state function, however, the states assumed little responsibility for it before the 1860s. Prior to the Civil War, the states largely ignored those children whose parents could not afford private schools. At best, some states maintained pauper schools to provide rudimentary skills for indigent children.

The problem of state responsibility for education came to a head in 1874 with the *Kalamazoo* case. This famous decision upheld the right of school districts in Michigan to levy and collect taxes for the operation of secondary schools, thus paving the way for a free public school system. Nevertheless, the transition from private to public education was quite complicated. Haphazard financial assistance from public sources, such as revenue from federal land grants, had to be replaced by more reliable funds. The creation of school districts with the power to levy taxes for school support took many years. Next, legislation had to be passed in all states requiring local communities to make provisions for the education of those whose parents could not afford it. Finally, the states took many years eliminating tuition charges, assuming all school costs, and discontinuing the pauper schools. It was not until the first decades of the twentieth century that completely free schools as we know them today came into existence.[21]

As the system has evolved over the years, the state has maintained the legal responsibility to provide education for its citizens, but most of the operating responsibility has been delegated by the state to local school districts or systems and finally to boards of education and local administrators. State departments of education provide broad leadership, planning, and supervision; but for practical purposes, education falls within the province of local school districts. Today there are over 17,000 local school districts varying in size, taxing ability, urbanization, and many other factors. This dissimilarity among districts, coupled with the American fondness for local control, inherently limits attempts to assure equal educational opportunity for

[21] Percy E. Burrup, *The Teacher and the Public School System* (New York: Harper and Row, 1967), pp. 313–314.

all citizens. The emphasis upon local control of education has meant that very small local units are making the principal educational decisions. Because of this desire for local control, the number of districts is extremely large and the expenditures per child vary greatly from one district to the next.[22]

Given the prevalence of the traditional school system, what are the existing structural arrangements and practices which provide the money for the public schools? In general, the schools are financed by taxes on real property. In the United States in 1970–1971, about 52 percent of school revenue was provided from local sources, 41 percent from state sources, and 7 percent from the federal government. There is wide variation among the states in respect to the proportion of funds derived from local, state, and federal sources. For example, in New Hampshire 86 percent of the school funds is derived from local taxes, 10 percent comes from the state, and 4 percent comes from the federal government. North Carolina, in sharp contrast, gets 19 percent from local sources, 66 percent from the state, and 15 percent from the federal government. The recent trend seems to be toward greater state and federal aid and less revenue coming from the local districts.

As mentioned above, the state, acting through its legislature, creates school districts as organizational entities and delegates to these districts the responsibility for governing and operating the schools. In a similar way, the state delegates its financial obligations to local school districts. In other words, the state requires local districts to levy taxes to raise funds for the schools. These funds generally are obtained through a tax on local real estate. In fact, school districts receive about 98 percent of their local tax revenue from taxes on property. Thus, the amount of money available for education depends upon the value of the real estate in the district and the amount of the tax levy. A district with low property value—a poor district—may well have less revenue than a wealthy district even if its taxing rate is higher.

The other major source of funds for the public schools, is, of course, the state itself. Among the many types of taxes which provide school revenue at the state level are the sales tax, the income tax, and the motor vehicle and gasoline tax. The major problem faced by the

[22] Clifford L. Dochterman, *Understanding Education's Financial Dilemma* (Denver: Education Commission of the States, 1972), p. 5.

states is how to apportion the funds collected in a fair manner to the local school districts. All states try to provide their local districts with a minimum of funds and then to equalize opportunity among districts with some sort of so-called equalization formula. In theory, the poorer districts should receive more state money and the wealthier districts less. This ideal is hard to achieve, however, because there are no intrastate real estate assessing standards. Neither are there any effective measures for determining the ability of local districts to support their schools. Consequently, there are wide variations in state expenditures per pupil. When these variations are combined with the inadequacies of the local tax structures, it is easy to understand why the entire system has been the center of recent controversy. The compound effect of both the local and state inadequacies is an enormous discrepancy between class size, teacher salaries, and school facilities in wealthy districts and those in poorer ones.

Note that the previous discussion—like that which follows—assumes that the quality of education depends directly upon its cost. In other words, the more money spent on education in a particular district, the more likely it is that the children are getting a better education. This correlation between cost and quality underlies the thinking of every existing school system, and nearly all systems of finance permit districts to apply varying tax rates and spend varying amounts per pupil in order to implement local aspirations and meet local needs.

The cost-quality relationship has been the basis of our state equalization formulas for decades, yet in a sense it has led to discrimination rather than equalization. There is no question that states have tried to help poor districts without limiting the per pupil expenditures or, more technically, the "offerings" of wealthy districts. In so doing, they have employed state aid plans and practices which have created situations of discrimination because of the imbalance in expenditures within states. For example, the underlying *flat grant* state aid plan still employed in many states is actually a nonequalizing system. In other words, the flat grant has no impact at all on *district wealth,* which is defined as the dollar value of a given tax source per pupil (such as the assessed valuation per pupil of real estate in a given district).[23]

[23] John E. Coons, William H. Clune, and Stephen Sugarman, "Educational Opportunity: A Workable Constitutional Test for State Financial Structures," *California Law Review,* April, 1969, pp. 312–316.

The flat grant is an absolute number of state dollars paid to a district on a per pupil basis. Rich and poor districts both get flat grants; thus, the offerings, or per pupil expenditures, of the districts are raised but the gap between rich and poor is left unchanged. In short, the "flat grant" is simply nonequalizing.[24]

Another typical state aid arrangement, known as the *foundation plan,* is a guarantee to the district that if it will make a determined "effort" by taxing itself at a specified minimum level, the state will give it a certain number of dollars per pupil. The state dollar minimum will be forthcoming only if the district fails to reach a state-guaranteed figure on its own. Suppose, under the foundation plan, the state guarantees $500 per pupil for a one-percent district effort. Furthermore, the poorest district has an assessed valuation per pupil of $10,000 and the richest district has an assessed valuation per pupil of $100,000. Each taxes at a specified minimum qualifying level of one percent. The first district thus raises $100 per pupil locally and is given $400 per pupil by the state to reach the guaranteed minimum. The second district raises $1,000 locally with the same one-percent tax rate effort and receives no state aid. In this case the foundation plan has a partially equalizing effect because it reduces, but does not eliminate, the disparity between the two districts.[25]

Combinations of the flat grant and foundation plan exist in many states, and they usually tend to be anti-equalizing in their effect. In other words, often when the two aid plans are combined, as in California and Illinois, state dollars serve to exaggerate wealth differentials and in effect provide a wealthy district with a bonus for being rich. These grossly unfair state aid plans are now being tested in court; the results of the court test in California are described below.

In studying the traditional school finance structures, we have seen that their vulnerability lies mainly in their failure to equalize educational expenditures among rich and poor communities. If we grant that there is a positive relationship between cost and quality in education, then the amount of money available, in affecting the quality of education, must also help determine the equality of educational opportunity being provided by a particular district. Equality and quality are interrelated: equality is not guaranteed when quality

[24] *Ibid.*
[25] *Ibid.*

is absent. It is this principle that was enunciated by the California Supreme Court in *Serrano* v. *Priest* [26] and by the three-judge Texas Federal Court in *Rodriguez* v. *San Antonio Independent School District*.[27]

Our discussion of the *Serrano* and *Rodriguez* cases, however, should not make us think that the dollar is the only requirement for equality in education. Desegregation (racial mix) has already been introduced as a possible requirement for equality, and there are numerous other plausible criteria. Also, we do not claim that large amounts of money infused into a school system would guarantee measurably increased educational output. Social scientists are still researching these relationships. Nevertheless, in our capitalistic society quality is generally reflected in cost. Thus, even though per pupil expenditure does not tell the whole story of quality and equality, it is an important index of differences in school districts. Today it is fairly certain that poor districts are providing a poorer quality of education than wealthy districts, and this phenomenon represents discrimination against poor people. Certainly the *Serrano* and *Rodriguez* cases, which illustrate the challenge to traditional patterns of school finance structure, relied on the finding that wide variations in expenditures and in ability to support education are a major obstacle to substantial equality of educational opportunity.

The principles and legal theory underlying the *Serrano* and *Rodriguez* decisions have had an impact, as we will see, not only upon persons directly concerned with school finance but also upon general public attitude toward the quest for equal educational opportunity in our nation. The basic constitutional arguments in *Rodriguez*, the case that reached the Supreme Court, were actually those developed earlier in *Serrano*. For this reason, the historic *Serrano* case is presented below to illustrate the Equal Protection Clause doctrine which was eventually rejected by the Court. Even though the Supreme Court reversed the *Rodriguez* decision in 1973, the eloquent *Serrano* arguments have become the basis of a reform movement in public school financing. Rather than discourage reformers, the reversal of *Rodriguez* has already stimulated attorneys to develop new constitutional theories to pursue their court battles.

[26] *Serrano* v. *Priest,* California Supreme Court, 96 Cal. Rptr. 601.

[27] *Rodriguez* v. *San Antonio Independent School District,* 337 F. Supp. 280 (Western District of Texas).

The Serrano Case

Judicial intervention in educational decision making was more conspicuous in 1971 than in any year since the historic *Brown* decision. Only 4 months after the United States Supreme Court ordered the use of busing to desegregate the Charlotte-Mecklenburg public schools, the California Supreme Court threw educational systems throughout the country again into turmoil. The Charlotte-Mecklenburg decision, as we have seen, touched off a controversy that promises to continue until all school districts—Northern and Southern —are desegregated in accordance with the *Brown* decree. The landmark decision of the California Supreme Court in *Serrano* v. *Priest* has already triggered a revolution in educational finance that may have as significant implications for equal opportunity as those which resulted from *Brown*. The *Serrano* decision said, simply, that the level of spending for a child's public education should not depend on the wealth of his school district or family. In the words of the court:

> We are called upon to determine whether the California public school financing system, with its substantial dependence on local property taxes and resultant wide disparities in school revenue, violates the Equal Protection Clause of the Fourteenth Amendment. We have determined that this funding scheme invidiously discriminates against the poor because it makes the quality of a child's education a function of the wealth of his parents and his neighbors. Recognizing as we must that the right to an education in our public schools is a fundamental interest which cannot be conditioned on wealth, we can discern no compelling state purpose necessitating the present method of financing. We have concluded, therefore, that such a system cannot withstand constitutional challenge and must fall before the Equal Protection Clause.[28]

The court's decision stirred parents, educators, legislators, politicians, and taxpayers alike. Local school administrators were left wondering where their next dollar would come from. Legislators were confused over the leadership they might provide to local school districts. Politicians, depending upon their level of government, were preparing for questions regarding their stands on the many subissues raised by the decision. Taxpayers, of course, feared more and higher

[28] *Ibid.*, p. 604.

taxes. The U.S. Commissioner of Education, a former big-city superintendent, was elated by the decision. He said:

> . . . the California decision, if upheld by the Supreme Court, would
> have a national impact. . . . It may expedite a long-sought solution
> to the issue of equal schooling among communities within a state.
> The ruling would lead to greater federal financing of public schools
> to equalize the quality of education among the states. Furthermore,
> the states' financial burden of expenditures for public schools would
> increase if the California decision obtains throughout the nation.
> . . . Finally, the decision would especially affect cities.[29]

It is clear that the Commissioner felt that the effects of the
Serrano case would be positive and that any revamping of support
structure for education would eventually benefit the large cities where
the disparities are greatest. The *New York Times* editorial following
the decision was a bit more cautious:

> Equality of educational opportunity has become ever more crucial
> in contemporary terms of human rights and economic well-being.
> State support in its present form merely builds a floor—often too
> low—under local school budgets; it does not effectively narrow the
> gap between rich and poor localities. . . . There is nothing sacred
> in the traditional reliance on property taxes to finance the schools.
> . . . Any adequate revision of present equalization formulas will,
> if it truly aims at closing the gap between rich and poor districts,
> move toward virtually full state financing. This is the proper course,
> provided it is not fastened upon as a way to level expenditures down
> to a lowest common denominator of support for educational medi-
> ocrity.[30]

Ironically, the decision drew some of its most favorable reactions
from the defendants, especially the California Superintendent of Public Instruction:

> The opinion of the Court conforms to my own view of a most seri-
> ous problem in education. We've been stating all along that the
> method by which we have financed public schools is inequitable and
> unfair and that the quality of a child's education should not depend
> on where he lives in the state.[31]

[29] "Wild Impact Seen in Schools Ruling," *New York Times,* September
1, 1971, p. 23.
[30] "Equal Rights to Learn," *New York Times,* September 2, 1971, p. 32.
[31] "Coast Court Questions the School Tax," *New York Times,* August 31,
1971, p. 23.

Most observers agreed that the court made possible a redistribution of resources in favor of poor communities and, at the same time, cleared the way for state governments to lift from hard-pressed communities the major burden of financing education. Transcending all the above remarks was an urgency of purpose and a recognition that the impact of the ruling was in a class with that of the *Brown* case.

In arriving at its conclusion that the quality of a child's education should not depend upon the wealth of his parents or his neighbors, the court viewed the California finance structure in light of the Equal Protection Clause. For the first time, traditional finance patterns were tested against the Fourteenth Amendment, which had been used successfully to strike down Southern school desegregation. Education was viewed as a "fundamental societal interest" by the court in its argument to declare the California school system unconstitutional. Thus *Serrano* attempted to establish, in a manner similar to the holding in *Swann,* that education is a human right which is not to be influenced by either place of birth or family means.

The logic of the California court in arriving at its decision illustrates one line of reasoning used by those seeking relief from the discrimination which they feel is inherent in many of the established structures and procedures in our society. The public school finance system is just one of those structures. In showing that quality in education is dependent upon financial support and that lack of wealth in a district must not be allowed to deprive children of a quality education, the court illustrated many of the variables and concepts under consideration in this book.

First, in considering the *Serrano* case, the court studied the finance system in California. It found that, as in other states, the major source of school revenue is the local real estate tax. Also as with other states, the districts' tax bases vary widely throughout the state. In general, the majority of the money is raised locally by combining the value of the real property in a particular district with that district's willingness to tax itself for education. The money not raised locally comes to the district by means of a typical state aid program. Not surprisingly, the court found wide disparities in the revenue available to individual districts and, consequently, in the level of per pupil expenditures. The court chose as its example the communities of Baldwin Park and Beverly Hills. The former spent $577 to educate each child while the latter expended $1,232 per child. In spite of this tremendous difference, and through a fault in the state aid system, both Baldwin Park and Beverly Hills received a flat grant. It is this type of discrepancy which led the plaintiff to claim that the school finance scheme violates the Equal Protection Clause of the Fourteenth Amendment.

The disparity between the districts, however, is not itself sufficient for the court to conclude that pupils failed to receive equal protection before the law. In order to rule that the school finance system was inadequate, the court had to be convinced that there was inequality of *educational opportunity*. In other words, the wide disparities among districts were not in themselves unconstitutional.

The court's reasoning in the *Serrano* case focused upon the fact that wealth (through property) seemed to play a part in the determination of school aid. Indeed, the relation of wealth to equal educational opportunity was of utmost concern to John Serrano in early 1968. Serrano had two extremely bright and capable sons whose potential he felt was going untested. The Serrano family lived in East Los Angeles in a poor, mainly Mexican-American community. In their neighborhood, the number of poor and minority children was increasing rapidly. As the neighborhood changed in composition, the resources available to the local school were being spread thinner and thinner. It was apparent to Serrano that class sizes were getting larger, teacher time for his children was becoming scarce, and even textbooks and equipment seemed to be in short supply. When Serrano finally went to the school to discuss his observations with the principal, he learned that the school authorities were despondent over the existing conditions and that they saw little hope for improvement in the near future. The principal told Serrano that, in his opinion, the district probably could not provide his sons with the education they needed to achieve at their learning capacity. The family decided that a good education was essential for the children regardless of cost or sacrifice. Accordingly, Serrano mortgaged his personal property and moved to Whittier, California, a neighboring but more affluent community. In Whittier, the boys found the educational challenge they needed.[32]

The plight of the Serrano family is not unusual in our country. What is unusual, however, is the considerable sacrifice that this family underwent in order to secure an adequate education for the boys. The experience moved Serrano to think seriously about questions such as

[32] Dochterman, *op. cit.*, p. 9.

these. Should parents be asked to make the type of personal sacrifice he did in order to obtain a decent education for their children? Should not good education be available to all rather than be a function of the wealth of a child's parents and neighbors? Is not education a "fundamental interest" of the nation, a right which should not be conditioned on wealth? Should the state be allowed to maintain a school finance system which depends upon a local property tax reflecting the differences in local wealth? [33]

These somewhat broad questions, formulated by Serrano, contain the essence of the argument presented later to the California Supreme Court in a suit filed against state and local officials. The use of local wealth as a basis for a state school finance structure was the primary issue. In the words of the court:

> Plaintiffs contend that the school financing system classifies on the basis of wealth. We find this proposition irrefutable. . . . Over half of all educational revenue is raised locally by levying taxes on real property in the individual school districts. Above the foundation program minimum, the wealth of a school district . . . is the major determinant of educational expenditures. . . . Districts with small tax bases simply cannot levy taxes at a rate sufficient to produce the revenue that more affluent districts reap with minimal tax effort. For example, Baldwin Park citizens who paid a school tax of $5.48 per $100 of assessed valuation, were able to spend less than half as much on education as Beverly Hills residents, who were taxed only $2.38 per $100.[34]

After establishing that wealth cannot be used as a basis for the California school finance system, the court went on to strike down all arguments presented by the defense regarding this point. One particular refutation by the court directly confronts the issue of wealth and inequality:

> But, say defendants, the expenditure per child does not accurately reflect a district's wealth because that expenditure is partly determined by the district's tax rate. Thus, a district with a high total assessed valuation might levy a low school tax, and end up spending the same amount per pupil as a poorer district whose residents opt to pay higher taxes. This argument is also meritless. Obviously, the richer district is favored when it can provide the same educational quality for its children with less tax effort. Furthermore, as a

---

[33] *Ibid.*, p. 10.
[34] California Supreme Court, *op. cit.*, p. 608.

statistical matter the poorer districts are financially unable to raise their taxes high enough to match the educational offerings of wealthier districts. Thus, affluent districts can have their cake and eat it too: they can provide a high quality education for their children while paying lower taxes. Poor districts, by contrast, have no cake at all.[35]

Another aspect of the Fourteenth Amendment challenge to the traditional school finance system in California is the assertion that education is a "fundamental societal interest" and, as such, must be available to all on an equal basis. The *fundamental interest* argument has deep historical roots. The concept has been applied to the rights of defendants in criminal cases as well as to voting privileges. Education as a fundamental interest also has long legal standing, but perhaps this concept is best expressed in the *Brown* decision. In that case the Supreme Court recognized that education is a major determinant of a person's chances for success in our society and that education influences a child's political socialization in all respects. According to the Court in *Brown:*

> Today, education is perhaps the most important function of state and local government. Compulsory school attendance laws and the great expenditures for education both demonstrate our recognition of the importance of education to our democratic society. It is required in the performance of our most basic public responsibilities, even service in the armed forces. It is the very foundation of good citizenship. Today it is a principal instrument in awakening the child to cultural values, in preparing him for later professional training, and in helping him to adjust normally to his environment. In these days, it is doubtful that any child may reasonably be expected to succeed in life if he is denied the opportunity of an education. Such an opportunity, where the state has undertaken to provide it, is a right which must be made available to all on equal terms.[36]

To embellish its argument that education is a fundamental interest, the court in *Serrano* continued:

> We are convinced that the distinctive and priceless function of education in our society warrants, indeed compels, our treating it as a "fundamental interest."
>
> First, education is essential in maintaining what several com-

[35] *Ibid.*, p. 612.
[36] *Ibid.*, p. 617.

mentators have termed "free enterprise democracy"—that is, preserving an individual's opportunity to compete successfully in the economic marketplace, despite a disadvantaged background. Accordingly, the public schools of this state are the bright hope for entry of the poor and oppressed into the mainstream of American society.

Second, education is universally relevant. . . .

Third, public education continues over a lengthy period of life. . . . Few other government services have such sustained, intensive contact with the recipient.

Fourth, education is unmatched in the extent to which it molds the personality of the youth of society.[37]

As a result of the above reasoning, the court was convinced that education was a fundamental societal interest. As such it could not, of course, be denied in quality to anyone because of the accident of place of birth or individual wealth. Nevertheless, one significant contradiction remained for the court to resolve: whether local control of education might be curtailed by judging the current school support scheme invalid. Local control in education has been a basic tenet of our democracy for generations. As the traditional school finance structures are challenged, scholars and politicians alike have begun to ask whether there can be local control if fiscal control becomes centralized. The assumption is that if finance systems such as that in California are struck down as unconstitutional, the funding arrangements for schools will become increasingly centralized. Many people at one time considered local control to be synonymous with equality of opportunity because they felt it produced variety, competition, experimentation, and citizen participation. But the court in *Serrano* seems to be saying that equality of opportunity can only be guaranteed if the financing of education is removed from local control and returned to the state level of government. Thus, if equality of opportunity and local control cannot be accommodated in a single system, there is a contradiction. The court resolved this matter by observing that "far from being necessary to promote local fiscal choice, the present financing system actually deprives the less wealthy districts of that option." [38] The court concluded that "no matter how the state decides to finance its system of public education, it can still leave (most of the current) decision-making power in the hands of local

[37] *Ibid.*, p. 619.
[38] *Ibid.*, p. 620.

districts." [39] In other words, the court denied that centralized finance would limit local control of education.

Serrano illustrates one of the most significant recent historical developments in the search for equal educational opportunity. It was an attempt to show, through an interpretation of the Equal Protection Clause of the Fourteenth Amendment, (1) that education is a "fundamental right" and (2) that traditional school finance patterns are unlawful because they classify pupils on the basis of their collective affluence and make the quality of a child's education dependent upon the resources of his school district and "upon the pocketbook of his parents." [40]

When the Supreme Court in the *Rodriguez* case struck down arguments based on the Equal Protection Clause, such as the "fundamental societal interest" or "fundamental right" notion, it nullified as well that portion of the *Serrano* case based on the Fourteenth Amendment. The Court did not deny the great importance of education to our society, but it did note that education is not a right either explicitly or implicitly guaranteed by the Constitution.

In an effort to construct new legal challenges following the Supreme Court decision in the *Rodriguez* case, reformers have turned their attention to school finance cases which can be based on state constitutions, because the Supreme Court has no jurisdiction over such state decisions. The interpretation of the state supreme court is usually final. Thus, in the case of *Robinson* v. *Cahill,* the Supreme Court of New Jersey held that the New Jersey system of school finance denied taxpayers the equal protection of the laws. Because the decision was based on the New Jersey constitution, it was immune from *Rodriguez* and other U.S. Supreme Court decisions—despite its striking similarity to the *Serrano* case.

In addition to challenges at the state level, lawyers have begun to recast the "fundamental right" theory in terms of the "great importance to our society" argument, thereby recognizing that education is not a right of each citizen. This is a very complex legal approach based on the cost–quality relationship in education as well as the question of local control. Still other legal challenges are certain to emerge as reform lawyers study the *Rodriguez* decision. These developments are examined in Chapter 5.

[39] *Ibid.*
[40] *Ibid.,* p. 623.

Chapter 3 has presented two dramatic illustrations of the struggle for equality in education. The first traced the development of school desegregation doctrine, while the second presented a challenge to the long-established funding structure of American education. Both are historic illustrations which promise to affect education and the struggle for equality in our society for many years.

Chapter 4

Perspectives on Equal Educational Opportunity

Equality of educational opportunity is a complex concept for many reasons, several of which have been discussed in preceding chapters. The concept is indeterminate. Yet perhaps much of the reason that it defies definition is that it is essentially prescriptive rather than descriptive. *Equality of educational opportunity* does not describe an actual state of affairs. It deals with "oughts"—what *should* be, what is *desired,* what is hoped for—and, of course, people inevitably disagree over what *ought* to be. The man who defines equality takes a moral stand. His moralizing may be good—even necessary—but it makes our coming to grips with the issue of equality of educational opportunity and arriving at a universal definition of the concept extremely difficult.

Another factor contributing to the complexity of equal educational opportunity is its many-sidedness. Like so many other issues, it can be analyzed from any number of perspectives. Which of the many analytical possibilities and perspectives should be included in a book such as this? Which should be emphasized? Which should be underplayed or even ignored?

The selections which follow reflect a variety of scholarly perspectives through which equal educational opportunity can be analyzed. They include philosophical, legal, economic, historical, and sociological analyses. The selections do not exhaust the perspectives through which this issue can be studied, nor does each article exhaust the possibilities within the perspective it represents. But they do represent those perspectives which have influentially shaped educational policies in the United States. Above all, they: (1) *represent* some of the major analytical perspectives through which the issue can be examined, (2) *analyze* the several ways in which the concept of equality of educational opportunity can be interpreted, (3) *portray* the shifts in interpretation of this concept throughout our educational history, (4) *examine* legal interpretations, (5) *analyze* the legal history of this concept, (6) *emphasize* the increased influence of the courts in defining this concept and its practical implications, and (7) *indicate* the current and prevailing interpretation of equal educational opportunity.

The Philosophical Context

The Concept of Equality in Education
B. PAUL KOMISAR & JERROLD R. COOMBS

The first selection approaches the concept of equality of educational opportunity by analyzing the term *equality*. What meanings, relevant to educational opportunity, are attached to *equality*? The authors point out that *equality* can be, and has been, interpreted in two ways: "equal as same" and "equal as fitting." They show how these two conceptions are usually tied to two different uses of language—descriptive and ascriptive.

The authors' analysis leads them to conclude that the term *equality*, rightly understood, has no fixed meaning, that it shifts in meaning given different contexts. Accordingly, they reject the "equal as same" conception because it assumes specific meanings appropriate in all contexts. Furthermore, they conclude that the principle of equality is a second-order principle; it is derived from first-order, or prior, ethical principles. Given these conclusions, the authors remind us that definitions of *equality* do not dictate our educational preferences. Rather, our educational preferences should suggest our meanings for *equality*.

SOURCE: *Studies in Philosophy and Education,* Vol. III, No. 3 (Fall, 1964), pp. 223–244. Reprinted, with some editing, by permission of the publishers and authors.

By addressing themselves to "equal as same" and "equal as fitting," the authors examine the reasoning behind the traditional "equal inputs" approach to equal opportunity. This approach uses the "equal as same" conception. Moreover, in their treatment of the "equal as fitting" conception, the authors help us to understand the arguments flowing from the Coleman study, that equal educational opportunity should be measured in terms of "educational outputs": how students will achieve in school.

B. Paul Komisar is Professor of Education at Temple University. He has written numerous articles which have appeared widely in professional and scholarly journals. He is also co-editor of the book, *Psychological Concepts in Education.* Jerrold Coombs is Professor of Education at the University of British Columbia. He has written for several professional and scholarly journals.

In the course of this paper we advance and try to justify the following claims: There are two concepts of equality—"equal as same" and "equal as fitting" tied usually to two different uses of language—descriptive and ascriptive. The sameness concept has a determinate definition and a singular meaning in all contexts of application. Equality in the fittingness sense has an indeterminate definition; its meaning shifts across contexts and language users.[1] Since the principle of equal opportunity employs the fittingness concept, it is not possible to give it a unique and definite interpretation without prior ethical commitments. Therefore, the equality principle is a second-order principle, derivative with respect to the necessary first-order ethical premises. Nor can the equality principle itself confer distinctiveness on one philosophy of education *vis-à-vis* any other philosophy. Philosophies with different commitments can, all the same, champion their own version of equal opportunity. . . .

I. *Two Concepts of Equality*

A. THE SAMENESS CONCEPT

Let us begin putting meat on these abstract bones by contrasting two speech acts—one descriptive, the other ascriptive. Consider first

---

[1] I.e., the sameness concept can be defined in the accepted way—more or less in terms of the necessary and sufficient conditions for applying or assessing applications of the term. The fittingness concept is not susceptible to definition in this way. The difference is roughly analogous to the divergence in definitional strategy one would follow with "brown" and "good" as applied to shoes.

a common sort of case wherein we say of students that they are of equal height or ability or have read an equal number of books. This we dub the descriptive use of "equal" and put it on a par with reports of hair color and the like.

What is the sense of the term "equal" when it is so employed? In these cases "equal" means "same" as in "same height" or "same IQ." One forewarning is in order, however. As Chappell [2] has recently noted, the term "same" has itself a dual use. We can refer to an object as "the same one we saw yesterday." Here the force of "same" is to identify as *one* thing what might appear on hasty, *prima facie* grounds to be distinct things. This is the *identifying* function of "same." But the term also serves a comparative purpose, in which it is presupposed that there are multiple objects and a comparison is made of them for this or that purpose (though not all purposes), with respect to certain characteristics (though not all characteristics). It is in this latter role that we take "same" as synonymous with "equal." Now our definition:

To say that X and Y are equal with respect to some characteristic C, is to:

1. *presuppose* that an appropriate (valid) scale for measuring units of C has been correctly applied to X and Y under standard conditions; and to
2. *presuppose* that the scale applied to X is equivalent or identical to the scale applied to Y; and further to
3. *presuppose* that the units of measurement employed have a degree of fineness suitable to the context; and, then, to
4. *assert* that the resultant scores or measurements in both applications are the same.

We need not tarry here very long. Equality as sameness gives us little trouble. Our main reason for specifying this concept is to contrast it with another sense of equality yet to come. There are those, however, who would make all uses of "equal" cleave to this sameness sense, and the temptation for such a move lies in the sameness concept itself.

Given two speakers sharing the above definition, there need not be *automatic* agreement in recognizing instances of sameness. That is,

[2] V. C. Chappell, "Sameness and Change," *Philosophical Review,* LXIX (July, 1960), 351–362.

descriptive claims of equality are not *completely* rulebound. One is given one's head to a limited extent; there is room for individual judgment in even such a hardheaded task as determining whether two characteristics are the same.

The source of this freedom is criterion 3 of the definition. Thus we may say of two students that they fared equally well (or fared the same) in a course of instruction when they received the same letter grade (A or B, etc.), despite discrepancies in their test scores or their dissimilar performance at varying stages in the instruction. But in such a circumstance we could not say that their test scores were necessarily the same. A college admissions officer might want measurements on a finer scale before allowing the two candidates to be "equal in school achievement." A shift to an unexpected level of precision is the stuff of contrived melodrama.

> "Yes, but they are not precisely equal," says Villain to Goodheart, who never imagined we were going to use calipers on cauliflower. So Goodheart loses the bet and coughs up his soul, his deed or daughter (for even tastes of Villains run in different directions). Goodheart's intentions were of the best but the moral is not to let your logic slide.

Consequently, there is a place for context, individual perspective to make a difference. Claims of equality are not *just* reports, not "a mere reading off of the facts." They reflect, to some degree, judgments of the speaker that can vary from case to case and speaker to speaker, depending on purpose, seriousness of concern, and kinds of scales available. There is a chink here in the wall of complete determinateness, but next we are considering another concept of equality wherein whole sections of this wall are absent. Our concern is that the critic not confuse a chink with a breach.

B. The Fittingness Concept

Consider a second range of speech acts in which we invoke "equality" as the operative term.

 (a) "The teacher gave equal treatment to both sides of the dispute."
 (b) "This school offers equal opportunity to all students."
 (c) "Both candidates were given an equal chance of admission to college."

1. These assertions differ from those made with the sameness concept in several respects.

First, note that these assertions have the force of judgments rather than reports. They avow that some practice was proper to the subjects at hand: they are expressions of approval (or disapproval in claims of inequality). Since we usually do not make a judgment of propriety or impropriety without cause, it is not surprising to find that these assertions have another function. This second function is most clearly seen in the negative case. A claim of unequal treatment constitutes a rebuke, censure of the perpetrator of it. It carries with it the presumption that the agent was responsible. Of course the responsibility can frequently be disclaimed ("I was made to change his grade"), passed on ("The school board mandated this") or its existence denied altogether ("Really, this is the only thing we can do"). But even when such disclaimers are justified, when responsibility cannot be assigned or assigned definitely, there remains what one writer has called the "evaluative residue." [3] "All right, the unequal treatment may not have been your fault, but it's a shoddy way to treat the student all the same."

The situation is less simple with respect to a positive claim. For if a claim of inequality (impropriety) is censure, what is the force of a claim of equality (propriety)? Given a suitable contextual plot, the positive claim may exonerate an agent of presumed wrong doing ("No, he did treat the students equally") or it may give official certification to an alleged propriety ("We find there is equal opportunity here" announced by some suitable committee or office).

We found above that this use of "equal" has affinities with evaluation. Nonetheless, a claim of equal treatment is not usually praise. "You presented all viewpoints brilliantly" is commendation. "You gave ten minutes to each position" is descriptive. A claim of equal treatment hangs uneasily between. It is not praise because it is a requirement of the *concept* of teaching that the teacher be fair, impartial, just. It is not description for we are passing on the legitimacy of the teacher's behavior.

2. There are two quick forays to make before the undergrowth thickens. Let us preface the first by stipulating that the approving, legitimizing, censuring, etc., acts be called the ascriptive functions of "equal." The sameness concept usually does not have these functions. The report that students have equal grades or read an equal number

---

[3] V. C. Walsh, "Ascriptions and Appraisals," *Journal of Philosophy*, LV (November 20, 1958), 1,062 ff.; and in *Scarcity and Evil* (Englewood Cliffs, N.J.: Prentice-Hall, Inc., 1961), p. 108.

of books is not of itself approval or disapproval, censure or exoneration. Of course we may take it as such, if we care to, by suitable additions to the context.

This brings us to another point: we do not need additional information to detect that "This teacher treats students unequally" is obloquy. We want to emphasize that it is the word *"equal"* which has the ascriptive functions we are discussing. That is, we are considering the ascriptive uses of the term itself, not the presence of the term in an otherwise ascriptive speech act. *"Equal"* is the operative term making the statement "This student was not given equal treatment" a rebuke. If the operative term were to be replaced, the whole force of the assertion would be altered. It is easy enough to note that "You should have players of equal (same) height" is a prescription. But "equal" does not make it so. It's more discerning to see with Benn and Peters, that:

> In social and political theory, however, "equality" is more often prescriptive than descriptive. In this sense, "all men are equal" would imply not that they possess some attribute or attributes in the same degree but that they ought to be treated alike.[4]

That is, the ascriptive functions (and Benn and Peters' prescriptive function as well) are built by convention into the very meaning of the term "equal." The functions don't simply arise from the syntactical form of the assertion. This is the point that is not grasped by those who analyze the concept of equality: the ascriptive functions *are part of the meaning* and must be accounted for in any definition we give.

So there is no doubt that the sameness concept can enter into ascriptive and prescriptive speech acts. It is likewise clear that the fittingness concept can be used purely descriptively, when its approving, censure, etc. functions have been revoked or neutralized. But in both "You should group students of equal ability" and "He said there is equal opportunity here" the term "equal" is not the operative one regulating the kind of speech act involved.

Our point, put in its most forceful manner, is that the fittingness concept of equality has ascriptive and prescriptive functions built into it. These are not part of the sameness concept. So the differences we have been discussing are truly differences between the concepts

[4] S. I. Benn and R. S. Peters, *Social Principles and the Democratic State* (London: Allen & Unwin, 1959), p. 108.

themselves. They are not differences between various speech acts in which "equal" is merely present.

3. It is this last point that is the sticky one, and it is surely time to stop dawdling over the ascriptive *functions* of "equal" and get to the main question. Granted that when the term is applied in contexts of the sort being discussed, it will have the force of approval or rebuke, etc. However, what is the *sense* of the term in these contexts? This sense of "equal" is *fittingness*. To say that certain treatment is equal treatment is to be saying that it is fitting to the subjects exposed to it. It is difficult, however, to pin this sense down with a definition; for the criteria of fittingness, unlike those for sameness, shift with the ever-moving sands of context. We will offer a general defining formula to fix the concept in place. But it should be borne in mind that it is the ascriptive functions, not the criteria for application, that are common to all contexts in which the fittingness concept is applied.

Skipping further preliminaries, we offer this definition of the fittingness of equality:

(a) The provisions or practices being adjudged equal be in accordance with rightful rules properly applied.
(b) The rules employed be selected with reference to the appropriate characteristics of the subjects, correctly described.

4. The definition stands in need of further explication. But criticism being more delightful than explanation, we will postpone discussion of our own definition in order to give protracted attention to an alternative view of the meaning of the fittingness concept. The view we refer to goes something like this:

> When I say "This teacher gave equal treatment" I may very well be approving the teacher's demeanor and what not, but nonetheless I am approving the treatment (of X and Y) because it is the same treatment (X and Y). So we can say that "equal" has the *sense* of sameness despite differences in *functions* or *use*. On this view there is one concept of equality not two, albeit in some speech acts the single concept has ascriptive and prescriptive appendages. But even with a full complement of barnacles and weeds, a boat is a boat for all that.

We want to oppose this single-meaning view, which we call the sameness thesis. "Equal," we will say, has not only taken on new functions but shifted its sense as well; and it is false to claim that sameness is identical with or essential to equality in the fittingness sense. . . .

II. *The Fittingness Concept and the Equality Principle*

Having assayed and rejected varied attempts to define equality in terms of sameness, we turn now to an explication of our own definition. Earlier we cited the following rules as constituting a definition of "equality" in its fittingness sense:

a. The provisions or practices being adjudged equal be in accordance with rightful rules, properly applied.
b. The rules be employed with reference to appropriate characteristics of the subjects, correctly described.

A. INDETERMINACY

Ponder now the state of our system. If equality were defined in terms of sameness, then there would be at least one constant criterion for the application of the term in each and every context. But the upshot of our discussion in the previous section was negative with respect to this hope. The definition offered here in place of sameness is indeterminate. It is indeterminate with respect to the content of the rules to be followed and the characteristics of the subjects that are relevant.

Furthermore, the definition stands in constant danger of redundancy on the score that relevancy of subject characteristics and propriety of rules are functions of one another. That is, whether a candidate's religion is relevant in college admissions is dependent on the presence or absence of a rule about treatment of candidates with respect to this characteristic. And whether we have such rules is dependent on the importance we attribute to the characteristic.

B. PRIMACY OF ETHICAL JUDGMENT

This indeterminacy in the definition of the fittingness concept is apparently analogous to that encountered in connection with the sameness concept. With regard to the sameness concept, the selection of a suitable scale for gainsaying measures of things to be compared is a matter of practical judgment. In applying the fittingness concept, however, one is choosing the morally right rules to adhere to in a given case. This is a *moral* judgment.

It is commonly recognized that assent to equality is a moral act. What we here assert is that the decision as to what *constitutes* equality in concrete cases is likewise a moral decision and a logically necessary one. Allegiance to the equality principle as such is an empty gesture. The principle is a secondary one, depending on logically prior moral commitments to make it meaningful. For example, it is meaningless to support the idea that school subsidies should be distributed to communities on an equal basis. It is not until a commitment is made as to what constitutes rightful allocation that assent to the equality principle becomes significant. Therefore no philosophy of education is identified or made controversial by its belief in educational equality. What is distinctive about an educational philosophy is the particular way it interprets this belief, the judgments and commitments it makes along the way. For to round out this topic on a note of redundancy, the definition of equality does not dictate our educational preferences. Rather it is the case that our educational preferences constitute *our* meaning for equality.

C. ESSENTIALLY CONTESTED

Thus it is that the specific criteria or rules by which we determine a treatment to be equal are not part of the definition of the concept. As illustration, consider the distribution of state funds to local districts on an "equal" basis. A rule (read "formula") which allocates funds on the basis of local tax *effort* is no more or less "true equality" than rules which dispense moneys to compensate for deficiencies in local tax resources or which give the same amount to each local district or which reward districts manifesting greatest educational improvements; or any combination of these. Any of these can be defended as the right, and hence fitting, way to distribute subsidies. The same holds true for, say, the allocation of teaching talent to students of differential ability. The best teachers might be allocated to the most able students; to the least able, or assigned on some compromise basis. There is nothing in the linguistic conventions which render any one rule as the "real" or "true" meaning of "equal treatment."

We would borrow from Gallie at this point and speak of "equality" in its fittingness sense as an essentially contested concept, i.e., as one of the "concepts the proper use of which inevitably involves

the growth and development of the individual. No reference to equal intellectual capacity or to any other native endowments is intended. The intended reference is the *chance* to get an education, *of whatever amount and kind* one's endowments make possible. It is the chance that is to be equalized.[8]

The illusion is created here that the criteria specifying what is equal treatment in some context are simply "read off" from the facts of the environment and student's characteristics. (As, for example, equal right can be "read off," merely from the facts.) But a student's endowments make different kinds of education possible. Which should we give the student a chance to get? And which of his endowments do we judge to be appropriate to encourage? The authors state that fair play is the sense of equal opportunity, but they ignore the fact that this is a moral notion. What is equal treatment is a matter of moral choice, not factual reporting, and this yields contesting, not uniform views.

Equal Educational Opportunity: The Durable Injustice

THOMAS F. GREEN

Professor Green limits his analysis of equal educational opportunity to arguments of justice. The author notes that educational equality can be analyzed in terms of social utility, but since social utility and justice can conflict, he limits his analysis solely to questions of justice. In so doing, Green implies what Komisar and Coombs in the preceding selection made explicit: the equality principle is a second-order principle, derived from prior ethical principles.

[8] William O. Stanley, B. Othanel Smith, Kenneth D. Benne, and Archibald W. Anderson, *Social Foundations of Education* (New York: The Dryden Press, Inc., 1956), p. 228. Some italics added.

SOURCE: *Philosophy of Education 1971: Proceedings of the Twenty-Seventh Annual Meeting of the Philosophy of Education Society—Dallas, April 4–7, 1971.* Edited by Robert D. Heslep. Published for the Philosophy of Education Society by *Studies in Philosophy and Education,* 1971, pp. 121–143. Reprinted by permission of the publisher and the author.

In his analysis, Professor Green deals more with injustice than with the concept of justice. He reasons that it is impractical, if not impossible, to formulate a principle of justice at once general enough to cover all the demands of justice in an educational system and yet specific enough to constitute a clear guide to practice.

For the purposes of his analysis Green regards the educational system as a system for the distribution of certain goods and benefits. He does not dwell upon the nature of such goods and benefits, but notes that the distributive point of view permits in-depth analysis of equality and inequality. Thus he provides us with a framework for judging the justice of, for example, the disparities between income and wealth discussed earlier. More importantly, with his model he can ask a fundamental question in the equal opportunity conflict: what would constitute an acceptable or unacceptable inequality in the distribution of educational goods and benefits?

Within the context of this question, Green considers the adequacy of the traditional *input* approach to equal educational opportunity. He then examines some major assumptions of the emerging approach, stimulated by the Coleman Report, which is to consider equal educational opportunity by looking at the consequences of schooling: how well or poorly pupils achieve in school in light of the resources or lack of them which they bring to school.

Green points out that this approach, which he calls the *benefit view of equal education opportunity,* calls for "a school with an extraordinarily powerful pedagogical system. Indeed, it requires the development of a school system that is immensely powerful *relative* to those other institutions, such as the family, that constitute the environment for learning in the early years." Given America's current values and family structures, Green doubts that the benefit view will be a workable alternative within the foreseeable future.

In analyzing the distribution of educational goods and services, Professor Green contrasts the criteria of *merit* and *need.* His observations have implications for such issues as tracking and ability grouping, which were discussed briefly in Chapter 2.

Green's paper, like that of Komisar and Coombs, reflects a relatively recent development in the discipline of philosophy of education: a growing tendency to avoid the construction of cosmic schools of educational philosophy in favor of using philosophical tools, particularly linguistic analysis, to examine major educational concepts and crucial policies.

Professor Green is Co-Director of the Center for Educational Policy Studies at Syracuse University. He is the author of numerous articles and books.

For the next decade, and beyond, the attainment of equal educational opportunity will probably be among the most fundamental and intractable issues confronting American education. It is likely, also, to be a basic problem in most countries of the western world. The issues are not likely to go away, nor are they likely to be overcome without direct and serious attention. But what precisely are the issues of equal educational opportunity? In what follows, I intend to examine at least two formulations of the problem, formulations, moreover, that have actually occurred in the course of recent policy debate. Furthermore, these formulations will be rendered within rather strict and clear limits so that it may be easier to assess the prospects of arriving at a satisfactory resolution.

I. *Some Methodological Limits*

It is immensely important to keep these limits in mind. Otherwise, much of the analysis will be misunderstood. In the first place, I wish to limit the analysis to arguments of justice. Justice and utility can conflict. The claim that a certain policy should be adopted because it is socially beneficial can always be rebutted on the grounds that, nonetheless, it is unjust; and, conversely, any claim that a certain policy should be adopted because it is just, can always be rebutted on the ground that, nonetheless, it is not socially useful. I have no doubt, then, that there are arguments for equal educational opportunity derived solely from claims of social utility. My point is not that such arguments are unimportant, but simply that they are not central in the following analysis.

Thus, if we consider the conflicting claims of justice and utility, then the following analysis is limited by its focus on the idea of justice. But if, on the other hand, we consider the ideas of justice and injustice, then the focus of the analysis will fall more heavily on the idea of injustice. This emphasis is important for many reasons. To begin with, it may be impossible—or at any rate impractical—to formulate a principle of *justice* at once sufficiently general to cover the demands of justice in the educational system and at the same time sufficiently specific to actually constitute a guide to practice. It is not impractical or impossible, however, to set forth the assumptions of policy and features of practice that permit the claims of *injustice* to arise.

. . . The claims of utility are likely to enter quickly into any argument on the side of justice. The claims that a specific practice or policy is just will seldom constitute sufficient grounds for its adoption. But, on the other hand, the claim that a specific policy or practice is unjust might often constitute sufficient grounds for its abandonment and for the abandonment of any alternative that is likewise unjust. The force of such an argument will depend greatly, of course, on the magnitude of the injustice.

In short, reason may regard the evil of injustice as greater than the good of justice. Thus, in discussions of policy and practice we tend to give greater normative weight to the claims of injustice than to the claims of justice. . . .

There is a third and related limitation. . . . The educational system is the kind of social system that, among other things, distributes certain goods and benefits, certain honors and awards. I believe that nowhere in fact does there exist anything we could call an educational system that does not perform such a distributive function in some way. Indeed, I doubt that such an educational system can exist. It may be a defining feature of what we *mean* by an educational system that it perform a distributive function.

It needs to be explained, however, that in the following analysis educational goods and benefits should be distinguished from other benefits of a non-educational sort that happen to be associated with education. For example, I do not mean to include income, occupational opportunity, or social class standing as educational goods and benefits. I know well that these are associated in varying degrees of strength with educational attainment. Nonetheless, I regard them as goods and benefits *linked* to educational benefits, but not themselves educational benefits. By educational goods and benefits, I mean such things as knowledge, skills, taste, and certificates. I shall take the view that these are the things distributed by the educational system (not to be confused with the school system). Though they are not the only goods distributed by the system, these goods happen, for purely contingent reasons, to be associated with certain other goods and benefits of the society that are non-educational in nature.

Social issues of equality and inequality can be usefully formulated in relation to some distribution of goods and benefits. It is doubtful that *all* issues of equality can be formulated in this way, because there are other forms of justice than distributive justice. Still, the distributive point of view will carry us far in understanding issues of equality and inequality. Equality of income, for example, would exist within a society if its economy distributed the same income to every individual. Experience suggests that it is unreasonable to expect such a state of affairs to exist or to exist for very long, even in those societies that have made the attainment of equal income a fundamental objective. Typically, we get an unequal distribution of income. The question of justice, indeed the questions of social policy concerning equality, arise when we ask whether the unequal distribution is acceptable.

The phrase "acceptable inequality" deserves some explanation. There are two features of distributions generally that are of interest. First, if we assume that in all likelihood there will be some inequality in the distribution, say, of income, then we may ask whether the range of that distribution offends our sense of justice. Thus, we may discover that at the one end of the distribution there are those as rich as Croesus and at the other end those who are impoverished beyond imagination. Thus, our sense of injustice may be aroused not because there are too many rich and too many poor, but simply because the distance between them is too great. . . . But secondly, if we are not offended by the range in the distribution of income, we may still find offense in the distribution within that range. There may be injustice of a different kind, arising not because the poor are too poor and the rich too rich, but simply because there are too many rich or poor. Thus, by an "unacceptable inequality" I mean to refer to some distribution of goods and benefits in which either the range or the distribution within that range is viewed as unacceptable, on grounds of justice.

There is another extremely important reason for limiting the discussion of equal educational opportunity to such a distributive perspective. The focus on distribution amounts to a kind of methodological injunction to be specific in thinking about goals and alternatives. . . . We are strongly tempted to transform the formulation of educational ideals into principles of social organization, and conversely to move too quickly from the adoption of social principles to their formulation as educational ideals. It seems to me, moreover, that we are often inclined to reason in this way without attending to the constraints that would be imposed by taking a distributive point of view. For example, it is often argued that the educational system needs to develop in larger numbers young adults with a high tolerance for ambiguity, low dispositions for sterotypic thinking, high capacities and dispositions for creativity, and strong capabilities for independent thinking. Yet, the distributive point of view forces one to ask just what distribution of these traits we are seeking in such ideals. . . . Any society all of whose members have a "high tolerance for ambiguity" would have a great deal of difficulty getting some rather basic things done. Such a society would be extremely unstable. One might reply, "Nonetheless, we need a great many more people like that." And with that, I would not argue. I wish only to point out that the distributive view will help immensely to demarcate the limits of educational ideals. I believe that none of the goods sought in education are without some limit when we imagine them distributed in certain ways. None of them are unqualified goods. But if there are unqualified educational goods, that fact also will be discoverable through applying a distributive view.

II. *Inequality and the Grounds for Distributing Educational Benefits*

What then would constitute an acceptable or unacceptable inequality in the distribution of educational goods and benefits? The charge of injustice cannot be lodged against every unequal distribution. . . . We do not worry, for example, if people come out of the educational system with different abilities or competencies or knowing different things or even with different honors and awards. We expect the educational system to make discriminations of these sorts. We do not require that different people should know the same things. Neither would we be upset if it turned out that on the whole philosophers are paid more than those who know a lot about English literature or if physicists are paid more than those that know a lot about mathematics. These are inequalities in the results of the educational system and in subsequent economic "chances" related to those educational results. But such differential results present no serious problems of equality or inequality.

On the other hand, we would probably regard it as a serious problem if we found that certain social *groups* taken as aggregates are differentially treated by the system. For example, it could be regarded as a serious social problem if the educational system, on the whole, teaches whites more than blacks, the rich more than the poor, males more than females, or the middle class more than the lower class. It can be legitimately asked, however, why the existence of this distributive inequality is more serious than the existence of the other. Both have to do with the same goods and benefits—knowledge at specifiable levels in specific areas together with the subsequent opportunities associated with possession of that knowledge. The educational system must distribute its benefits or goods in some way. Why should the distribution become unacceptable when associated with some groups, but not when associated with others?

The answer is clear, but seldom made explicit. We are inclined to believe that the educational system must distribute its benefits unequally in a way corresponding to the unequal distribution of certain capacities that, in ordinary parlance, we associate with the term "ability." If educationally relevant abilities are unequally distributed in the total population, then it seems perfectly justified that the distribution of educational benefits should be unequal in a corresponding way. But presumably, being poor, black or lower class has no relation whatever to one's abilities or to one's capacity to learn. . . . Unless it is assumed that only the rich, white, and middle-class have the capacity to learn, it will follow that any disproportionate distribution of educational goods to such groups will constitute an unacceptable inequality.

The same point can be put more directly in another way. Suppose we ask whether, in principle, there can be any criteria sufficient to define a group of people that can justifiably be permitted to benefit differentially from the educational system. What would those criteria be? On the surface, it appears that there can be only three—ability, choice, and tenacity. For the moment, I would like to consider tenacity as a kind of choice. Thus, it appears to be a justifiable result if the educational system distributes minimal benefits to any population that either chooses not to benefit from the system or is, in some sense, uneducable. The ability to benefit from the educational system on the part of some group together with the choice not to do so would seem sufficient grounds for distributing minimal benefits to that group. Consider, for example, the Mennonites. Presumably Mennonite children have the ability to advance farther within the educational system than they typically do. But for religious and cultural reasons they choose not to. This choice would clearly justify an unequal distribution of educational goods and benefits unrelated to ability. But that result cannot be regarded as an endemic feature of the distributive behavior of the educational system. It is rather a consequence of choice on the part of a certain population.

But furthermore, regardless of the choice exercised by any specific population, the educational system would appear justified in distributing minimal benefits to any group that can be shown to be uneducable, i.e., unable to benefit from the system. Thus, it seems true *prima facie* that the ability to benefit and the inability to benefit seem to be the only criteria that can be used to regulate the system in distributing its benefits in a grossly unequal manner. Clearly, a minimal distribution of educational benefits to any specific population would not be justified if there is the ability to benefit, the desire to do so, and yet the lack of power to choose to do so. Thus, given roughly equal power to choose to benefit from the system, continuing large differentials in the distribution of educational goods seem justified only on grounds of large corresponding inequalities in the distribution of ability.

Perhaps this is the reason why we regard it as acceptable where educational benefits are differentially distributed to philosophers and to physicists or to mathematicians and literary critics. These differences are presumably based upon identifiable and corresponding distributions of abilities together with an exercise of choice. But when these same goods and benefits are distributed according to social class, economic status, sex, or race, we have an unacceptable distribution because it is assumed that such demographic differences are unrelated to the distribution of ability. Thus, the attainment of equal educational opportunity can be viewed as the effort to redistribute the benefits of the educational system *on grounds that are educationally relevant,* and those grounds appear to be grounds of ability.

III. *Two Theories of Equal Opportunity*

This way of formulating the problem does not leave the idea of "equality" altogether undefined. There are important distributive differences between the traditional view that equal opportunity has to do essentially with equal access to schooling and the more contemporary view that relates equal opportunity more closely to equality of achievement. Any approach that relates equality of educational opportunity to the distribution of educational benefits will fit only the second of these two views. The point needs clarification.

The traditional and still widely shared view is that equality of educational opportunity is attained when there is roughly equal opportunity for different segments of the population to compete for the benefits of the educational system. It is a minimum condition of this view that there be provided for every person within the society some school with approximately comparable curricula, facilities, staff, and management. If there are children for whom no school at all exists, then those children do not have equal educational opportunity. Moreover, if the schools available for some youngsters are significantly deficient in the scope of curriculum, the competence of the staff, or the adequacy of facilities, then the children who attend those schools do not have equal educational opportunity. Viewed in this way, equal opportunity consists of two elements. First, it requires access to some school for anyone who wishes to secure the benefits of schooling; but secondly, it requires that the schools available should have approximately equal inputs, i.e., teachers, materials, and facilities.

Given such a view, it can be argued that whether persons wish to benefit from the educational system or whether they successfully secure the benefits of the system is a matter left entirely to the individual. The result will depend upon the talents, choices, and tenacity of the individual. Equal *opportunity* will have been provided although persons may not equally use such opportunities. Thus, the fact that certain social groups may not benefit equally from the system has nothing to do with the existence or non-existence of equal opportunity. On this view, how the educational system distributes its *benefits* among the population has little to do with equal opportunity and much to do with the choices, abilities, and tenacity of individuals. Thus, equal educational opportunity, on this view, has much to do with the distribution of inputs to the system; it has little or nothing to do with the distribution of outputs. I shall refer to this view as the resource view of equal educational opportunity.

In our understanding of equal educational opportunity, we have moved away from a view of equal resources to a view of equal achievement. I shall refer to this view as the benefit view of equal educational opportunity. Imagine two sets of schools of approximately comparable staff, facilities, and instructional materials. By the traditional concept they would be providing equal educational opportunity to their respective students. Suppose, however, that such systems of schools in fact produce enormous disparities of achievement between the children attending the two different systems. What would we say if those disparities increased the longer the children stayed in school? It would be immensely difficult to maintain the conviction that no inequality of opportunity exists. . . .

The point can receive a perfectly general and precise formulation. There are three kinds of limiting cases concerned with the distribution of educational benefits when those benefits are construed as achievement. They are represented by the diagrams in Figure I. These diagrams assume the existence of two social groups—no matter how defined—who begin their education at somewhat different levels of learning. According to the benefit view of equal opportunity, *I* is the paradigmatic case of inequality; *III* is the paradigmatic case of equality; and *II* is a borderline case. Thus, it can be set down as a kind of definition that any society will have attained a condition of equal educational opportunity when (1) the range of the distribution of benefits and (2) the distribution within that range is approximately the same for each relevant social group within the student population.

There are four important points that need to be made about this definition. First, it does not mean that everyone must reach the same level of achievement. It means only that the *range* of achievement and the distribution *within* that range should be about the same for each social group. Secondly, it should be clear that equal opportunity in the benefit sense is compatible with and may even require unequal opportunity in the resource sense.[1] This is the point that most vividly illustrates the difference between the two views of equal opportunity. Third, it seems too much to claim that equal benefit is what we *mean* by equal educational opportunity; but it is not too much to say that its attainment would be a sufficient condition for the claim to have achieved equal educational opportunity. For under these conditions, the disadvantaged of society would no longer be *educationally* dis-

---

[1] It is interesting to observe in operation this difference between the traditional and contemporary views of educational equality. Under Title I of the Elementary and Secondary Education Act, the Congress has appropriated funds especially targeted for the education of the disadvantaged. It has been known for a long time, however, that within school districts in the United States it often happens that substantially larger local resources have been allocated to schools attended by the advantaged and substantially smaller resources to schools attended by the disadvantaged. In other words, within school districts there have been unequal inputs between schools. In 1970, the Office of Education advanced the view that in order to qualify for additional funds under Title I, local school districts would have to first attain a condition of "comparability" between schools of the district. The assumption is that in order to attain equality of educational opportunity it will be necessary to allocate disproportionately greater resources to the education of the disadvantaged, but that before such additional funds can be secured, the local district must attain equality of educational opportunity in the traditional sense. Thus the traditional definition and the achievement definitions of equal educational opportunity both come into play in this particular policy action.

FIGURE I   Model Cases in the Distribution of Some Educational Benefits

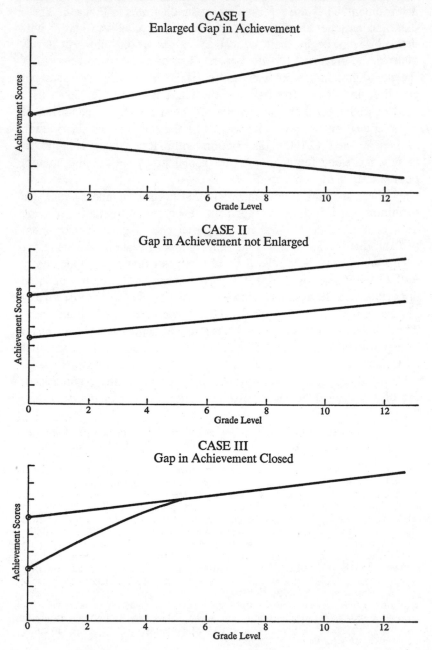

CASE I
Enlarged Gap in Achievement

CASE II
Gap in Achievement not Enlarged

CASE III
Gap in Achievement Closed

advantaged. We would have reached a point at which neither social class, income, race, nor sex would be a barrier to educational achievement. Thus, even though the benefit view does not capture all that we *mean* by equal educational opportunity, still it seems to set forth sufficient conditions for its attainment in the distributive behavior of the system.

Finally, equal opportunity, in the benefit sense, constitutes a kind of ideal. But that ideal will stand differently related to the demands of justice and injustice and therefore differently related to the formulation of policy depending upon how the assumptions of that ideal are formulated.

IV. *The Assumptions of the Benefit View*

I shall deal with four assumptions. The first, and most serious, . . . contains several related claims. To begin with, it seems *prima facie* true that the benefit view can be made credible only on the assumption that educationally relevant abilities are randomly distributed throughout the population. I have already argued that there are apparently only three criteria sufficient to define a social group that can justifiably be permitted to benefit disproportionately from the system. Those criteria must be ability, choice, and tenacity. There is a tendency to add a fourth, namely, works or achievement. But works can be viewed, for the moment at least, as a special class of abilities, namely, those abilities displayed in success in certain kinds of achievement. Thus, given roughly equal resources to choose to benefit from the system, I argued that continuing large differentials in the distribution of educational goods could only be justified on grounds of large corresponding inequalities in the distribution of ability. If the distribution of benefits must be based upon ability, and if *any* distribution of those benefits strongly associated with race, class, income, or sex is unjust, then clearly we are assuming that educationally relevant abilities are not distributed according to race, class, income, or sex. It must be assumed, in short, that though the society may be stratified by such factors, ability is not; or, in other words, ability is randomly or nearly randomly distributed in the population with respect to those variables.

It should be noted that this assumption concerning the distribution of abilities is necessary in any argument attempting to show that the current distribution of the educational system is *unjust, provided that* the argument also accept the view that the distribution of benefits should accord with the distribution of ability. Though such an argument may strongly support the claim that a certain distribution of benefits is *unjust;* still it is visibly insufficient to support the *justice* of a corresponding unequal distribution. In other words, it is tempting to conclude that if we could empirically identify two groups that differ substantially in their possession of some educationally relevant property, then justice would permit us to distribute educational benefits disproportionately to the two groups. If it could be established, for example, that as a matter of empirical fact educationally relevant properties, such as intelligence and ability, are not randomly distributed but are in fact concentrated within certain social classes . . . or certain racial groups, then it seems possible to conclude that the educational system would be justified in distributing benefits disproportionately to members of those groups that are so blessed. Still, this conclusion would be unwarranted. . . . Even if it could be demonstrated that there is a population in which educationally relevant abilities are in short supply, still, it does not follow from that alone that the educational system would be justified in distributing a disproportionately small share of benefits to that group. For even though a given social group is less adequately endowed with the relevant abilities, still, justice can demand that we bring them to the same level of achievement.

This counter-argument, however, clearly involves giving up the view that the system should distribute its benefits on the basis of ability. It requires the introduction of a different principle of justice. Instead of justice according to merit or works, it introduces the notion of justice according to need. I wish to defer discussing this additional direction of thought. For the moment we may. . . . explore the assumptions of the benefit view of equal opportunity first by holding constant the principle that educational goods should be distributed on the basis of ability. Only then will I consider the view that they should be distributed on the basis of need or on some other principle. I wish to do this because I believe that *in fact* most contemporary efforts to bring about more equal educational opportunity do take the view that educational goods and benefits should be distributed in relation to ability.

That educationally relevant abilities are randomly distributed in the population is, of course, an empirical rather than a logical claim. Whether it is true is a question of fact. It can be doubted. But though the *truth* of this assumption is a matter of fact, its place in the arguments for educational opportunity is not. It is an assumption that is logically necessary in any argument claiming to show that the distribution of educational goods and benefits along lines of race, class, income, or sex is unjust. Thus the status of this first assumption is rather odd. It constitutes a factual claim. Yet, even if it could be demonstrated to be factually false, it would have to be believed in order for the current benefit view of equal educational opportunity to make any sense.

It might be objected that I have been taking an unduly simplistic view of "educationally relevant" abilities. The view that educational benefits should be distributed according to abilities may appear to assume that there is some well defined and readily identifiable, perhaps even accurately measurable, set of abilities that we can designate as educationally relevant. But suppose that we are unable to define or identify, much less measure, any such set of abilities. Then, it might be supposed that this entire approach is rendered irrelevant to the real issues of educational policy that confront us.

This kind of objection stems from a fundamental misunderstanding. The fact is that the logical function of the assumption that abilities are randomly distributed is such that the assumption will be required in arguments for equal educational opportunity *no matter how abilities are defined, identified, or measured.* The consequences for practice will be very different, of course, depending upon what abilities and what range of abilities any society tends to adopt as "educationally relevant." But the essential point is that no matter how those abilities are defined, no matter how numerous they be or how complex their measurement, it will still be an assumption of the benefit view of educational equality that those abilities are randomly distributed throughout the society.

The remaining three assumptions have to do with the role of schools in attaining equal educational opportunity in the benefit sense. The claim contained in these assumptions is simply that (2) the school can be made an effective institution to counter the effects of out-of-school environment (3) in a sustained way so as to (4) bring about a rate of learning for the disadvantaged that is greater than the rate of learning for the advantaged. . . .

There are only three possible ways that equal educational achievement can be attained between any two social groups that begin their schooling with important differences in the average levels of achievement. We can attain the desired result either by lowering the rate of learning for the advantaged, increasing the rate of learning for the disadvantaged, or some combination of both.

V. *Meeting the Problem: An Assessment*

We may rule out the first and third of these schema as representing any reasonable expectation. In both cases the attainment of the goal would require us to adopt explicit policies aimed at lowering the educational achievement of children in the advantaged class. It would be unreasonable to expect such a course of action to be adopted. Furthermore, it would be undesirable, perhaps even immoral. It can be argued that the middle class in America has from time to time accepted policies that *in fact* have the consequence of lowering the achievement rates of their children. But though policies having that consequence may have been adopted, I know of no reason to suppose that they were adopted for that purpose. . . . It follows that there is one and only one way by which we can hope to attain the goal of equal educational opportunity in the achievement sense, and that is by increasing the rate of learning for the educationally disadvantaged so that it is greater than the rate of learning of the advantaged. This is the fourth of the assumptions involved in the benefit view of equal opportunity. The possibility of doing this is an assumption implicit in the very notion of adopting equal educational opportunity in the benefit sense as a serious social goal. . . .

The question then is whether it is a reasonable expectation to attain the state of affairs set forth in that schema. On the surface, at least, it seems to be a goal perfectly within reach. Surely it is a state of affairs toward which we should strive, and there are indeed many efforts already under way to move in that direction. For example, if we know that inequities in levels of learning relevant to good school performance exist already at the beginning of school, then it seems reasonable to attempt to make up for such differences during the pre-school years. Thus, such a program as Head Start seems a perfectly reasonable component in any set of policies aimed at achieving equal educational opportunity, and indeed all sorts of other efforts at early-childhood education for the disadvantaged would be important in any effort to attain such a social goal. In fact, we have reason to believe, from experience with Head Start, that such efforts to narrow the initial gap in learning levels can be successful. . . .

However, we also have reason to believe that the effects of such a head start soon dissipate when the child reaches the regular school. Thus, we must recognize that the attainment of equal educational opportunity requires not simply that the school, or the pre-school, be successful in counteracting the effects of environment, but that it be successful in this effort *over a long span of time;* and this is the third of the assumptions contained in the benefit view of equal opportunity. About this assumption we have less reason to be hopeful.

We may summarize: The benefit view of equal educational opportunity seems to assume as a practical goal that the school can be successful in counter-acting the effects of environment on learning, not simply for a short time, but for a long time, so as to increase the rate of learning for the disadvantaged. Otherwise the disadvantaged will not catch up. Thus, the benefit view of equal educational opportunity requires a school with an extraordinarily powerful pedagogical system. Indeed, it requires the development of a school system that is immensely powerful *relative* to those other institutions, such as the family, that constitute the environment for learning in the early years. Furthermore, the power of the school relative to such other institutions would have to be exercised in the lives of children for a *very* long time, probably at least through the first six years of schooling.

It seems to me extremely doubtful that the necessary components for such an achievement will be permitted to occur in American society in the foreseeable future. But quite beyond that judgment, there are substantial reasons to doubt that even if it did occur, it would make very much difference to the attainment of equal educational opportunity in the benefit sense. For if the necessary pedagogy is developed and the essential resources are assembled to accelerate the rate of learning for the disadvantaged, it would be reasonable to expect that the first social group in American society to adopt such effective measures would be the parents of the advantaged class.

. . . It would not be surprising, for example, to discover that the mere promulgation and dissemination of the idea of giving some children a "head start" was accompanied by a rapid increase in early-childhood education among the advantaged groups of American society. After all, if the idea of having a head start is good for the children of poverty, it will be good too for the children of affluence whose parents will be better able to provide it. . . . Thus, it seems reasonable to expect that if there are developed the techniques of pedagogy and the social resources sufficient to close the achievement gap between advantaged and disadvantaged, those techniques and resources will be used by the advantaged to maintain their advantage, and equal opportunity expressed as equal benefit will not be attained.

There are at least two possible counter-arguments as to how this particular pattern of change can be thwarted and equal opportunity achieved. In the first place, it can be argued that accompanying the development of effective schools for the disadvantaged it will be necessary to employ political measures sufficient to prevent the advantaged groups in society from maintaining their advantage. It is difficult to see precisely what those measures might be, but it is not difficult to see that such measures would probably have to be repressive against the American middle class to such a degree that would make them unlikely to be adopted, much less to actually succeed.

Similarly, it seems likely that in order to achieve equal educational opportunity in the achievement sense within the foreseeable future, it will be necessary to develop schools into such total institutions as to seriously call into question any accustomed ideas we may have about the proper relation between the school and the family. Such a course would seriously jeopardize the structure of family life itself. . . . As James Coleman has put it,

> the relative intensity of the convergent school influences and the divergent out-of-school influences determines the effectiveness of the educational opportunity. In this perspective, complete equality of opportunity can be reached only if all the divergent out-of-school influences vanish, a condition that would arise only in the advent of boarding schools; given the existing divergent influences, equality of opportunity can only be approached but never fully reached. The concept becomes one of degree of proximity to equality of opportunity. This proximity is determined, then, not merely by the *equality* of educational inputs, but by the *intensity* of the school's influence relative to the external divergent influences. That is, equality of output is not so much determined by equality of the resource inputs, but by the power of these resources in bringing about achievement.

Coleman remarks that "complete equality of opportunity can be reached only if all the divergent out-of-school influences *vanish*," and the attainment of that object has to do with "the *intensity* of the school's influence relative to the external divergent influences." In these remarks, he is clearly correct. The direction of this change is *toward* the establishment of the school as a total institution, i.e., an institution whose social processes are uninfluenced by forces external to its control. . . . For these reasons alone, it is unlikely that this path toward equal educational opportunity will be successful.

The second kind of counter-development may seem more hopeful because it appears to be less drastic. Yet its greater hopefulness, even so, may be a consequence simply of its greater obscurity. It might be argued that the kind of pedagogy and the kind of school needed to accelerate achievement for the disadvantaged must turn out so that even though it may prove more effective for the disadvantaged, still it will not be sought by the middle class or by the educationally advantaged. In other words, it might happen that the kind of pedagogy and curriculum that will permit the educationally disadvantaged to "catch up" quickly in verbal skills, for example, may be inappropriate or may appear to be undesirable to the educationally advantaged. There are two conditions set forth in this conjecture. The first is that educational processes are developed that permit the disadvantaged to "achieve" at the levels of the advantaged and by the same measures. The second condition is that such processes be unwanted or inappropriate for the children of the educationally advantaged. Under these two conditions, there is some hope that the advantaged will not be disposed to take actions sufficient to maintain their advantage, and thus the disadvantaged will be permitted to "catch up." This kind of strategy constitutes a strong argument for "community control" in some form and for pluralism, but within powerful limits.

It is conceivable that a kind of educational theory and pedagogy can be developed that is effective in increasing the "achievement" levels of the "disadvantaged," but which at the same time is not likely to be adopted by the "advantaged." Such a development, however, . . . is likely to be opposed by the advantaged as unacceptable for anyone.

VI. *Distribution Independent of Ability*

If unequal opportunity in the benefit sense is an injustice, then it is a durable one indeed. But this dark prognosis results from holding constant certain factors already in process of change. In the first place, it results from examining the distributive behavior of the currently existing system without considering the fact that that system itself might change. But, more important, this somewhat dismal future stems from adhering strictly to the view that the distribution of educational goods and benefits should accord with the distribution of "educationally relevant" abilities.

It is possible, however, to take an entirely different view. It might be argued that the educational system should not distribute its benefits in meager amounts to those of meager abilities anymore than that the health system should lavish its energies on the healthy. Justice demands precisely the opposite. We should not try to make the healthy sick, but neither should we withhold the benefits of medicine from the ill and injured. We might regard the unequal capacity to secure the benefits of education in just that light, not as something to be unequally rewarded but as something to be overcome. In short, if we take the view that every social group should benefit approximately equally from the educational system, we need not be assuming that "educationally relevant" abilities are randomly distributed in the population. On the contrary, it can be argued that if there are those endowed with lesser abilities, it should be the responsibility of the educational system to organize itself so that despite their lesser abilities, nonetheless, they profit as much as any other group. To the extent that ignorance and even stupidity are thought of as diseases or physical handicaps, it does not violate our sense of justice to compensate for them. We can give according to need. This, in short, is the view that neither benefits nor resources should be distributed by the system in accordance with "educationally relevant" abilities *no matter how those abilities are defined.*

But what precisely is the nature of this view that benefits should be distributed independently of abilities? In the first place, the idea that educational benefits should be distributed by the system independently of ability is actually not a view about the grounds for the distribution of *benefits*. It is a view, on the contrary, about the grounds for the distribution of *resources*. It is a view that takes a particular distribution of educational benefits as a given target and then, on that basis, argues for a particular distribution of resources. . . .

In introducing this view, what we are dealing with is the movement from a standard of justice according to merit or works to a view of justice according to need. Thus, *in addition* to denying an old distributive principle, we shall introduce a new one, namely distribution according to need. But how, from this point of view, shall we understand the term "need"? The view that educational benefits should be distributed according to need really turns out to be a view that educational *resources* should be distributed in whatever way is needed to accomplish a particular distribution of benefits. Need is thus defined as whatever resources are needed to yield such a result. This, then, is an argument concerned essentially with criteria for the distribution of educational resources, not benefits.

. . . The view of justice according to need that we have been considering does not escape the idea that the distribution of educational benefits should accord with the distribution of abilities. When the distribution curves . . . [of any two groups] match, it is not assumed that educational benefits *within* groups X and Y will be based upon anything other than abilities. It is only denied that the distribution of benefits *between* the two groups should be based upon their respective shares of "educationally relevant" abilities. Thus, the idea of justice according to need does not, in this case, entirely escape the principle that educational benefits should be distributed on the basis of abilities. The idea, in this particular form, restricts the application of that principle but does not abandon it. And where it prohibits the application of that principle no other basis for distribution of *benefits* is put in its place.

In this first formulation, then, the idea of justice according to need provides a principle for the distribution of outlay rather than output. Moreover, it is a view concerned with attaining a particular distribution of benefits within a given range. It does not go so far as to suggest that the range of the distribution itself should be changed. . . .

The distributive version of justice according to need has received its most cogent formulations in the problem of redistributing income. In that context, arguments for redistribution generally arise when the range of distribution is too large. When there are some who have not enough to secure the barest essentials of life and others who have more than any person can rationally choose to spend or invest, then our sense of injustice is aroused and arguments for redistribution are likely to be advanced. The principle is that in such circumstances we should find the means of taking from the top end of the distribution in order to raise the share of those at the bottom. Thus, the aim is to narrow the range in the distribution of income.

The distribution of educational benefits is not in all respects like the distribution of income. Still, there are interesting parallels. For example, we cannot, strictly speaking, take knowledge from those who have a lot and give it to those who don't. But still, it is not hard to imagine a society in which the range in the distribution of knowledge and skills is so great as to present serious social problems. In that case, we could not speak of taking educational benefits from the educationally rich to give to the educationally poor. But we would probably seek to narrow the range of the distribution somewhat by either advancing those at the bottom or holding back those at the top.

Thus, in the ethics of redistribution the striking parallel between education and income is to be found in the idea that there should be a floor and a ceiling. Just as our sense of injustice may demand the creation of a minimum level of income, so it may also demand establishment of a minimum level in the receipt of educational benefits. It certainly must be true in principle that there are levels of educational achievement and points in the system of schooling where educational benefits should be distributed on grounds of need, quite apart from any considerations of social utility or any claims of merit or ability. This would be a view of distribution according to need somewhat different from the one discussed earlier. Here need is defined not as *resources* needed to attain an equalization of distribution between social groups, but as minimum educational *benefits* needed for life in a particular society.

There are some immensely interesting features of this view of justice according to need. In the first place, although the first version was clearly a principle related to equal opportunity in the benefit sense, this version is not. It states simply that the educational system must distribute its benefits so that a certain share is secured by each person regardless of his abilities. That is to say, there must be a level of educational achievement that everyone attains and that level is not determined by the performance of the person of least abilities.

Other premises are needed, however, in order to render this a principle of equal opportunity. For example, it can be the case in a society that everyone attains a certain minimum level of achievement, but not at all during anything approaching the same period of time. Thus, if we view the distribution of educational benefits across generations, then this principle of distribution according to need is compatible with gross inequalities between social groups and within social groups at any *specific* period of time. An additional premise is needed, stating that the educational system must distribute its resources so that everyone attains or exceeds a certain level of benefits *at approx-*

imately the same age. If this additional condition is satisfied then it will follow that equal educational opportunity in the benefit sense will have been attained *at the level of minimum achievement;* for if it is satisfied, then it will follow that educational benefits will be distributed at some minimum level of need without regard to race, sex, or economic and social status and that this state of affairs will have been attained at about the same time for every member of each age cohort. On strictly conceptual grounds, this principle of justice according to need does not *by itself* constitute a principle of distribution sufficient to establish equal educational opportunity in the benefit sense. But with this additional condition, it does.

In the second place, this latter version of distribution independent of abilities and according to need is perfectly compatible with the principle of distribution according to ability, *provided the two principles are applied at different levels of the system.* This fact is of vastly greater import than it may seem at first blush. Unless this second version of justice according to need is restricted in its application to certain initial levels of the system, then it would no longer suffice as a principle of distribution at all. That is to say, if the demand is made and satisfied without restriction to distribute educational benefits equally to all persons at approximately the same age, then it becomes not a principle for equalization of a distribution within a certain range, but a principle for the elimination of the range itself. Thus, there are strong *prima facie* reasons to believe that no principle for the distribution of educational benefits according to need and unrelated to the distribution of abilities can be applied unrestrictedly to all levels of the educational system. Distribution according to merit or works must come into play.

Thus, the principle of justice according to need turns out, in one of its formulations, not to be a principle for the distribution of benefits at all and, in another of its formulations, not to be applicable without restriction to all levels of the system. In either case, the principle that educational benefits should be distributed in accord with the distribution of "educationally relevant" abilities gets reintroduced. It seems an intractable feature of education itself. Education is endemically unequal in the way it distributes its benefits. Some distributions will be acceptably unequal and some will not. At the juncture of educational theory and social policy two questions seem paramount. First, which distributions are unacceptably unequal and on

what grounds? And secondly, what non-educational goods and benefits on grounds of justice and utility ought to be linked to the distribution of educational goods and benefits?

Responsibility of the Schools:
A Sociologist's Perspective

Responsibility of the Schools in the Provision of Equal Educational Opportunity
JAMES S. COLEMAN

The author of this paper is perhaps the leading figure, certainly the
leading sociologist, among those studying the issue of equal
educational opportunity. Professor Coleman's study, commissioned
by the Congress through the Civil Rights Act of 1964, remains
the only nationwide survey of race and education in the United States.

In this selection, Coleman traces the development of the
concept of equality of educational opportunity in the United States.
He puts into perspective the conflicting views in today's controversy
and indicates how some of the findings of his study are influencing
contemporary interpretations of equal educational opportunity.

Coleman points out that the *effects* of resource inputs, rather
than a mere definition of inputs, now constitute the basis for
assessing equal opportunity. In this sense, Coleman, Komisar and
Coombs, and Green are in agreement. Indeed, as noted earlier,
Coleman's study has been the major influence in this development.
As Green pointed out, however, this kind of interpretation requires
a basic change in the concept of the school itself. Green doubts that
Americans can make this change; but Coleman, who also
recognizes that the shift in interpretation demands a corresponding
change in the concept of the school, is much more optimistic.

James S. Coleman is Professor of Social Relations at Johns
Hopkins University. He has written widely on adolescence and

SOURCE: *NASSP Bulletin*, May, 1968, pp. 179–190. Reprinted, with some
editing, by permission of the publisher and the author.

the sociology of education. His book, *The Adolescent Society* (New York: Free Press of Glencoe, 1961) marked him as one of the foremost authorities in this country on the sociology of adolescence.

I want to focus attention on a general concept or idea and on the way in which that concept, as held by people in society, has changed over recent history and is likely to change in the future. That concept is "equality of educational opportunity."

When public schools began in the United States, equality of opportunity meant several things:

1. Providing a *free education* up to a given level which constituted the principal entry point to the labor force.
2. Providing a *common curriculum* for all children, regardless of background.
3. Partly by design and partly because of low population density, providing that children from diverse backgrounds attend the *same school*.
4. Providing equality within a given *locality*, since local taxes provided the source of support for schools.

This conception of equality of opportunity is still held by many persons; but there are some assumptions in it which are not obvious.

One of the most important of these is that opportunity lay in exposure to a given curriculum. The amount of opportunity is then measured in terms of the level of curriculum to which the child is exposed. The higher the curriculum made available to a given set of children, the greater their opportunity.

The most interesting point about this assumption is the relatively passive role of the school and community, relative to the child's role. The school's obligation was to "provide an opportunity" by being available, within easy geographic access of the child, free of cost (beyond the value of the child's time), and with a curriculum that would not exclude him from higher education. The obligation to "use the opportunity" was on the child or the family, so that his role was defined to be the active one, with the responsibility for achievement upon him.

This concept of equality of opportunity has been implicit in most educational practice throughout most of the period of public education in the nineteenth and twentieth centuries. However, there have been several challenges to it, serious questions raised by new conditions in public education.

Challenges

Two of the most important challenges to the basic concept came from opposing directions: The Southern states in the United States, in the face of Negro demands for equality of opportunity during the reconstruction period, devised the concept of "separate but equal." And the Supreme Court countered this in 1954 with the doctrine that legal separation by race inherently constitutes inequality of opportunity. Thus the Southern states challenged the assumption that equality depended on the opportunity to attend the same school. This challenge was, however, consistent with the overall logic of the original concept, for the idea of attendance at the same school was not the most essential part of the logic. The logic, or inherent idea, was that opportunity resided in exposure to a curriculum, and the community's responsibility was to provide that exposure, the child's to take advantage of it.

It was the pervasiveness of this underlying idea which created the difficulty for the Supreme Court. It was evident that even when identical facilities and identical teacher salaries existed for racially separate schools, "equality of educational opportunity" in some sense did not exist. But the source of this inequality remained an unarticulated feeling. In the decision of the Supreme Court, this unarticulated feeling began to take form. The essence of it was that the *effects* of such separate schools were, or were likely to be, different. Thus the concept of equality of opportunity which focused on effects of schooling began to take form. The actual decision of the court was in fact a confusion of two unrelated premises: this new concept, which looked at results of schooling, and the legal premise that the use of race as a basis for school assignment violates fundamental freedoms.

But what is important for the evolution of this concept of equality of opportunity is that a new and different assumption was introduced—the assumption that equality of opportunity depends in some fashion upon effects of schooling. By so doing it brought into the open the implicit goals of equality of educational opportunity—that is, goals having to do with the *results* of school—to which the original concept was somewhat awkwardly directed. That these goals were in fact behind the concept can be verified by a simple mental experiment: suppose the early schools had operated for only one hour a week, attended by children of all social classes. This would have met the explicit assumptions of the early concept of equality of opportunity, since the school is free, with a common curriculum, and attended by all children in the locality. But it obviously would not have been accepted, even at that time, as providing equality of opportunity, because its effects would have been so minimal. The additional educational resources provided by middle- and upper-class families, whether in the home, by tutoring, or in private supplementary schools, would have created severe inequalities in results.

Thus the dependence of the concept upon results or effects of schooling, which had lain hidden until 1954, came partially into the open with the Supreme Court decision. Yet this was not the end, for it created more problems than it solved. It might allow one to assess gross inequalities, such as that created by dual school systems in the South or by a system like that in the mental experiment I just described. But it allows nothing beyond that. Even more confounding, since the decision did not use effects of schooling as a criterion of inequality, but only as justification for a criterion of racial integration, then integration itself emerged as the basis for a new concept of equality of educational opportunity. Thus the idea of effects of schooling as an element in the concept was introduced but immediately overshadowed by another, the criterion of racial integration.

Definitions of Inequality

The next stage in the evolution of this concept was, I believe, the Office of Education Survey of Equality of Educational Opportunity. This survey was carried out under a directive in the Civil Rights Act of 1964 to the Commissioner of Education to assess the "lack of equality of educational opportunity" among racial and other groups in the United States. The evolution of this concept, and the existing disarray which this evolution has created, made the very definition of the task exceedingly difficult. It was obvious that no single concept of equality of educational opportunity existed, and that the survey must give information relevant to a variety of different concepts.

One of these was the traditional concept, with inequality defined in terms of differences of the community's input to the school, such as per-pupil expenditure, school plants, libraries, quality of teachers, and other similar quantities. A second definition of inequality lay in the racial composition of the school, following the Supreme Court's decision that segregated schooling is inherently unequal. By the first of these two concepts, the question of inequality through segregation is excluded, while by the second, there is inequality of education within a school system so long as the schools within the system have different racial composition. Yet neither of these definitions gives a suggestion of just how relevant any of these factors might be for school quality. Both are definitions of inequality in terms of resources provided in the school, with no attention to the relevance of these resources for learning.

A third and fourth concept take exactly the opposite approach, looking at effects of school. The first of these may be defined in terms of effects of the school for individuals with *equal backgrounds and abilities*. In this definition, equality of educational opportunity is equality of results, given the same individual input. With such a definition, inequality might come about either from differences in the school inputs or racial composition, but the test lies in the effects of these conditions.

The fourth type of inequality, again based on effects of school, is defined in terms of consequences of the school for individuals of *unequal* backgrounds and abilities. In this definition, equality of educational opportunity is equality of results given *different* individual inputs. The most striking examples of inequality of background here would be children from households in which a language other than English, such as Spanish or Navaho, is spoken. Other examples would be low-achieving children from homes in which there is a poverty of verbal expression or an absence of experiences which lead to conceptual facility.

Such a definition taken in the extreme would imply that equality of educational opportunity is reached only when the results of schooling (achievement and attitudes) are the same for the average member of racial and ethnic minorities as for the average member of the dominant group. These four definitions of equality for which the survey was designed split sharply into two groups: The first two concern *input* resources: first, those brought to the school by the actions of the school administration—facilities, curriculum, teachers; and second, those brought to the school by the other students, in the educational backgrounds which their presence contributed to the school. The last two definitions concern the *effects* of schooling.

When the report emerged, it did not give four different measures of equality, one for each of those definitions. But it did focus sharply on this dichotomy, in chapter 2 giving information on inequalities of input, relevant to the first and second definitions, and in chapter 3, giving information on the relation of input to results, relevant to the third and fourth definitions.

Assessing Effectiveness

Though not directly relevant to our discussion here, it is interesting to note the major results of this report. Examining the relation of school inputs to achievement results showed that it is precisely those input characteristics of schools that are *most alike* for Negroes and whites that are *least effective* for their achievement. Differences between schools attended by Negroes and those attended by whites were in the following increasing order: least differences, facilities and curriculum; next, teacher quality; and greatest differences, educational backgrounds of fellow students. This is precisely the same order as the effects these characteristics had on achievement of Negro students: facilities and curriculum, least effects; teacher quality, next; and backgrounds of fellow students, most effects.

I suggest that, by making the dichotomy between inputs and results explicit and by focusing attention not only on inputs but on results, the Office of Education Report brought into the open what had underlain all the ideas of equality of educational opportunity but had remained largely hidden: the concept implied *effective* equality of opportunity, that is, equality in those elements that are effective for learning. The reason this had lain half-hidden, obscured by definitions that involve inputs, is, I suspect, because educational research has until recently been unprepared to demonstrate what elements are effective.

The controversy that has surrounded the Report indicates that such measurement of effects is still subject to sharp disagreement. But the crucial point is that effects of inputs have come to constitute the basis for assessment of school quality (and thus equality of opportunity), rather than the mere definition of particular inputs being the measures of quality (e.g., that, by definition, small classes are better than large or higher-paid teachers are better than lower-paid ones).

But then, what would full equality of educational opportunity be if there were equality of effects, independent of the child's background? Clearly, achievement of groups that began at a different point should show a convergence, so that even though two population groups begin school with different levels of skills on the average, the average of the group that begins lower moves up to coincide with that of the group that begins higher.

Yet there are serious questions about this definition of equality of opportunity. It implies that over the 12 years of school there are no other influences, such as the family environment, which affect achievement, even though these influences may differ greatly for the two population groups. Concretely, it implies that white family environments, predominately middle class, and Negro family environments, predominately lower class, will produce no effects on achievement that would keep these averages apart. Such an assumption seems highly unrealistic, especially in view of the general importance of family background for achievement.

However, if such possibilities are acknowledged, then how far can the effects extend before there is inequality of educational opportunity? Can there be a constant difference throughout the school years? Or increasing differences?

A New Concept of Equality

The unanswerability of such questions begins to give a sense of a new concept of equality of educational opportunity—because these questions concern the *relative intensity* of two sets of influences: those which are alike for the two groups, principally in school, and those which are different, such as those in the home or neighborhood. If the school's influences are not only alike for the two groups but are very strong, relative to the divergent influences, then the two groups will move closer together. If those influences are very weak, then the groups will move apart. Or more generally, the relative intensity of the convergent school influences and the divergent out-of-school influences determines the proximity of the educational system to providing equality of educational opportunity. That is, equality of output is not so much determined by equality of the resource inputs, but by the power of these resources in bringing about achievement.

This, then, I suggest is the place where the concept of equality of educational opportunity presently stands—an evolution that might have been anticipated a century and a half ago when the first such concepts arose, yet one which is very different from the concept as it first developed. This difference is sharpened if we examine a further implication of the current concept. In describing the early concept, I indicated that the role of the community and the educational institution was a relatively passive one, that of providing a set of free public resources. The responsibility for profitable use of those resources lay with the child and his family. But the evolution of the concept has reversed these roles.

The implication of the concept as I have described it here is that the responsibility to create achievement lies with the educational institution, not with the child. The difference in achievement at grade 12 between the average Negro and the average white is, in effect, the degree of inequality of opportunity; and the reduction of that inequality is a responsibility of the school. This shift in responsibility follows logically from the shift of the concept of equality of opportunity from school resource inputs to effects of schooling. When that shift came about in the past several years, the school's responsibility shifted from increasing its "quality" and equalizing the distribution of this "quality" to the quality of its students' achievements. Yet how is this responsibility to be realized? I suggest that it may be realized through a change in the very concept of the school itself, from being the agency within which the child is taught to being the agent responsible for seeing that the child learns—a responsibility in which the school's own facilities may play only a part.

Legal Aspects Based on Court Cases

Separate but Equal
ALBERT P. BLAUSTEIN &
CLARENCE CLYDE FERGUSON, JR.

The two illustrations in Chapter 3 revealed how interpretation of the Equal Protection Clause of the Fourteenth Amendment has affected the struggle for educational equality during the last 75 years. The most

SOURCE: Albert P. Blaustein and Clarence C. Ferguson, Jr., *Desegregation and the Law: The Meaning and Effect of the School Segregation Cases* (New Brunswick, N.J.: Rutgers University Press, 1957), pp. 95–113. Reprinted by permission of the publisher and authors.

dramatic change in interpretation, of course, took place in 1954 when the Supreme Court, in *Brown* v. *Board of Education,* reversed the "separate but equal" doctrine of 1896. In this selection, Albert Blaustein and Clarence Ferguson analyze the legal history of the changing interpretation of the Fourteenth Amendment. The authors emphasize the many questions raised by the "separate but equal" concept and the underlying problem of determining criteria for measuring equality. They show how the numerous court cases following *Plessy* attempted to clarify the meaning of *equal protection* and to provide remedies for existing inequalities. The authors' main objective here is to trace the legal interpretation of the concept of equal educational opportunity. Their analysis ends with *Brown* v. *Board of Education* because it was there that the Court decided that integrated schools are a necessary condition for equality. Theoretically, the *Brown* decision made measurement of equality possible. As we will see in subsequent readings, however, the implementation of this *Brown* doctrine continues to be a frustrating societal goal.

At this point the reader might return to Chapter 3 to review the desegregation and school finance controversies which have been used throughout this book as illustrations of the struggle for equality in education.

This selection is taken from *Desegregation and the Law,* a classic work in the field of school law which provides an excellent legal-historical analysis of the school desegregation cases prior to and including the Brown case. Both Albert Blaustein and Clarence Ferguson are distinguished legal scholars. Blaustein is at present Professor of Law, Rutgers University at Camden. Ferguson is the former Dean of the Howard University Law School and is at present serving as an Assistant Secretary of State in Washington, D.C.

In 1895, an era of aggressive Negro leadership ended with the death of Frederick Douglass, a Negro spokesman and a close companion of the Radical Republicans who dominated Congress during the post-Civil War period. In that same year, Negro leader Booker T. Washington delivered a major speech in Atlanta, calling for a new program of racial coexistence based upon the concept of racial separation. And, in 1895, the Supreme Court docketed the case which was to establish the "separate but equal" doctrine in constitutional law.[1]

Homer Plessy, one-eighth Negro and seven-eighths white, was arrested in Louisiana when he refused to ride in the "colored" coach

[1] *Plessy* v. *Ferguson,* 163 U.S. 537, 16 Sup. Ct. 1138, 41 L. Ed. 256 (1896).

of a railroad train as required by the Louisiana statutes. He then instituted an action to restrain enforcement of these statutes on the grounds that they violated the Thirteenth and Fourteenth Amendments. The defendant, Ferguson, was the Louisiana judge designated to conduct the trial of Plessy on criminal charges. Plessy's plea to prohibit Ferguson's hearing the case was denied in the Louisiana courts. The Supreme Court affirmed.[2]

As it did in the *Slaughter-House* and *Civil Rights Cases* the Court brushed aside all arguments based on the Thirteenth Amendment. Debate on the Fourteenth Amendment raised more difficult legal problems. Unlike the cases which had involved the power of Congress to forbid discrimination, *Plessy* v. *Ferguson* posed the issue of the power of the state to require racial separation. The state action requirement, which had been read into the Fourteenth Amendment by the Court, had been fully satisfied. Louisiana had acted affirmatively in ordering segregation by race on public carriers. A new problem on the meaning of the Fourteenth Amendment was squarely before the nine men—and the opinion of the Supreme Court comprised the basic precedent for the arguments of the South in *Brown* v. *Board of Education.*

The "object" and purpose of the Fourteenth Amendment, according to the Court, was to secure the "absolute equality of the two races before the law." But, wrote Justice Henry Billings Brown, "in the nature of things it could not have been intended to abolish distinctions based on color, or to enforce social, as distinguished from political equality, or a commingling of the two races upon terms unsatisfactory to either." [3] In reaching this conclusion the Court did not indicate whether or to what extent it had followed the intent of the framers. But this was not important. The majority was obviously seeking to present its own particular viewpoint, and the method of analysis employed would have made such an inquiry irrelevant. Once the justices assumed that "in the nature of things" distinctions based on color could not have been intended to be prohibited, then the actual intent of the framers could play no part in their constitutional interpretation.

Plessy argued that state-enforced segregation stamped Negroes with a badge of inferiority. The high court disagreed, saying that such

---

[2] *Ibid.*
[3] *Id.,* at 163 U.S. 543, 16 Sup. Ct. 1140, 41 L. Ed. 258.

laws did not necessarily imply the inferiority of either one of the races. Following this point of view, Plessy could suffer no damage as a result of mere separation so long as the facilities furnished were equal to those from which he was excluded.

Counsel for Plessy asserted that if separation by race were held valid, a legislature might enact, with impunity, statutes designed solely to annoy a particular class. Legislation requiring Negroes and whites to walk on separate sides of the street, or an act requiring a railroad to provide separate cars for passengers with red, black and blond hair would all be valid, argued Plessy's lawyer. The Court concluded that classifications of this type were far different from state-required segregation.

"[T]he case reduces itself to a question whether the statute of Louisiana is a reasonable regulation," declared the high court, "and in respect to this, there must be a large discretion on the part of the legislature. In determining the question of reasonableness it is at liberty to act with respect to the established usages, customs and traditions of the people, and with a view to their comfort, and the preservation of the public peace and good order." [4] Implicit in the analysis made by the Court is the proposition that a legislative classification based on race alone may be justified under the Fourteenth Amendment, as long as some court deems it *reasonable*.

The conclusion that the Louisiana statute was reasonable was based upon the then existing traditions, customs and usages of the people, evidence of which was found by the Court in the school segregation statutes passed by the various states and District of Columbia. Particular reliance was placed upon the 1849 case of *Roberts* v. *City of Boston*,[5] in which the Supreme Judicial Court of Massachusetts upheld school segregation under the state constitution. Charles Sumner, later a leader among Radical Republicans, had been attorney for the plaintiff in the Roberts case. He argued that school segregation violated the Massachusetts constitutional declaration that all men were created free and equal. According to Sumner's reasoning, "free and equal" meant that all men were entitled to equal protection of the laws, and requiring Negroes to attend separate schools deprived them of that protection. Sumner's argument was the first formulation of the equal protection of the laws concept.

---

[4] *Id.*, at 163 U.S. 550, 16 Sup. Ct. 1143, 41 L. Ed. 260.
[5] *Roberts* v. *City of Boston*, 5 Cush. (59 Mass.) 198 (1849).

The Court in the Plessy case had ignored the impact of the Fourteenth Amendment itself on Massachusetts and other states. It did not recognize, as had the Supreme Court of Michigan in 1890, that the Roberts case "was made in the *ante bellum* days before the colored man was a citizen, and when, in nearly half the Union, he was but a chattel." Concluded the Michigan court, "it cannot now serve as precedent." [6] *Roberts* v. *City of Boston* was not strictly a precedent for the Plessy decision, but it was considered as evidence of customs and traditions of the American people. Although *Plessy* v. *Ferguson* did not involve education, there is no doubt that the Supreme Court had bestowed its blessings on state-maintained segregated school systems.

As in the *Civil Rights Cases,* John Marshall Harlan was the sole dissenter. "Our constitution," he declared, "is color blind, and neither knows nor tolerates classes among citizens." And, he continued, "In my opinion the judgment this day rendered will, in time, prove to be quite as pernicious as the decision in the *Dred Scott* case." [7]

With the Plessy decision, the separate but equal formula became the law of the Constitution. *Plessy* v. *Ferguson* is cited again and again as the case which established this doctrine. And yet, oddly enough, there are no words in the Court's opinion which declare that segregation is to be permitted where equal facilities are provided. Such words were to come from later lower court decisions which attempted to give meaning to the Plessy principle. What happened in the Plessy case was that the judges upheld what they believed to be the "reasonableness" of the Louisiana transportation laws without providing guidance for the other courts which had to decide these subsequent segregation cases. The principle propounded by the nine men of 1896—that a state could compel "reasonable" racial segregation—was strictly judge-made law, giving a hitherto unknown meaning to the Fourteenth Amendment. It was basic law, but it left unanswered two critical questions: What are the criteria for measuring equality? What is the proper judicial remedy where inequality is found to exist?

In view of the ultimate holding in *Plessy* v. *Ferguson,* the Court was not required to reach the second question. While logically it should have considered the first question in arriving at its decision,

---

[6] *Ferguson* v. *Gies,* 82 Mich. 358, 364, 46 N.W. 718, 720 (1890).
[7] *Supra,* note 1, 163 U.S. 559, 16 Sup. Ct. 1146, 41 L. Ed. 263.

there is nothing in the opinion which shows any attempt to formulate a standard of equivalence. This failure probably lies in the fact that the Court classified the right to ride an unsegregated train and attend an unsegregated school as inherently *social*. And the Supreme Court had already concluded that the Amendment was designed to protect political rights only. On the basis of this type of analysis Plessy had no right to invoke the Amendment at all, even if there were in fact inequality.

In view of later decisions on segregation there is no valid distinction between social and political rights where the racial segregation is state-imposed. Regardless of the distinction which might be made by a layman between political and social rights, once those rights are affected by state action they become political in nature. Failure of the Court to grasp this fact has led lawyers as well as laymen to the mistaken assumption that the absence of a state command to separate the races is the logical equivalent of a command to commingle. This in turn has led to the observation that "If one race be inferior to the other socially, the Constitution of the United States cannot put them upon the same plane." [8] The assertion was completely irrelevant. Plessy was merely requesting freedom from a state-imposed requirement that he ride in a separate railroad car; he was not requesting a ruling that whites and Negroes be compelled to ride together. What Plessy was requesting may sound like the same thing as an order to commingle, but it is in reality something quite different. That difference is spelled out in numerous opinions which have been handed down since the Plessy decision. An individual may with impunity choose his social peers by the application of any criteria he desires—color, religion, education, wealth or hair styling. Once the state enters the picture, however, the choice is no longer personal or social. Discrimination becomes a political matter. It follows that a state may not behave as if it were a country club when it enacts laws affecting voting, jury service or public education.

Three years after *Plessy* v. *Ferguson,* the Court faced its first school segregation case, *Cummings* v. *Board of Education.*[9] The Negro plaintiffs had asked for an injunction closing the white schools of Richmond County, Georgia, until a separate school was provided for Negro children. At the beginning of the litigation, plaintiffs

[8] *Id.,* at 163 U.S. 552, 16 Sup. Ct. 1143, 41 L. Ed. 261.
[9] *Cummings* v. *Board of Education,* 175 U.S. 528, 20 Sup. Ct. 197, 44 L. Ed. 262 (1899).

contended that under the separate but equal ‚doctrine complete failure to provide a high school resulted in obvious inequality. Then, during the oral argument, the Negro parents asserted for the first time that state-maintained separate schools were unconstitutional. As a matter of technical legal procedure, the contention came too late. "It was said at argument," Justice Harlan responded for the Court, "that the vice in the common school system of Georgia was the requirement that the white and colored children of the State be educated in separate schools. But we need not consider that question in this case. No such issue was made in the pleadings." [10] The nine men then held that the remedy requested was improper, since closing all the schools would not eradicate the wrong, and the suit was dismissed. Thus in its first education case, the Supreme Court not only avoided passing on the validity of separate but equal, but also failed to indicate any appropriate standards for measuring equality.

The 1899 Cummings case was cited by ex-Justice Byrnes in 1956 as the first of six earlier Supreme Court opinions upholding the separate but equal doctrine in public education.[11] Byrnes, however, omits discussion of the very similar case of *Berea College* v. *Kentucky*,[12] decided in 1908. For, in this case, as in the Cummings case, the Supreme Court had before it a question of segregated schools—and in the Berea case, as in the Cummings case, the Court avoided direct consideration of the separate but equal doctrine.

In the Berea case, the Supreme Court had under analysis the "Day Law" of Kentucky, which stated that whites and Negroes could not be taught together in any private school unless that school maintained separate buildings for each race at least twenty-five miles apart. The Court sustained the law on the narrow ground that a corporate charter (and that would include the one held by Berea College) was subject to the reasonable regulations of the legislature which granted that charter. The effect of the ruling was to allow the "Day Law" to stand, without the necessity of reconsidering separate but equal. As in *Plessy* v. *Ferguson,* Justice Harlan registered a dissent.

The second of the cases cited by Byrnes as authority for the

[10] *Id.,* at 175 U.S. 543, 20 Sup. Ct. 200, 44 L. Ed. 266.
[11] James F. Byrnes, "The Supreme Court Must Be Curbed," *U.S. News and World Report,* May 18, 1956, p. 52.
[12] *Berea College* v. *Kentucky,* 211 U.S. 45, 29 Sup. Ct. 33, 53 L. Ed. 81 (1908).

validity of the separate but equal doctrine is the important 1927 decision of *Gong Lum* v. *Rice.*[13]

Martha Lum, a Chinese resident of Mississippi, objected to a school board order requiring her to attend a school maintained for members of the colored race. Since there were no separate schools for Mongolians, she contended that she was entitled to attend the white schools. Homer Plessy, who was seven-eighths white, initially argued essentially the same point; he asserted that he should be entitled to the benefits of being white and not subjected to the disabilities of being Negro. In *Plessy* v. *Ferguson,* the Supreme Court avoided decision as to whether Plessy was white or Negro. In the Gong Lum case it accepted the finding of the Mississippi courts that for purposes of the public education laws, all those who were not white belonged to the "colored race."

Legally, Martha Lum might just as well have been Negro. Thus the stage was set for a direct ruling on the validity of separate but equal in public education. Was legislation requiring racially segregated schools unconstitutional as an automatic denial of the equal protection of the laws?

"Were this a new question," wrote Chief Justice Taft, "it would call for very full argument and consideration, but we think that it is the same question which has been many times decided to be within the constitutional power of the state legislature to settle without intervention of the federal courts under the Federal Constitution." [14] The Chief Justice then cited fifteen cases in support of his assertion, but in none of the cases had the Supreme Court spoken.

Speaking for the Court, Taft then referred to the Plessy case as having approved the decision in *Roberts* v. *City of Boston*. This was in large measure inaccurate. The Roberts case, it will be remembered, arose before the Fourteenth Amendment was in existence. And in *Roberts* v. *City of Boston,* the Plessy Court had found not a precedent, but only some evidence of "custom, usage and tradition" which justified the classification by race. On the other hand, the fifteen lower court cases cited by Taft were precedents; they did hold that separate but equal facilities satisfied the requirements of the equal protection clause. The Supreme Court of 1927, however, refused to accord those precedents express approval. They merely held that

[13] *Gong Lum* v. *Rice,* 275 U.S. 78, 48 Sup. Ct. 91, 72 L. Ed. 172 (1927).
[14] *Id.,* at 275 U.S. 85, 48 Sup. Ct. 93, 72 L. Ed. 177.

Martha Lum could be classified as colored *"assuming* the cases above cited to be rightly decided" [15] (emphasis supplied).

While the separate but equal rule did come before the Court again during the first forty years following *Plessy* v. *Ferguson,* it was upheld only in the transportation cases. Certainly, questions as to the constitutionality of the doctrine were not reconsidered by the Court in the only three school cases which had arisen during that period. Failure to act resulted in the continuation of separate school systems all over the South and in some parts of the North. It was clear that such schools would continue to exist until the Supreme Court squarely faced the issue. For all practical purposes, the separate but equal concept had achieved *de facto* constitutionality in the field of public education as a minimum constitutional requirement.

But this was the extent of the decisional law as formulated by the United States Supreme Court. There still remained the question of how to measure equality; there still remained the question of a proper judicial remedy when and if inequality was found to exist.

These questions arose again and again as the lower federal courts struggled to reach judgment in subsequent school segregation cases. The federal district judges could not find the answers in the Plessy, Cummings and Gong Lum decisions, and they obviously could not ask the Supreme Court to explain its prior opinions. All that the lower courts could do was to apply the Plessy principle as they understood it—and answer the questions themselves. From the amalgam of their decisions came the expression and amplification of the separate but equal dogma. Yet, despite the number of lower court cases which were to consider the issue of school segregation, the courts were significantly unsuccessful in fashioning definite criteria to measure equality.

In 1912, per capita expenditure for Negro schools was $1.71, as compared to the figure of $15 for all schools.[16] But measurement in terms of dollars and cents alone is not necessarily the best guide in evaluating a state's educational offerings. In the Cummings case, the Court had found no vice in the disparity of expenditures in the dual school system. Nor was it feasible to demand identical school facilities as a requirement of equality, since absolute duplication would

[15] *Ibid.*
[16] See Herbert Hill and Jack Greenberg, *Citizen's Guide to De-Segregation* (Boston, 1955), p. 45.

be an impossibility. All that the courts could or did say was that separate but equal required "substantial" equality.

Defining substantial equality was itself a formidable task. Even when the issue presented was one of physical inequality in the tangibles—buildings, books and equipment—inconsistent judgments followed.[17] When more subtle standards were argued before the courts—quality of instruction, school supervision and curricula content—even greater divergence of opinion resulted.[18]

Fiscal differences, while easily proved as matters of fact, gave rise to difficult collateral legal questions involving tax incidence and tax classification.[19] Separate but equal raised many more problems than it solved.

The remedy for correcting such inequality was similarly left to the lower courts. The Supreme Court had already indicated in the Cummings case that closing down all the schools was not an appropriate solution. No further guidance was given by the high tribunal as to the proper relief. The lower courts fashioned remedies which varied from ordering immediate admission to white schools to vague directions to educational authorities to equalize the schools.[20]

Writing in 1954, Robert A. Leflar, dean of the Arkansas Law School, and Wylie Davis concluded: "It is generally conceded that the experiment, so far as it depended in areas of governmental regulation upon a judicial guaranty of 'separate but equal' facilities for Negroes and other minority races in this country has failed to effectuate the theory underlying it. Until recently," they continued, "the governmental conduct required in public education by the 'separate but equal' rule has seldom been clear, and even when clear, has seldom been forthcoming." [21]

The cases of Plessy, Cummings and Berea were certainly not

---

[17] See *Butler* v. *Wilemon*, 86 F. Supp. 397 (Tex. 1949); *Moore* v. *Porterfield*, 113 Okla. 234, 241 Pac. 346 (1925); *Lowery* v. *School Trustees*, 140 N.C. 33, 52 S.E. 267 (1905).

[18] See *Reynold* v. *Board of Education*, 66 Kan. 672, 72 Pac. 274 (1903); *Williams* v. *Zimmerman*, 172 Md. 563, 192 Atl. 353 (1937); *Carter* v. *School Board*, 182 F.2d 531 (4th Cir. 1950).

[19] *E.g.*, *Davenport* v. *Cloverport*, 72 Fed. 689 (Ky. 1896); *Lowery* v. *School Trustees, supra*, note 17.

[20] See *Miller* v. *Board of Education*, 106 F. Supp. 988 (D.C. 1952); *Williams* v. *Board of Education*, 79 Kan. 202, 99 Pac. 216 (1908); *cf. Wrighten* v. *Board of Trustees*, 72 F. Supp. 948 (S.C. 1947).

[21] Robert A. Leflar and Wylie H. Davis, *Public School Segregation*, 67 Harv. L. Rev. 377, 392 (1954).

definitive as to constitutional requirements in public education. In *Brown* v. *Board of Education,* the Supreme Court recognized that the Gong Lum case had not decided the ultimate constitutional question. The plaintiff in that case, observed Chief Justice Warren, "contended only that state authorities had misapplied the doctrine by classifying him [sic] with Negro children and requiring him [sic] to attend a Negro school."

This certainly does not mean that because the first three education cases did not technically validate the doctrine of separate but equal, the Court in 1954 was forced to decide as it did in *Brown* v. *Board of Education.* Just as the Supreme Court limited its reading of those three cases to restrict them to their technical holdings, so it could have, on the other hand, read them expansively. Counsel for the Southern states urged the broader interpretation.

The Supreme Court might have concluded that after fifty years of failure to declare separate but equal *invalid,* it was too late to raise the argument anew in 1954. John W. Davis urged the Court to adopt this position during oral argument: "[S]omewhere, sometime, to every principle comes a moment of repose when the decision has been so often announced, so confidently relied upon, so long continued, that it passes the limits of judicial discretion and disturbance." [22]

On some occasions such argument has been persuasive. The constitutional doctrine which extended the protection of the Fourteenth Amendment's due process clause to corporations became established in much the same manner as did separate but equal doctrine in the field of public education. [23] In 1937, forty-eight years after corporations first received the benefits of due process, only Justice Black was willing to disturb the legal principles upon which states and incorporated associations had so long relied. [24] Lawyer Davis contended that judicial statesmanship required the Court to accept the settled practices of the South: "And we said in effect—and I am bold enough to repeat it here now—that, in the language of Judge Parker in his opinion below, after that had been the consistent

[22] John W. Davis, Oral argument in *Brown* v. *Board of Education* (private printing), p. 18.

[23] *Santa Clara County* v. *Southern Pacific Ry. Co.,* 118 U.S. 294, 30 L.Ed. 118 (1886); *Minneapolis Ry. Co.* v. *Beckwith,* 129 U.S. 26, 9 Sup. Ct. 207, 32 L. Ed. 586 (1889).

[24] *Connecticut General Co.* v. *Johnson,* 303 U.S. 77, 85, 58 Sup. Ct. 436, 439, 82 L. Ed. 673, 678 (1938).

history for over three quarters of a century, it was late indeed in the day to disturb it on any theoretical or sociological basis." [25] John W. Davis, as chief proponent of the Southern argument, was unable to persuade Chief Justice Warren's Court.

Why did the Supreme Court, fifty-five years after its first educational decision in the Cummings case, decide to call for "very full argument and consideration" of the question of the constitutionality of school segregation? A portion of the answer is found in four other opinions of the Court, and in a case decided by the highest court of Maryland. Interestingly enough, all but one of these cases involved segregation in law schools, while the one exception was concerned with separate facilities in graduate education. In each of these five cases the court ordered integration to achieve the requirement of equality.

In 1935 a graduate of Amherst College, Donald Murray, was denied admission to the University of Maryland Law School solely because of his race. In Murray's suit against the University, he was represented by Thurgood Marshall, just two years at the bar. University officials offered Murray a scholarship to attend any law school which would accept him, but he claimed a right to attend the state-supported school in Maryland.

The Maryland Court of Appeals decisively answered the two critical questions involved in the application of the separate but equal doctrine.[26] The first of these questions related to the measure of equality; the second was concerned with the proper remedy.

As to the first problem, the court held that Maryland's offer of an out-of-state tuition scholarship was inadequate as a matter of dollars and cents. Murray would have to bear the costs of living away from home. Further, the Court of Appeals agreed with Murray's other arguments. "And as petitioner points out," said the Court of Appeals in regard to non-Maryland law schools, "he could not there have the advantages of study of law of this state primarily, and of attendance on state courts, where he intends to practice." [27] For these two reasons, the Court concluded that Maryland's treatment of Murray not only constituted a factual inequality, but was below the standard of "substantial" equality required by the equal protection clause.

[25] *Supra*, note 22.
[26] *Pearson* v. *Murray*, 169 Md. 478, 182 Atl. 590 (1936).
[27] *Id.*, at 169 Md. 486, 182 Atl. 593.

The opinion was equally decisive as to the proper remedy. "[Since in] Maryland now the equal treatment can be furnished only in the one existing law school, the petitioner, in our opinion," declared the high court, "must be admitted there. We cannot find the remedy to be that of ordering separate schools for Negroes." [28] And Murray entered Maryland Law School.

Not so fortunate was Lloyd Gaines, who sought and was denied admission to the state-supported law school at the University of Missouri. Seven of the nine men of the United States Supreme Court eventually held in 1938 that Gaines must be offered a legal education in Missouri, and that in the absence of a separate equal school there, he had the right to attend the "white" law school.[29] Gaines was never to enjoy the fruits of his victory. He disappeared shortly after the opinion was rendered, and diligent search has failed to uncover his whereabouts.

The Gaines case was the beginning of a revolution in the Supreme Court approach to educational problems. True, separate but equal was not overturned. In fact, the Court was expressly giving content to the "equal" requirement of the formula. But in giving substance to the doctrine, the Supreme Court began to consider the intangible factors obviously present in legal education. "Petitioner insists," wrote Chief Justice Hughes in the Gaines case, "that for one intending to practice in Missouri there are special advantages in attending a law school there, both in relation to the opportunities for the particular study of Missouri law and for the observation of the local courts, and also in view of the prestige of the Missouri law school among the citizens of the State, his prospective clients." [30] And, as had the state tribunal in the Murray decision, the Supreme Court concluded that the offer of tuition in an out-of-state law school could not duplicate these advantages.

Neither the Gaines nor the Murray situations involved a separate Negro law school within the state. Thus the only effective remedy for Gaines and Murray was the immediate admission to the state-supported law school.

This was desegregation even under the separate but equal formula.

[28] *Id.,* at 169 Md. 488, 182 Atl. 594.
[29] *Missouri ex rel. Gaines* v. *Canada,* 305 U.S. 337, 59 Sup. Ct. 232, 83 L. Ed. 208 (1938).
[30] *Id.,* at 305 U.S. 349, 59 Sup. Ct. 236, 83 L. Ed. 213.

Justices James C. McReynolds and Pierce Butler disagreed with Hughes' analysis in the Gaines case. They suggested arguments which the South was to use in *Brown* v. *Board of Education.* "For a long time," wrote McReynolds in his dissent, "Missouri has acted upon the view that the best interests of her people demand separation of whites and Negroes in schools. Under the opinion just announced, I presume she may abandon her law school and thereby disadvantage her white citizens without improving petitioner's opportunities for legal instruction; or she may break down the settled practice concerning separate schools and thereby, as indicated by experience, damnify both races." [31]

In 1950, fifteen years after the Gaines case, Herman Sweatt was denied admission to the University of Texas Law School on racial grounds. Unlike Maryland and Missouri, which offered to educate Negro lawyers in other states, Texas established a separate law school. The equality of this new law school was in issue. By the time that the Sweatt case reached the Supreme Court, it was clear that the legal education cases were directly related to the problems of general public education. "Friends of the Court" appeared on both sides, offering their legal views. In addition to the briefs filed by the parties directly concerned, *amici curiae* briefs in support of Sweatt were submitted by the United States government and by a committee of law school teachers among others. The attorneys general of eleven Southern states prepared prosegregation arguments. It was urged that the Court should repudiate *Plessy* v. *Ferguson* in its application to school segregation; it was also urged that the Court make a specific statement recognizing the principle of separate but equal in all areas of public education.

The Supreme Court, however, was not yet ready to make a clear statement adopting either of these divergent positions. It readily found substantial inequality existed between Texas's white and colored law schools in regard to the "tangibles"—size of faculty, number of library volumes, physical plant and location.[32] "What is more important," declared the Court, "the University of Texas Law School possesses to a far greater degree those qualities which are incapable of objective measurement but which make for greatness in a law school." [33]

---

[31] *Id.,* at 305 U.S. 353, 59 Sup. Ct. 238, 83 L. Ed. 215.
[32] *Sweatt* v. *Painter,* 339 U.S. 629, 70 Sup. Ct. 848, 94 L. Ed. 1114 (1950).
[33] *Id.,* at 339 U.S. 634, 70 Sup. Ct. 850, 94 L. Ed. 1119.

The Court had little difficulty in dealing effectively with the formulation of criteria of equality in legal education. As a court of lawyers, it was thoroughly familiar with the aims and objectives of legal education. It could and did speak from its collective experience. No sociologists were needed to remind the Court that, "The law school cannot be effective in isolation from the individuals and institutions with which the law interacts. Few students and no one who has practiced law would choose to study in an academic vacuum, removed from the interplay of ideas and exchange of views with which the law is concerned." [34] So far as the law was concerned, the Court's obvious and undisputed premise was that the professional society in which lawyers circulated was of necessity nonsegregated. There are no colored court systems, nor colored governments. Education for an integrated society must of necessity be nonsegregated to be effective. In the Murray, Gaines and Sweatt cases, the courts ultimately found that integration was the constitutional measure of the states' obligation in legal education.

Two years before the Sweatt decision, the Court had used the Gaines formula in ordering the immediate admission of a Negro applicant to the University of Oklahoma Law School. In that case, *Sipuel* v. *Board of Education*,[35] the nine men issued a *per curiam* decision (a brief opinion of the whole Court with minimum explanation) noting that the inequality was patent. Since no provision had been made for Negro legal education either in state or out-of-state, immediate admission to the one Oklahoma-supported law school was deemed the proper remedy.

This was not, however, the only *possible* remedy. While the Cummings case had rejected the proposal to close down all schools where inequality existed, the Supreme Court might have ordered the state to provide a separate law school which would meet the tests of the then standard of substantial equality.[36] This could only have been done before the Sweatt decision, since that case pointed out the impossibility of segregated equality in a nonsegregated society. But the Supreme Court would not render such a judgment.

The Court (and the judges of Maryland) held that the rights

---

[34] *Ibid.*

[35] *Sipuel* v. *Board of Education*, 332 U.S. 631, 68 Sup. Ct. 299, 92 L. Ed. 604 (1948).

[36] See *Fisher* v. *Hurst*, 333 U.S. 147, 68 Sup. Ct. 389, 92 L. Ed. 1149 (1950).

of the Negro plaintiffs under the Constitution were both "personal and present." And since they were "present," the law could not ask Gaines, Sipuel and Sweatt to await the establishment of new law schools. Immediate admission to existing schools was the only adequate remedy.

On the same day that the Sweatt case was decided, the Court also gave judgment in *McLaurin* v. *Board of Regents*.[87] Following the decision in the Sipuel case, McLaurin had been admitted to the Graduate School of the University of Oklahoma. Desegregation, however, stopped at the point of admittance. McLaurin was assigned a special "colored" seat in each classroom, a special table was provided for him in the library, and he was required to dine in a segregated portion of the school cafeteria. The Supreme Court struck down such discriminatory practices in these words: "There is a vast difference—a Constitutional difference—between restrictions imposed by the state which prohibit the intellectual commingling of students, and the refusal of individuals to commingle when the state presents no such bar." [88]

Justice Brown in the Plessy case had assumed that an absence of a state command to separate the races was the logical equivalent of a state command to commingle. In deciding the McLaurin case, however, the Supreme Court erased this assumption from constitutional analysis. Notwithstanding the McLaurin decision, Senator Ervin still argued in 1956 that Southerners "realize that if a valid law requiring desegregation should be adopted, they would no longer have the freedom to select their associates. They would be forced to associate by legal formula rather than personal preference." [89]

Despite the far-reaching import of the McLaurin decision and the law school cases, the Court purported not to disturb the separate but equal doctrine. "Broader issues have been urged for our consideration," said Chief Justice Vinson in *Sweatt* v. *Painter*, "but we adhere to the principle of deciding constitutional questions only in the context of the particular case before the Court." [40] There was no need for the Court to re-examine separate but equal in order to reach its decisions. This principle of judicial self-restraint is well established.

---

[87] *McLaurin* v. *Board of Regents*, 339 U.S. 637, 70 Sup. Ct. 851, 94 L. Ed. 1149 (1950).
[88] *Id.*, at 339 U.S. 641, 70 Sup. Ct. 853, 94 L. Ed. 1154.
[89] Sam Ervin, Jr., "The Case for Segregation," *Look*, April 3, 1956, p. 32.
[40] *Supra*, note 32, 339 U.S. 631, 70 Sup. Ct. 849, 94 L. Ed. 1118.

The Supreme Court has often said that it "has no jurisdiction to pronounce any statute, either of a state or of the United States, void, because irreconcilable with the Constitution, except as it is called upon to adjudge the legal rights of litigants in actual controversies. In the exercise of that jurisdiction, it is bound by two rules, to which it has rigidly adhered: one, never to anticipate a question of constitutional law in advance of the necessity of deciding it; the other never to formulate a rule of constitutional law broader than is required by the precise facts to which it is to be applied." [41] Professor Freund has characterized this as the most salient proposition of constitutional law next to Marshall's dictate on constitutional interpretation.[42]

The Supreme Court in *Sweatt* v. *Painter* did not accede to the demands of Sweatt's counsel to overrule separate but equal. Wrote Chief Justice Vinson, "We cannot agree with respondents that the doctrine of *Plessy* v. *Ferguson* should be reexamined in the light of contemporary knowledge respecting the purposes of the Fourteenth Amendment and the effects of racial segregation." [43] The Court had yet to reach the ultimate question: Is racial segregation in public schools unconstitutional *per se?*

Ex-Justice Byrnes, citing Cummings, Gong Lum, and the four decisions of the Supreme Court dealing with law school and graduate education, believed that the Supreme Court had already answered this question. He argued that all six of these cases are authority for the validity of the separate but equal doctrine. But in none of these six cases—nor in the Berea or Murray cases which Byrnes had not considered—was the issue squarely before the courts. In all of these cases, decision was rendered without reaching the specific determination of whether a racial classification was unconstitutional *per se.*

But the specific question was not avoided in *Brown* v. *Board of Education.* The nine men of 1954 had turned back the clock to prior decisions and concluded that separate but equal was ripe for reexamination. Did separation itself result in an inequality which deprived Negroes of their "personal and present" rights as guaranteed by the equal protection clause?

"In the instant cases," declared Chief Justice Warren, "that

[41] *Liverpool, New York & Philadelphia S.S. Co.* v. *Commissioners,* 113 U.S. 33, 39, 5 Sup. Ct. 352, 355, 28 L. Ed. 899, 901 (1885).

[42] Paul A. Freund, *On Understanding the Supreme Court* (Boston, 1951), p. 46.

[43] *Supra,* note 32, 339 U.S. 635, 70 Sup. Ct. 851, 94 L. Ed. 1120.

question is directly presented. Here, unlike *Sweatt* v. *Painter,* there are findings below that the Negro and white schools involved have been equalized with respect to buildings, curricula, qualifications and salaries of teachers, and other 'tangible' factors. Our decision, therefore, cannot turn on merely a comparison of these tangible factors in Negro and white schools involved in each of the cases. We must look instead to the effect of segregation itself on public education."

The criteria by which the Supreme Court measures constitutional equality had been changed.

The History of the *Swann* Litigation

F. RICHARD BERNASEK

In the *Brown* decision, the Supreme Court theoretically decreed an end to state-imposed segregation. As we have seen in Chapter 3 and the preceding articles, however, the details of enforcing the mandate in *Brown* make eliminating dual school operations a frustratingly difficult problem. Numerous schemes for desegregating dual districts have been ruled illegal by the courts, and busing pupils to achieve forced integration has never been popular. In fact, for more than a decade after the *Brown* decree, few legal precedents were handed down to give lower courts and school boards guidelines for enforcing integration. Indeed, the Supreme Court's landmark busing decision (in *Swann* v. *Charlotte-Mecklenburg*) was delayed for years until the legal guidelines became clear enough for the Court to reach a decision concerning this very controversial issue (see Chapter 3, pp. 42–48). F. Richard Bernasek's historical-legal sketch analyzes the shift in judicial thought regarding implementation of the *Brown* decision. In his insightful review of the cases preceding the Supreme Court's ruling on the *Swann* case, he analyzes the legal thinking which led the Court to order the use of a very unpopular busing scheme to remove the remains of state-enforced segregation.

When F. Richard Bernasek wrote this article he was a senior at the University of Kansas Law School and Editor of the *Kansas Law Review.* Now he is a practicing attorney in Dallas, Texas.

    SOURCE: F. Richard Bernasek, "The Permissibility and Necessity of Busing School Children to Attain Integrated Schools: Charlotte-Mecklenburg Board of Education—A Case Study," *Kansas Law Review,* Vol. 20, May, 1971, pp. 165–178.

Prior to 1965, the County School Board of Mecklenburg County, North Carolina, assigned pupils to schools on the basis of their residential location in a geographic zone. While each student was given an unlimited right to transfer to any school within the district, transportation was not furnished to those electing to transfer. Under this system of pupil assignment, only about 2,200 of the 23,000 Negro students in the district attended integrated schools. Plaintiffs brought desegregation action against the school board, complaining that attendance zones had been intentionally gerrymandered to prevent racial mixing in the schools.[1] To support their allegation plaintiffs relied on evidence indicating that slight extensions of some of the zone boundaries would have resulted in a significantly greater amount of racial balance in some schools.

The district court found that the "question . . . is not what is best for all concerned but simply what are the plaintiffs entitled to have as a matter of constitutional law."[2] The court went on to hold that (1) the school board had no duty to set attendance boundaries for the purpose of achieving racial mixing, (2) there was no evidence of intentional gerrymandering by the school board. The court based its conclusion that no gerrymandering had occurred on evidence that zone boundaries had been fixed along "natural geographic boundaries."[3]

On appeal to the Fourth Circuit the decision of the district court was affirmed.[4] Speaking for the court, Judge Clement Haynsworth approved the district court's determination that the Constitution, as interpreted in *Brown,* permitted consideration of natural geographic boundaries in fixing attendance zones. He emphasized that the school board had no duty to consciously achieve a maximum racial mixture through its zoning policy. Judge Haynsworth concluded further that the school board had gone beyond its constitutional duty by providing a system of free transfer to help reduce the effects of segregated hous-

[1] *Swann* v. *Charlotte-Mecklenburg Bd. of Educ.,* 243 F. Supp. 667 (W.D.N.C. 1965).

[2] *Id.* at 668.

[3] For cases in which the courts have found attendance zones to have been intentionally gerrymandered to perpetrate segregated schools see *Clemons* v. *Board of Educ. of Hillsboro, Ohio,* 228 F.2d 853 (6th Cir.), *cert. denied,* 350 U.S. 1006 (1956); and *Webb* v. *School District No. 90, Johnson County,* 167 Kan. 395, 206 P.2d 1066 (1949).

[4] *Swann* v. *Charlotte-Mecklenburg Bd. of Educ.,* 369 F.2d 29 (4th Cir. 1966).

ing. This decision effectively narrowed the plaintiff's avenue of relief from de facto segregation to situations involving intentional gerrymandering by the school board to prevent school integration. Rejecting any inference of gerrymandering generated by the school board's failure to make slight and easily implemented boundary changes, the court pointed to the adherence to natural geographic boundaries as conclusive proof of good faith. Racial housing patterns often follow natural and man-made physical boundaries; under this decision a school board could easily exclude members of minority races from "white" schools by simply following these natural boundaries. Practically, the court's burden of proving gerrymandering is impossible to meet.[5]

Two years after the Fourth Circuit decision, the Supreme Court decided *Green* v. *County School Board of New Kent County* [6] wherein the school board maintained a segregated school system in a county which had no residential segregation. Students were bused to enable operation of racially separate schools. Reacting to the 1964 Civil Rights Act,[7] the board had adopted a plan of "freedom of choice" in order to remain eligible for federal financial assistance.[8] Under this plan, students in the first and eighth grades were required to choose which of two schools they desired to attend. Thereafter, every year each student was given a choice of which school he would attend the following year. If no choice was made the student was reassigned to the same school. After three years under the plan, only 15% of the black students were electing to attend the formerly all white school. Eighty-five percent of the county's black students remained in the other, all black, school.

Noting that the New Kent School System was precisely the kind

---

[5] *See* Kaplan, *Segregation Litigation and the Schools—Part II: The General Northern Problem,* 58 Nw. U.L. Rev. 157 (1963). "Although many Negro leaders have asserted that, in almost all cities, gerrymandering, or racially motivated zoning, has been the rule rather than the exception, this is extremely difficult and expensive to establish." *Id.* at 157.

[6] 391 U.S. 430 (1968).

[7] 41 U.S.C. §§ 2000d–2000d-4 (1964) which basically provides that no person shall be subjected to discrimination on the basis of race in any program receiving federal financial assistance.

[8] The HEW "Guidelines," 45 C.F.R. §§ 181.1–181.76 (1967), permitted boards which maintained a system of freedom of choice to remain eligible for financial assistance. HEW participation in school desegregation is treated comprehensively in Comment, *The Courts, HEW, and Southern School Desegregation,* 77 Yale L.J. 321 (1967).

of system which *Brown II* had ordered dismantled, the Supreme Court declared the board's "freedom of choice" plan constitutionally unacceptable. The Court ordered the school board to take "whatever steps might be necessary to convert to a unitary system in which racial discrimination would be eliminated root and branch." [9] The school board's duty was "to come forward with a plan that promises realistically to work, and promises realistically to work *now*." [10] The Court went on to say that a good faith plan which showed promise of dismantling the dual system would be permissible, but that "availability to the board of a more promising course of action [might] indicate a lack of good faith. . . ." [11]

The thrust of *Green* was to establish an affirmative duty to take effective action to dismantle existing dual systems. Practically, this duty went beyond proof of nongerrymandered attendance zones, to establishing a plan which would further racial balance in the schools. To be acceptable, a plan would have to enable some racial mixing.

The *Green* effectiveness test failed to establish any criteria for determining how much racial mixing was required before a plan promised to be effective in establishing a unitary system. From the factual circumstances of the case it is apparent that something more than token representation of black students in a few white schools was required. Implicit in the decision was that school boards would have to take affirmative action to obtain racial mixture in order to meet the *Green* requirements. As in *Brown,* the broad language in *Green* could have been applied to de facto segregation in which no state compulsion was evident, but the Court made no express reference to such a system.

Relying on *Green,* the *Swann* plaintiffs brought a motion for further relief seeking greater speed in desegregating the Charlotte-Mecklenburg schools.[12] Noting that approximately 14,000 of the District's 24,000 Negro students still attended schools that were all, or nearly all, black, the district court found that the schools were not desegregated. After citing extensively from *Green,* the district judge determined that the meaning of the constitutional guaranty of equal education had intensified: "The duty now appears as not simply a negative duty to refrain from active legal discrimination, but a duty

---

[9] 391 U.S. 430, 437–38.
[10] *Id.* at 439.
[11] *Id.*
[12] *Swann* v. *Charlotte-Mecklenburg Bd. of Educ.,* 300 F. Supp. 1358 (W.D.N.C. 1969).

to act positively to fashion affirmatively a school system as free as possible from the lasting effects of such historical *apartheid*." [18]

The Court concluded that government action had contributed significantly to residential segregation in the county. Local zoning laws, urban renewal programs, and state enforcement of restrictive covenants had had an effect on the residential pattern upon which the school board had superimposed its attendance zones. This fact, coupled with the school board's building program and pupil assignment system, provided what the court considered to be sufficient reason for placing an affirmative duty on the board to correct the resulting de facto segregation.

The school board was ordered to submit a plan which would desegregate the schools completely by the Fall of 1970. If the use of free transfer was to be retained, the board was to provide transportation to students who requested a transfer from a school in which their race was in the majority to one in which they were in the minority. Although the Court implied that a substantial amount of racial mixing would be required to satisfy the Board's affirmative duty, it was unwilling to fix a ratio of attendance which would satisfy those requirements.

Like *Green,* this decision gave no guidelines for determining when an assignment system would be considered effective. It held the existing conditions to be unsatisfactory, but the board was left to determine for itself how far beyond existing conditions it was required to go. This enabled a certain amount of hedging by the board in formulating its plan.

The plan required by the district court's order was ruled on in August of 1969.[14] The plan proposed among other things: closing seven all black schools and transferring the students to suburban white schools; transferring about 1,200 black students from overly crowded schools; and reassigning about 200 white students to integrated schools. Noting that the plan would enable 4,200 black students to attend schools which would afford them a greater educational opportunity, the court approved the plan for one year even though it was reluctant to put the major burden of desegregation on the black community. The board was ordered to submit a further plan for desegregation for the 1970–71 school year with the goal of complete

---

[18] *Id.* at 1363.

[14] *Swann* v. *Charlotte-Mecklenburg Bd. of Educ.,* 306 F. Supp. 1291 (W.D.N.C. 1969).

desegregation to the maximum extent educationally possible. Although it is unclear exactly what the Court meant by the maximum extent educationally possible, the inference arising could be that the court was referring to situations in which all schools were balanced in a manner which was educationally most sound. The court had relied on expert testimony that the optimal racial mixture for both black and white achievement was somewhere around 70% white to 30% black.[15] Apparently this was the ratio the district judge expected to be attained.

The next U.S. Supreme Court decision which was to have a significant effect upon *Swann* was *Alexander* v. *Holmes County Bd. of Educ.*[16] The Court held that all deliberate speed was no longer a constitutionally acceptable rate for desegregating the schools, and that school boards were to cease immediately operation of dual school systems and to begin operation of unitary systems "within which no person is to be effectively excluded from any school because of race or color." [17] *Alexander* intensified the affirmative duty of effective desegregation imposed on school boards by *Green.* While providing a definition of a unitary school system (*i.e.* that no child in the system was effectively excluded from any school on racial grounds), *Alexander* did not specify the amount of racial mixing required.

The Charlotte-Mecklenburg Board's desegregation plan for the 1970–71 school year was considered by the district court after the *Alexander* decision.[18] The promised integration for the 1969–1970 school year had not been achieved. Only about 1,300 black students had been transferred to white schools, instead of the promised 4,200. Throughout the entire system over half the black students attended schools that were 98%–100% black. Stressing the urgency required by *Alexander,* the district court refused any extension of time to comply with its August 15th order. It also refused to approve the board's plan for the 1970–71 school year and appointed an expert, Dr. Finger, as consultant to prepare immediate plans and recommendations for desegregating the district's schools.

[15] *Id.* at 1297; in substantial accord with the evidence is U.S. Dep't of Health, Education, and Welfare, Equality of Educational Opportunity 28 (Summary Report 1966).
[16] 396 U.S. 19 (1969).
[17] *Id.* at 20.
[18] *Swann* v. *Charlotte-Mecklenburg Bd. of Educ.*, 306 F. Supp. 1299 (W.D.N.C. 1969).

After examining plans submitted by Dr. Finger and the school board, the court adopted the plan proposed by Dr. Finger.[19] The court's order, incorporating the Finger plan, required: (1) that the school board cease operating segregated schools, (2) that no school be operated in such a way that all or nearly all of its students were black, (3) that pupils of all grades would be assigned in such a way that as nearly as practical the various schools at various grade levels would have about the same proportion of black and white students, (4) that students assigned to schools further than 1½ miles from their homes, for the purpose of obtaining racial balance, were to be furnished transportation, (5) that the board continue assignment in the future in a manner which would prevent a return to imbalance, and (6) that no transfer would be allowed which had the effect of increasing racial imbalance in either of the schools affected by the transfer.

Two things about the court's order are notable. The first is the requirement of extensive busing to implement the plan; this clearly went beyond any previous requirement by the district court. In discussing the use of busing as a tool for achieving desegregation, the court determined that the cost of the increased busing required by the Finger plan would be only 1% of the school board's operating costs. It held further that the cost of such busing was not a legitimate reason to prevent its use in overcoming racial imbalance.

The second notable point is that the order provided a concrete definition of a unitary school. The board could meet its duty by eliminating all segregated schools and assigning pupils in a way that a specific black-white ratio would be attained in all schools. This left no room for speculation concerning what the school board was required to do.

The final important lower court decision was made by the Fourth Circuit Court of Appeals, where a 4–2 majority [20] vacated the district court's order as it applied to desegregating elementary schools and remanded the case for further consideration.[21] Speaking for the majority, Judge Butzner held: (1) that not every school in a

[19] *Swann* v. *Charlotte-Mecklenburg Bd. of Educ.*, 311 F. Supp. 265 (W.D.N.C. 1970).

[20] Although disagreeing with the majority opinion, Judge Bryan joined that opinion to create a clear majority for the decision to remand.

[21] *Swann* v. *Charlotte-Mecklenburg Bd. of Educ.*, 431 F.2d 138 (4th Cir. 1970).

unitary system need be integrated, (2) that school boards were required to use all "reasonable" means to integrate the schools, and
(3) that if black residential districts were so large that their schools
could not be integrated by reasonable means, then school boards
would be required to take further steps to assure that no ghetto
students were excluded from integrated schools because of their race.

The majority recognized the role that government action had
played in causing segregated neighborhood schools, and acknowledged the duty of the school board to alleviate the condition. However it also took notice of the fact that similar situations existed in
many United States cities, some of which had Negro ghettos so large
that no reasonable method could accomplish integration of the ghetto
schools. Using that fact as a premise, and reasoning that constitutional standards were to be applied uniformly throughout the country,
the court concluded that it was not necessary to eliminate all-Negro
schools, even in situations where large ghetto districts were not
present.

The Court determined that busing was a permissible tool for
achieving integration, and approved its use as required in the district
court's order as it applied to junior and senior high school attendance.
But after considering several factors, such as the age of the pupils,
the distance and time required for busing, the effect on traffic, and
the cost, it concluded that the increased use of busing as required in
the order's application to elementary schools was an unreasonable
burden on the school board. At the same time the Court of Appeals
approved the district court's finding that the school board's plan was
ineffective and unsatisfactory. On remand, the court suggested con-
sultation with HEW experts to develop alternative methods which
would be more effective than the board's plan and less burdensome
than the Finger plan.

The two dissenting judges criticized the majority's decision on
several grounds. First, they considered the Finger plan to be the only
effective method of accomplishing desegregation. In light of the
burden of establishing an effective method required in *Green,* they
reasoned that the Finger plan was the only plan constitutionally permissible. The dissent also emphasized that there was really no
middle ground between the two plans the majority had rejected. Any
plan which would achieve more effective integration than the board
plan would require extensive busing.

The other objections centered around the reasonableness test adopted by the majority. The dissent considered the cost and inconvenience of the Finger plan to be minor in light of what it accomplished, and consequently did not consider the plan to be unreasonable. They also considered the reasonableness standard to be a value judgment that desegregation was not worth the price, a conclusion they considered improper since desegregation was required by the Constitution. Finally, the two judges criticized the vagueness of the reasonableness standard.[22]

An Economic Perspective

Unequal Education and the Reproduction of the Social Division of Labor

SAMUEL BOWLES

In this selection, economist Samuel Bowles observes that available data suggest that our educational system did not evolve as part of some noble pursuit for equal opportunity, "but rather to meet the needs of capitalist employers for a disciplined and skilled labor force and to provide a mechanism for social control in the interests of political stability." He notes, further, that as the economic importance of skilled and well-educated labor has grown over the years, inequalities in the public school system have become increasingly important in perpetuating the social stratification system from one generation to another.

Bowles traces those developments in our educational history which link inequalities in education to the maintenance and perpetuation of the class structure in the United States. His analysis dramatically challenges our long-held faith that the American public education system ensures an open and democratic society. It should be noted, however, that his observations regarding the relationship between our schools and

[22] 431 F.2d at 156.

SOURCE: Samuel Bowles, "Getting Nowhere: Programmed Class Stagnation," *Society* (June, 1972). pp. 4249. Reprinted by permission of the publisher and the author.

the social-economic class system tend to agree with the findings of the Coleman Report.

Bowles concludes that as long as the social division of labor persists, "as long as jobs are structured so that some have power over many and others have power over nothing," inequality of opportunity will continue to be woven into the educational fabric of the United States. In this regard, the reader might find it interesting to return to the discussion of the functional necessity of social stratification in Chapter 2 (see pp. 29–30).

Samuel Bowles is Assistant Professor of Economics at Harvard University. He is also associated with the Harvard Center for Studies in Education and Development.

Education has long been the chosen instrument of American social reformers. Whatever the ills that beset our society, education is thought to be the cure. Most Americans share the faith—voiced by Horace Mann over a century ago—that education is the "great equalizer." With access to public schools, the children of every class and condition have an equal chance to develop their talents and make a success of themselves. It is our public system of education—so the conventional wisdom goes—that guarantees an open society where any citizen can rise from the lowliest background to high social position according to his ability and efforts.

The record of educational history in the United States and scrutiny of the present state of our colleges and schools lend little support to this comforting optimism. Rather, the available data suggest an alternative interpretation. Apparently our schools have evolved not as part of a pursuit of equality but rather to meet the needs of capitalist employers for a disciplined and skilled labor force and to provide a mechanism for social control in the interests of political stability. As the economic importance of skilled and well-educated labor has grown, inequalities in the school system have become increasingly important in reproducing the class structure from one generation to the next. In fact, the United States school system is pervaded by class inequalities which have shown little sign of diminishing over the last half-century. The evidently unequal control over school boards and other decision-making bodies in education does not provide a sufficient explanation of the persistence and pervasiveness of these inequalities. Although the unequal distribution of political power serves to maintain inequalities in education, their origins are to be found outside the political sphere in the class structure itself and in the class subcultures typical of capitalist societies. Thus unequal education has its roots in the very class structure which it serves to legitimize and reproduce.

In colonial America, as in most pre-capitalist societies of the past, the basic productive unit was the family. For the vast majority of male adults, work was self-directed and was performed without direct supervision. Though constrained by poverty, ill health, the low level of technological development and occasional interferences by the political authorities, a man had considerable leeway in choosing his working hours, what to produce, and how to produce it. While great inequalities in wealth, political power, and other aspects of status normally existed, differences in the degree of autonomy in work were relatively minor, particularly when compared with what was to come.

Parents as Teachers

Transmitting the necessary productive skills to the children as they grew up proved to be a simple task, not because the work was devoid of skill, but because the quite substantial skills required were virtually unchanging from generation to generation, and because the transition to the world of work did not require that the child adapt to a wholly new set of social relationships. The child learned the concrete skills and adapted to the social relations of production through learning by doing within the family.

All of this changed with the advent of the capitalist economy in which the vast majority of economically active individuals relinquished control over their labor power in return for wages or salaries and in which the non-labor means of production were privately owned. The extension of capitalist production (particularly the factory system) undermined the role of the family as the major unit of both socialization and production. Small farmers were driven off the land or competed out of business. Cottage industry was destroyed. Ownership of the means of production became heavily concentrated in the hands of the owners of capital and land. Increasingly, production was carried on in large organizations in which a small management group directed the work activities of the entire labor force. The social relations of production—the authority structure, the prescribed types of behavior and response characteristic of the work place—became increasingly distinct from those of the family.

The divorce of the worker from control over production—from control over his own labor—is particularly important in understanding the role of schooling in capitalist societies. The resulting social division of labor between controllers and the controlled is a crucial aspect of the class structure and will be seen as an important barrier to the achievement of social-class equality in schooling.

While undermining both family and church—the main institutions of socialization—the development of the capitalist system created at the same time an environment which would ultimately challenge the political order. Workers were thrown together in oppressive factories, and the isolation which had helped to maintain quiescence in earlier, widely dispersed peasant populations was broken down. With an increasing number of families uprooted from the land, the workers' search for a living resulted in large-scale labor migrations. Transient (and even foreign) elements came to constitute a major segment of the population and began to pose seemingly insurmountable problems of assimilation, integration, and control. Inequalities of wealth became more apparent and were less easily justified and less readily accepted. The simple legitimizing ideologies of the earlier period—for example, the divine right of kings and the divine origin of social rank—fell under the capitalist attack on the royalty and the traditional landed interests. The broadening of the electorate, first sought by the capitalist class in the struggle against the entrenched interests of the pre-capitalist period, soon threatened to become an instrument for the growing power of the working class. Having risen to political power, the capitalist class sought a mechanism to insure social control and political stability.

An institutional crisis was at hand. The outcome, in virtually all capitalist countries, was the rise of mass education. In the United States, the many advantages of schooling as a socialization process were quickly perceived. The early proponents of the rapid expansion of schooling argued that education could perform many of the socialization functions which earlier had been centered in the family and to a lesser extent in the church.

An ideal preparation for factory work was found in the social relations of the school, specifically in its emphasis on discipline, punctuality, acceptance of authority outside the family and individual accountability for one's work. A manufacturer writing to the Massachusetts State Board of Education from Lowell in 1841 commented:

> I have never considered mere knowledge . . . as the only advantage derived from a good education. . . . [Workers with more education possess] a higher and better state of morals, are more orderly and respectful in their deportment, and more ready to comply with the wholesome and necessary regulations of an establishment. . . . In times of agitation, on account of some change in regulations or wages, I have always looked to the most intelligent, best educated and the most moral for support. The ignorant and uneducated I have generally found the most turbulent and troublesome, acting under the impulse of excited passion and jealousy.

The social relations of the school would replicate the social relations of the workplace and thus help young people adapt to the social division of labor. Schools would further lead people to accept the authority of the state and its agents—the teachers—at a young age, in part by fostering the illusion of the benevolence of the government in its relations with citizens. Moreover, because schooling would ostensibly be open to all, one's position in the social division of labor could be portrayed as the result not of birth, but of one's own efforts and talents. And if the children's everyday experiences with the structure of schooling were insufficient to inculcate the correct views and attitudes, the curriculum itself would be made to embody the bourgeois ideology. Thomas Cooper, an American economist, wrote in 1828:

> Education universally extended throughout the community will tend to disabuse the working class of people in respect of a notion that has crept into the minds of our mechanics and is gradually prevailing, that manual labor is at present very inadequately rewarded, owing to combinations of the rich against the poor; that mere mental labor is comparatively worthless; that property or wealth ought not to be accumulated or transmitted; that to take interest on money lent or profit on capital employed is unjust. . . . The mistaken and ignorant people who entertain these fallacies as truths will learn, when they have the opportunity of learning, that the institution of political society originated in the protection of property.

The movement for public elementary and secondary education in the United States originated in the nineteenth century in states dominated by the burgeoning industrial capitalist class, most notably in Massachusetts. It spread rapidly to all parts of the country except the South. In Massachusetts the extension of elementary education was in large measure a response to industrialization and to the need for social control of the Irish and other non-Yankee workers recruited to work in the mills. The fact that some working people's movements had demanded free instruction should not obscure the basically coercive nature of the extension of schooling. In many parts of the country, schools were literally imposed upon the workers.

A system of class stratification developed within this rapidly expanding educational system. Children of the social elite normally attended private schools. Because working-class children tended to leave school early, the class composition of the public high schools was distinctly more elite than that of the public primary schools. And as a university education ceased to be merely training for teaching or the divinity and became important in gaining access to the pinnacles of the business world, upper-class families increasingly used their money and influence to get their children into the best universities, often at the expense of the children of less elite families.

Around the turn of the century, large numbers of working-class (and particularly immigrant) children began attending high schools. At the same time, a system of class stratification developed within secondary education.

The older democratic ideology of the common school—that the same curriculum should be offered to all children—gave way to the "progressive" insistence that education should be tailored to the "needs of the child." The superintendent of the Boston schools summed up the change in 1908:

> Until very recently [the schools] have offered equal opportunity for all to receive *one kind* of education, but what will make them democratic is to provide opportunity for all to receive such education as will fit them *equally well* for their particular life work.

In the interests of providing an education relevant to the later life of the students, vocational schools and tracks were developed for the children of working families. The academic curriculum was preserved for those who would later have the opportunity to make use of book learning either in college or in white-collar employment. This and other educational reforms of the progressive education movement reflected an implicit assumption of the immutability of the class structure.

Tracking by Social Class

The frankness with which students were channeled into curriculum tracks on the basis of their social-class background raised serious doubts concerning the openness of the class structure. The apparent unfairness of the selection and tracking procedures was disguised (though not mitigated much) by another "progressive" reform—"objective" educational testing. Particularly after World War I, the capitulation of the schools to business values and the cult of efficiency led to the increased use of intelligence and scholastic achievement testing as an ostensibly unbiased means of measuring school outputs and classifying students. The complementary growth of the guidance counseling profession allowed much of the channeling to proceed from the students' own well-counseled choices, thus adding an apparent element of voluntarism to the mechanisms perpetuating the class structure.

As schooling became the standard for assigning children positions in the class structure, it played a major part in legitimizing the structure itself. But at the same time it undermined the simple processes by which the upper class had preserved its position from one generation to the next—the inheritance of physical capital. When education and skills play an important role in the hierarchy of production, the inheritance of capital from one generation to the next is not enough to reproduce the social division of labor. Rather skills broadly defined and educational credentials must somehow be passed on within the family. It is in furthering this modern form of class structure that the school plays a fundamental role. Children whose parents occupy positions at the top of the occupational hierarchy receive more and better schooling than working-class children. Inequalities in years of schooling are particularly evident. My analysis of United States Census data indicates that if we define social-class standing by the income, occupation, and educational level of the parents, a child from the 90th percentile in the class distribution may expect on the average to achieve over four-and-a-half more years of schooling than a child from the tenth percentile. Even among those who had graduated from high school, children of families earning less than $3,000 per year were over six times as likely not to attend college as were the children of families earning over $15,000.

Because schooling is heavily subsidized by the general taxpayer, the longer a child attends school, the more public resources he has access to. Further, public expenditure per student in four-year colleges greatly exceeds that in elementary schools; those who stay in school longer receive an increasingly large *annual* public subsidy. In the school year 1969–1970, per-pupil expenditures of federal, state, and local funds were $1,490 for colleges and universities and $747 for primary and secondary schools. Even at the elementary level, schools in low income neighborhoods tend to be less well endowed with equipment, books, teachers, and other inputs into the educational process.

The inequalities in schooling go deeper than these simple measures. Differences in rules, expected modes of behavior and opportunities for choice are most glaring when we compare levels of schooling. Note the wide range of choice over curriculum, life style, and allocation of time afforded to college students compared with the obedience and respect for authority expected in high school. Differentiation also occurs within each level of schooling. One needs only to compare the social relations of a junior college with those of an elite four-year college, or those of a working-class high school with those of a wealthy suburban high school, for verification of this point. It is consistent with this pattern that the play-oriented, child-centered pedagogy of the progressive movement found little acceptance outside of private schools and public schools in wealthy communities.

Mirror of the Factory

These differences in socialization patterns do not arise by accident. Rather, they are the product of class differences in educational objectives and expectations held by parents and educators alike and of differences in student responsiveness to various patterns of teaching and control. Further, a teacher in an understaffed, ill-equipped school may be compelled to resort to authoritarian tactics whether she wants to or not. Lack of resources precludes having small intimate classes, a multiplicity of elective courses, specialized teachers (except disciplinary personnel), free time for the teachers and the free space required for a more open, flexible educational environment. Socialization in such a school comes to mirror that of the factory; students are treated as raw materials on a production line. There is a high premium on obedience and punctuality and there are few opportunities for independent, creative work or individualized attention by teachers.

Even where working-class children attend a well-financed school they do not receive the şame treatment as the children of the rich. Class stratification within a given school is achieved through tracking and differential participation in extracurricular activities; it is reinforced by attitudes of teachers and particularly guidance personnel who expect working-class children to do poorly, to terminate schooling early and to end up in jobs similar to their parents.

Not surprisingly, the results of schooling differ greatly for children of different social classes. On nationally standardized achievement tests, children whose parents were themselves highly educated outperform by a wide margin the children of parents with less education. A recent study revealed, for example, that among white high school seniors, those whose parents were in the top education decile were on the average well over three grade levels ahead of those whose parents were in the bottom decile.

Given class differences in scholastic achievement, class inequalities in college attendance are to be expected. Thus one might be tempted to argue that the data in Table 1 are simply a reflection of unequal scholastic achievement in high school and do not reflect any additional social-class inequalities peculiar to the process of college admission. This view, so comforting to the admissions personnel in our elite universities, is unsupported by the available data, some of which is presented in Table 2. Access to a college education is highly

TABLE 1   College Attendance in 1967 among High School Graduates, by Family Income

Family Income	Percent Who Did Not Attend College
Total	53.1
under $3,000	80.2
$3,000 to $3,999	67.7
$4,000 to $5,999	63.7
$6,000 to $7,499	58.9
$7,500 to $9,999	49.0
$10,000 to $14,999	38.7
$15,000 and over	13.3

Refers to high school seniors in October, 1965 who subsequently graduated. Bureau of the Census, *Current Population Report,* 1969. College attendance refers to both two- and four-year institutions.

TABLE 2 Probability of College Entry for a Male Who Has Reached
Grade 11

			SOCIOECONOMIC QUARTILES			
			Low			*High*
			1	*2*	*3*	*4*
	Low	1	.13	.15	.29	.36
Ability		2	.25	.34	.45	.65
quartiles		3	.48	.70	.73	.87
	High	4	.06	.12	.13	.26

Based on a large sample of U.S. high school students studied by Project
Talent at the University of Pittsburgh, 1966.

The socioeconomic index is a composite measure including family income, father's occupation and education, mother's education, and so forth.
The ability scale is a composite of tests measuring general academic aptitude.

unequal, even for students of the same measured academic ability.

And inequalities of educational opportunity show no signs of
abatement. In fact, data from a recent United States Census survey,
reported in Table 3, indicate that graduation from college is at least
as dependent on one's class background now as it was 50 years ago.
Considering access to all levels of education, the data suggest that the

TABLE 3 Among Sons Who Had Reached High School, Percentage
Who Graduated from College, by Son's Age and Father's Level of
Education

			Father's Education					
			SOME HIGH SCHOOL		HIGH SCHOOL GRADUATE		SOME COLLEGE OR MORE	
Son's Age in 1962	*Likely Dates of College Graduation*	*Less Than 8 Years*	*Per- cent Gradu- ating*	*Ratio to Less Than 8 Years*	*Per- cent Gradu- ating*	*Ratio to Less Than 8 Years*	*Per- cent Gradu- ating*	*Ratio to Less Than 8 Years*
25–34	1950–1959	07.6	17.4	2.29	25.6	3.37	51.9	6.83
35–44	1940–1949	08.6	11.9	1.38	25.3	2.94	53.9	6.27
45–54	1930–1939	07.7	09.8	1.27	15.1	1.96	36.9	4.79
55–64	1920–1929	08.9	09.8	1.10	19.2	2.16	29.8	3.35

Based on U.S. Census data for 1962 as reported in William G. Spady,
"Educational Mobility and Access: Growth and Paradoxes," *American Journal
of Sociology,* November, 1967.

Assumes college graduation at age 22.

number of years of schooling attained by a child depends upon the social-class standing of the father slightly more in the recent period than it did at the beginning of the century.

The pervasive and persistent inequalities in the United States system of education pose serious problems of interpretation. If the costs of education borne by students and their families were very high, or if nepotism were rampant, or if formal segregation of pupils by social class were practiced, or if educational decisions were made by a select few whom we might call the power elite, it would not be difficult to explain the continued inequalities in the system. The problem is to reconcile the above empirical findings with the facts of our society as we perceive them: public and virtually tuition-free education at all levels, few legal instruments for the direct implementation of class segregation, a limited role for contacts or nepotism in the achievement of high status or income, a commitment (at the rhetorical level at least) to equality of educational opportunity and a system of control of education which if not particularly democratic extends far beyond anything resembling a power elite. The attempt to reconcile these apparently discrepant facts leads us back to a consideration of the social division of labor, the associated class cultures, and the exercise of class power.

The social division of labor—based on the hierarchical structure of production—gives rise to distinct class subcultures, each of which has its own values, personality traits, and expectations. The social relations of production characteristic of advanced capitalist societies (and many socialist societies) are most clearly illustrated in the bureaucracy and hierarchy of the modern corporation. Occupational roles in the capitalist economy may be grouped according to the degree of independence and control exercised by the person holding the job. The personality attributes associated with the adequate performance of jobs in occupational categories defined in this broad way differ considerably, some apparently requiring independence and internal discipline, and others emphasizing such traits as obedience, predictability, and willingness to subject oneself to external controls.

These personality attributes are developed primarily at a young age, both in the family and to a lesser extent in secondary socialization institutions such as schools. Daily experience in the work place reinforces these traits in adults. Because people tend to marry within their own class, both parents are likely to have a similar set of these fundamental personality traits. Thus children of parents occupying a given position in the occupational hierarchy grow up in homes where child-rearing methods and perhaps even the physical surroundings tend to develop personality characteristics appropriate to adequate job performance in the occupational roles of the parents. The children of managers and professionals are taught self-reliance within a broad set of constraints; the children of production-line workers are taught conformity and obedience.

Melvin Kohn summarizes his extensive empirical work on class structure and parental values as follows:

> Whether consciously or not, parents tend to impart to their children lessons derived from the condition of life of their own class—and thus help to prepare their children for a similar class position. . . . The conformist values and orientation of lower- and working-class parents are inappropriate for training children to deal with the problems of middle-class and professional life. . . . The family, then, functions as a mechanism for perpetuating inequality.

This relation between parents' class position and child's personality attributes is reinforced by schools and other social institutions. Teachers, guidance counselors, and school administrators ordinarily encourage students to develop aspirations and expectations typical of their social class, even if the child tends to have deviant aspirations.

It is true that schools introduce some common elements of socialization for all students. Discipline, respect for property, competition, and punctuality are part of implicit curricula. Yet the ability of a school to appreciably change a child's future is severely limited. However, the responsiveness of children to different types of schooling seems highly dependent upon the personality traits, values, and expectations which have been developed through the family. Furthermore, since children spend a small amount of time in school—less than a quarter of their waking hours over the course of a year— schools are probably more effective where they complement and reinforce rather than oppose the socialization processes of the home and neighborhood. Not surprisingly, this relationship between family socialization and that of the schools reproduces patterns of class culture from generation to generation.

Among adults the differing daily work experiences of people reinforce these patterns of class culture. The reward structure of the workplace favors the continued development of traits such as obedience and acceptance of authority among workers. Conversely, those occupying directing roles in production are rewarded for the capacity to make decisions and exert authority. Thus the operation of the incentive structure of the job stabilizes and reproduces patterns of class culture. The operation of the labor market translates these differences in class culture into income inequalities and occupational hierarchies. Recent work by Herbert Gintis and other economists shows that the relation between schooling and economic success cannot be explained by the effect of schooling on intellectual capacity. Rather, the economic success of individuals with higher educational attainments is explained by their highly rewarded personality characteristics which facilitate entry into the upper echelons of the production hierarchy. These personality characteristics, originating in the work experiences of one's parents, transmitted in turn to children through early socialization practices, and reinforced in school and on the job, are an important vehicle for the reproduction of the social division of labor.

But the argument thus far is incomplete. The perpetuation of inequality through the schooling system has been represented as an almost automatic, self-enforcing mechanism, operating through the medium of class culture. An important further dimension is added to this interpretation if we note that positions of control in the productive hierarchy tend to be associated with positions of political influence. Given the disproportionate share of political power held by the upper classes and their capacity for determining the accepted patterns of behavior and procedures, to define the national interest and to control the ideological and institutional context in which educational decisions are made, it is not surprising to find that resources are allocated unequally among school tracks, between schools serving different classes and between levels of schooling. The same configuration of power results in curricula, methods of instruction, and criteria which, though often seemingly innocuous and ostensibly even egalitarian, serves to maintain the unequal system.

Illusion of Fair Treatment

Take the operation of one of these rules of the game—the principle that excellence in schooling should be rewarded. The upper class defines excellence in terms on which upper-class children tend to excel (for example, scholastic achievement). Adherence to this principle yields inegalitarian outcomes (for example, unequal access to higher education) while maintaining the appearance of fair treatment. Those who would defend the "reward excellence" principle on the grounds of efficient selection to ensure the most efficient use of educational resources might ask themselves this: why should colleges admit those with the highest college entrance examination board scores? Why not the lowest or the middle? According to conventional standards of efficiency, the rational social objective of the college is to render the greatest increment in individual capacities ("value added," to the economist), not to produce the most illustrious graduating class ("gross output"). Thus the principle of rewarding excellence does not appear to be motivated by a concern for the efficient use of educational resources. Rather it serves to legitimize the unequal consequences of schooling.

Though cognitive capacities are relatively unimportant in the determination of income and occupational success, the reward of intellectual ability in school plays an important role. The "objective" testing of scholastic achievement and relatively meritocratic system of grading encourages the illusion that promotion and rewards are distributed fairly. The close relationship between educational attainments and later occupational success further masks the paramount importance of race and social-class background for getting ahead.

At the same time, the institution of objectively administered tests of performance serves to allow a limited amount of upward mobility among exceptional children of the lower class, thus providing further legitimation of the operations of the social system by giving some credence to the myth of widespread mobility.

The operation of the "reward excellence" rule illustrates the symbiosis between the political and economic power of the upper class. Adherence to the rule has the effect of generating unequal consequences via a mechanism which operates largely outside the political system. As long as one adheres to the reward (academic) excellence principle, the responsibility for unequal results in schooling appears to rest outside the upper class, often in some fault of the poor —such as their class culture—which is viewed as lying beyond the reach of political action or criticism.

Thus it appears that the consequences of an unequal distribution of political power among classes complement the results of class culture in maintaining an educational system which has thus far been capable of transmitting status from generation to generation, and capable in addition of political survival in the formally democratic and egalitarian environment of the contemporary United States.

The role of the schools in reproducing and legitimizing the social division of labor has recently been challenged by popular egalitarian movements. At the same time, the educational system is showing signs of internal structural weakness. I have argued elsewhere that overproduction of highly educated workers by universities and graduate schools and a breakdown of authority at all levels of schooling are not passing phenomena, but deeply rooted in the pattern of growth and structural change in the advanced capitalist economy. These two developments suggest that fundamental change in the schooling process may soon be possible.

But it should be clear that educational equality cannot be achieved through changes in the school system alone. Attempts at educational reform may move us closer to that objective (if, in their failure, they lay bare the unequal nature of our school system and destroy the illusion of unimpeded mobility through education). Yet if the record of the last century and a half of educational reforms is any guide, we should not expect radical change in education to result from the efforts of reformers who confine their attention to the schools. My interpretation of the educational consequences of class culture and class power suggests that past educational reform movements failed because they sought to eliminate educational inequalities without challenging the basic institutions of capitalism.

Efforts to equalize education through changes in school finance, compensatory education, and similar programs will at best scratch the surface of inequality. As long as jobs are structured so that some have power over many and others have power over nothing—as long as the social division of labor persists—educational inequality will be built into U.S. society.

Chapter 5

The Continuing Quest
for Equality: Projections
on a Recurring Controversy

Throughout this book we have focused on the complexity of the issue of equal educational opportunity. We have emphasized the questions raised rather than the possible solutions for this serious social problem. Now, however, we turn from what *is* to opinions on what *should be*. Needless to say, the concept of educational equality is of interest not only to educators but also to politicians, jurists, and taxpayers alike. Despite recent progress toward defining equal opportunity in the courts and other arenas, however, the issue remains highly complex. The casual observer might innocently have assumed that the struggle for equality of educational opportunity was over as a result of the egalitarian decisions in *Swann, Serrano,* and similar court cases. But *Rodriguez* had a sobering effect on this premature thinking. Some were further misled by the attention being given to busing and school desegregation in general by Congress and the President. Certainly awareness of the issue has increased, but whether or not we are closer to ensuring quality and equality of schooling remains debatable.

We have studied certain factors that seem to be inherent in the basic concept of educational equality. We have observed that the Fourteenth Amendment is an integral part of any argument over educational equality as are the notions of neighborhood racial mix and the ability of a community to support its schools financially. For example, we have learned that the Supreme Court has not only reconfirmed the *Brown* desegregation decree but also ordered its implementation at all costs.

Now we turn to a sampling of the thinking of people with widely varying backgrounds and perspectives on the issue of equal educational opportunity. We begin with an article by Mary Jo Bane and Christopher Jencks, who argue that schools have few, if any, significant effects on the adult success of those who attend them. Next, William T. Blackstone, a philosopher, offers his prescription for the social change necessary to guarantee educational equality.

The following three selections, by Owen Fiss, William Greenbaum, and Thomas Shannon, predict the significance of the *Swann, Serrano,* and *Rodriguez* cases, respectively. Here we see how three legal experts interpret the specific court cases which have been featured throughout this book. Next, a national civil rights group takes issue with the *Swann* decision. Finally, a journalistic selection asserts that the emotionalism over busing and school desegregation is attributable to interfering parents who fear social and political change.

The Schools and Equal Opportunity
MARY JO BANE and CHRISTOPHER JENCKS

The authors report on the major finding of Jencks' controversial work, *Inequality: A Reassessment of the Effect of Family and Schooling in America.* They contend that schools have few long-term effects on the later "success" of those who attend them and that quality education will not reduce social and economic inequalities. The conclusions of Jencks and his associates will continue to be major objects of contention for years to come. They challenge long-held beliefs about the benefits of public education and, like the Coleman Report, hold that the quality of a school's "output" depends primarily upon the social and economic characteristics of the entering children.

Mary Jo Bane is a research associate at the Center for Educational Policy Research, Harvard University. Christopher Jencks is an Associate Professor of Education at Harvard. He is the author or co-author of numerous articles and books.

SOURCE: *Saturday Review of Education,* September 16, 1972, pp. 37–41. Reprinted by permission of the authors.

Americans have a recurrent fantasy that schools can solve their problems. Thus it was perhaps inevitable that, after we rediscovered poverty and inequality in the early 1960s, we turned to the schools for solutions. Yet the schools did not provide solutions, the high hopes of the early-and-middle 1960s faded, and the war on poverty ended in ignominious surrender to the *status quo*. In part, of course, this was because the war in Southeast Asia turned out to be incompatible with the war on poverty. In part, however, it was because we all had rather muddleheaded ideas about the various causes and cures of poverty and inequality.

Today there are signs that some people are beginning to look for new solutions to these perennial problems. There is a vast amount of sociological and economic data that can, we think, help in this effort, both by explaining the failures of the 1960s and by suggesting more realistic alternatives. For the past four years we have been working with this data. Our research has led us to three general conclusions.

First, poverty is a condition of relative rather than absolute deprivation. People feel poor and are poor if they have a lot less money than their neighbors. This is true regardless of their absolute income. It follows that we cannot eliminate poverty unless we prevent people from falling too far below the national average. The problem is economic inequality rather than low incomes.

Second, the reforms of the 1960s were misdirected because they focused only on equalizing opportunity to "succeed" (or "fail") rather than on reducing the economic and social distance between those who succeeded and those who failed. The evidence we have reviewed suggests that equalizing opportunity will not do very much to equalize results, and hence that it will not do much to reduce poverty.

Third, even if we are interested solely in equalizing opportunities for economic success, making schools more equal will not help very much. Differences between schools have very little effect on what happens to students after they graduate.

The main policy implication of these findings is that although school reform is important for improving the lives of children, schools cannot contribute significantly to adult equality. If we want economic equality in our society, we will have to get it by changing our economic institutions, not by changing the schools.

Poverty and Inequality

The rhetoric of the war on poverty described the persistence of poverty in the midst of affluence as a "paradox," largely attributable to "neglect." Official publications all assumed that poverty was an absolute rather than a relative condition. Having assumed this, they all showed progress toward the elimination of poverty, since fewer and fewer people had incomes below the official "poverty line."

Yet, despite all the official announcements of progress, many Americans still seemed poor, by both their own standards and their neighbors'. The reason was that most Americans define poverty in relative rather than absolute terms. Public-opinion surveys show, for example, that when people are asked how much money an American family needs to "get by," they typically name a figure about half what the average American family actually receives. This has been true for the last three decades, despite the fact that real incomes (incomes adjusted for inflation) have doubled in the interval.

During the Depression the average American family was living on about $30 a week. A third of all families were living on less than half this amount, which made it natural for Franklin Roosevelt to speak of "one-third of a nation" as ill-housed, ill-clothed, and ill-fed. By 1964 mean family income was about $160 a week, and the Gallup poll found that the average American thought a family of four needed at least $80 a week to "get by." Even allowing for inflation, this was twice what people had thought necessary during the Depression. Playing it safe, the Johnson administration defined the poverty line at $60 a week for a family of four, but most people felt this was inadequate. By 1970 inflation had raised mean family income to about $200 a week, and the National Welfare Rights Organization was trying to rally liberal support for a guaranteed income of $100 a week.

These changes in the definition of poverty were not just a matter of "rising expectations" or of people's needing to "keep up with the Joneses." The goods and services that made it possible to live on $15 a week during the Depression were no longer available to a family with the same real income ($40 a week) in 1964. Eating habits had changed, and many cheap foods had disappeared from the stores. Housing arrangements had changed, too. During the Depression many people could not afford indoor plumbing and "got by" with a privy. By the 1960s privies were illegal in most places. Those who still could not afford an indoor toilet ended up in buildings that had broken toilets. For these they paid more than their parents had paid for privies.

Examples of this kind suggest that the "cost of living" is not the cost of buying some fixed set of goods and services. It is the cost of participating in a social system. It therefore depends in large part on how much other people habitually spend to participate in the system. Those who fall below the norm, whatever it may be, are excluded. Accordingly, raising the incomes of the poor will not eliminate poverty if the cost of participating in "mainstream" American life rises even faster. People with incomes less than half the national average will not be able to afford what "everyone" regards as "necessities." The only way to eliminate poverty is, therefore, to make sure everyone has an income at least half the average.

Arguments of this kind suggest not only that it makes more sense to think of "poverty" as a relative rather than an absolute condition but that eliminating poverty, at least as it is usually defined in America, depends on eliminating, or at least greatly reducing, inequality.

Schooling and Opportunity

Almost none of the reform legislation of the 1960s involved direct efforts to equalize adult status, power, or income. Most Americans accepted the idea that these rewards should go to those who were most competent and diligent. Their objection to America's traditional economic system was not that it produced inequality but that the rules determining who succeeded and who failed were often unfair. The reformers wanted to create a world in which success would no longer be associated with skin color, economic background, or other "irrelevant" factors, but only with actual merit. What they wanted, in short, was what they called "equal opportunity."

Their strategy for achieving equal opportunity placed great emphasis on education. Many people imagined that if schools could equalize people's cognitive skills this would equalize their bargaining powers as adults. Presumably, if everyone had equal bargaining power, few people would end up very poor.

This strategy for reducing poverty rested on a series of assumptions that went roughly as follows:

1. Eliminating poverty is largely a matter of helping children born into poverty to rise out of it. Once families escape from poverty, they do not fall back into it. Middle-class children rarely end up poor.

2. The primary reason poor children cannot escape from poverty is that they do not acquire basic cognitive skills. They cannot read, write, calculate, or articulate. Lacking these skills, they cannot get or keep a well-paid job.

3. The best mechanism for breaking this "vicious circle" is educational reform. Since children born into poor homes do not acquire the skills they need from their parents, they must be taught these skills in school. This can be done by making sure that they attend the same schools as middle-class children, by giving them extra compensatory programs in school, by giving their parents a voice in running their schools, or by some combination of all three approaches.

Our research over the last four years suggests that each of these assumptions is erroneous:

1. Poverty is not primarily hereditary. While children born into poverty have a higher than average chance of ending up poor, there is still an enormous amount of economic mobility from one generation to the next. A father whose occupational status is high passes on less than half his advantage to his sons, and a father whose status is low passes along less than half his disadvantage. A family whose income is above the norm has an even harder time passing along its privileges; its sons are typically only about a third as advantaged as the parents. Conversely, a family whose income is below average will typically have sons about a third as disadvantaged as the parents. The effects of parents' status on their daughters' economic positions appear to be even weaker. This means that many "advantaged" parents have some "disadvantaged" children and vice versa.

2. The primary reason some people end up richer than others is not that they have more adequate cognitive skills. While children who read well, get the right answers to arithmetic problems, and articulate their thoughts clearly are somewhat more likely than others to get ahead, there are many other equally important factors involved. The effects of I.Q. on economic success are about the same as the effects of family background. This means, for example, that if two men's I.Q. scores differ by 17 points—the typical difference between I.Q. scores of individuals chosen at random—their incomes will typically differ by less than $2,000. That amount is not completely

trivial, of course. But the income difference between random individuals is three times as large, and the difference between the best-paid fifth and the worst-paid fifth of all male workers averages $14,000. There is almost as much economic inequality among those who score high on standardized tests as in the general population.

3. There is no evidence that school reform can substantially reduce the extent of cognitive inequality, as measured by tests of verbal fluency, reading comprehension, or mathematical skill. Eliminating qualitative differences between elementary schools would reduce the range of scores on standardized tests in sixth grade by less than 3 percent. Eliminating qualitative differences between high schools would hardly reduce the range of twelfth grade scores at all and would reduce by only 1 percent the disparities in the amount of education people eventually get.

Our best guess, after reviewing all the evidence we could find, is that racial desegregation raises black elementary school students' test scores by a couple of points. But most of the test-score gap between blacks and whites persists, even when they are in the same schools. So also: Tracking has very little effect on test scores. And neither the overall level of resources available to a school nor any specific, easily identifiable school policy has a significant effect on students' cognitive skills or educational attainments. Thus, even if we went beyond "equal opportunity" and allocated resources disproportionately to schools whose students now do worst on tests and are least likely to acquire credentials, this would not improve these students' prospects very much.

The evidence does not tell us why school quality has so little effect on test scores. Three possible explanations come to mind. First, children seem to be more influenced by what happens at home than by what happens in school. They may also be more influenced by what happens on the streets and by what they see on television. Second, administrators have very little control over those aspects of school life that do affect children. Reallocating resources, reassigning pupils, and rewriting the curriculum seldom change the way teachers and students actually treat each other minute by minute. Third, even when the schools exert an unusual influence on children, the resulting changes are not likely to persist into adulthood. It takes a huge change in elementary school test scores, for example, to alter adult income by a significant amount.

Equal Opportunity and Unequal Results

The evidence we have reviewed, taken all together, suggests that equalizing opportunity cannot take us very far toward eliminating inequality. The simplest way of demonstrating this is to compare the economic prospects of brothers raised in the same home. Even the most egalitarian society could not hope to make opportunities for all children appreciably more equal than the opportunities now available to brothers from the same family. Looking at society at large, if we compare random pairs of individuals, the difference between their occupational statuses averages about 28 points on the Duncan "status scale" (the scale runs from 0 to 96 points). The difference between brothers' occupational statuses averages fully 23 points on this same scale. If we compare men's incomes, the difference between random pairs averaged about $6,200 in 1968. The difference between brothers' incomes, according to our best estimate, probably averaged about $5,700. These estimates mean that people who start off equal end up almost as unequal as everyone else. Inequality is not mostly inherited: It is re-created anew in each generation.

We can take this line of argument a step further by comparing people who not only start off in similar families but who also have the same I.Q. scores and get the same amount of schooling. Such people's occupational statuses differ by an average of 21 points, compared to 28 points for random individuals. If we compare their incomes, making the additional assumption that the men have the same occupational status, we find that they differ by an average of about $5,300, compared to $6,200 for men chosen at random.

These comparisons suggest that adult success must depend on a lot of things besides family background, schooling, and the cognitive skills measured by standardized tests. We have no idea what these factors are. To some extent, no doubt, specialized varieties of competence, such as the ability to hit a ball thrown at high speed or the ability to persuade a customer that he wants a larger car than he thought he wanted, play a major role. Income also depends on luck: the range of jobs available when you are job hunting, the amount of overtime work in your plant, good or bad weather for your strawberry crop, and a hundred other unpredictable accidents.

Equalizing opportunity will not, then, do much to reduce economic inequality in America. If poverty is relative rather than absolute, equalizing opportunity will not do much to reduce poverty, either.

Implications for Educational Policy

These findings imply that school reform is never likely to have any significant effect on the degree of inequality among adults. This suggests that the prevalent "factory" model, in which schools are seen as places that "produce" alumni, probably ought to be abandoned. It is true that schools have "inputs" and "outputs," and that one of their nominal purposes is to take human "raw material" (*i.e.,* children) and convert it into something more "useful" (*i.e.,* employable adults). Our research suggests, however, that the character of a school's output depends largely on a single input, the characteristics of the entering children. Everything else—the school budget, its policies, the characteristics of the teachers—is either secondary or completely irrelevant, at least so long as the range of variation among schools is as narrow as it seems to be in America.

These findings have convinced us that the long-term effects of schooling are relatively uniform. The day-to-day internal life of the schools, in contrast, is highly variable. It follows that *the primary basis for evaluating a school should be whether the students and teachers find it a satisfying place to be.* This does not mean we think schools should be like mediocre summer camps, in which children are kept out of trouble but not taught anything. We doubt that a school can be enjoyable for either adults or children unless the children keep learning new things. We value ideas and the life of the mind, and we think that a school that does not value these things is a poor place for children. But a school that values ideas because they enrich the lives of children is quite different from a school that values high reading scores because reading scores are important for adult success.

Our concern with making schools satisfying places for teachers and children has led us to a concern for diversity and choice. People have widely different notions of what a "satisfying" place is, and we believe they ought to be able to put these values into practice. As we have noted, our research suggests that none of the programs or structural arrangements in common use today has consistently different long-term effects from any other. Since the character of a child's schooling has few long-term effects, and since these effects are quite unpredictable, society has little reason to constrain the choices available to parents and children. If a "good school" is one the students and staff find satisfying, no one school will be best for everyone. Since there is no evidence that professional educators know appreciably more than parents about what is good for children, it seems reasonable to let parents decide what kind of education their children should have while they are young and to let the children decide as they get older.

Short-term considerations also seem decisive in determining whether to spend more money on schooling or to spend it on busing children to schools outside their neighborhoods. If extra resources make school life pleasanter and more interesting, they are worthwhile. But we should not try to justify school expenditures on the grounds that they boost adult earnings. Likewise, busing ought to be justified in political and moral terms rather than in terms of presumed long-term effects on the children who are bused. If we want an integrated society, we ought to have integrated schools, which make people feel they have a stake in the well-being of other races. If we want a society in which people are free to segregate themselves, then we should apply that principle to our schools. There is, however, no compelling reason to treat schools differently from other social arrangements, including neighborhoods. Personally, we believe in both open housing and open schools. If parents or students want to take buses to schools in other neighborhoods, school boards ought to provide the buses, expand the relevant schools, and ensure that the students are welcome in the schools they want to attend. This is the least we can do to offset the effects of residential segregation. But we do not believe that forced busing can be justified on the grounds of its long-term benefits for students.

This leads to our last conclusion about educational reform. Reformers are always getting trapped into claiming too much for what they propose. They may want a particular reform—like open classrooms, or desegregation, or vouchers—because they think these reforms will make schools more satisfying places to work. Yet they feel obliged to claim that these reforms will also reduce the number of nonreaders, increase racial understanding, or strengthen family life. A wise reformer ought to be more modest, claiming only that a particular reform will not harm adult society and that it will make life pleasanter for parents, teachers, and students in the short run.

This plea for modesty in school reform will, we fear, fall on deaf ears. Ivan Illich is right in seeing schools as secular churches, through which we seek to improve not ourselves but our descendants. That this process should be disagreeable seems inevitable; one cannot abolish original sin through self-indulgence. That it should be immodest seems equally inevitable; a religion that promises anything less than salvation wins few converts. In school, as in church, we present the world as we wish it were. We try to inspire children with the ideals we ourselves have failed to live up to. We assume, for example, that we cannot make adults live in desegregated neighborhoods, so we devise schemes for busing children from one neighborhood to another in order to desegregate the schools. We all prefer conducting our moral experiments on other people. Nonetheless, so long as we confine our experiments to children, we will not have much effect on adult life.

Implications for Social Reform

Then how *are* we to affect adult life? Our findings tell us that different kinds of inequality are only loosely related to one another. This can be either encouraging or discouraging, depending on how you look at it. On the discouraging side, it means that eliminating inequality in one area will not eliminate it in other areas. On the encouraging side, it means that inequality in one area does not dictate inequality in other areas.

To begin with, genetic inequality is not a major obstacle to economic equality. It is true that genetic diversity almost inevitably means considerable variation in people's scores on standardized tests. But this kind of cognitive inequality need not imply anything like the present degree of economic inequality. We estimate, for example, that if the only sources of income inequality in America were differences in people's genes, the top fifth of the population would earn only about 1.4 times as much as the bottom fifth. In actuality, the top fifth earns seven times as much as the bottom fifth.

Second, our findings suggest that psychological and cultural differences between families are not an irrevocable barrier to adult equality. Family background has more influence than genes on an individual's educational attainment, occupational status, and income. Nonetheless, if family background were the only source of economic inequality in America, the top fifth would earn only about twice as much as the bottom fifth.

Our findings show, then, that inequality is not determined at birth. But they also suggest that economic equality cannot be achieved by indirect efforts to manipulate the environments in which people grow up. We have already discussed the minuscule effects of equalizing school quality. Equalizing the amount of schooling people get would not work much better. Income inequality among men with similar amounts of schooling is only 5–10 percent less than among men in general. The effect is even less if we include women.

If we want to eliminate economic inequality, we must make this an explicit objective of public policy rather than deluding ourselves into thinking that we can do it by giving everyone equal opportunity to succeed or fail. If we want an occupational structure which is less hierarchical and in which the social distance between the top and the bottom is reduced, we will have to make deliberate efforts to reorganize work and redistribute power within organizations. We will probably also have to rotate jobs, so that no individual holds power very long.

If we want an income distribution that is more equal, we can constrain employers, either by tax incentives or direct legislation, to reduce wage disparities between their best- and worst-paid workers. We can make taxes more progressive, and we can provide income supplements to those who do not make an adequate living from wages alone. We can also provide free public services for those who cannot afford to buy adequate services in the private sector. Pursued with vigor, such a strategy can make "poverty" (*i.e.,* having a living standard less than half the national average) virtually impossible. Such a strategy would also make economic "success," in the sense of having, say, a living standard more than twice the national average, far less common than it now is. The net effect would be to make those with the most competence and luck subsidize those with the least competence and luck to a far greater extent than they do today. Unless we are prepared to do this, poverty and inequality will remain with us indefinitely.

This strategy was rejected during the 1960s for the simple reason that it commanded relatively little popular support. The required legislation could not have passed Congress, nor could it pass today. That does not mean that it is the wrong strategy. It simply means that, until we change the political and moral premises on which most Americans now operate, poverty and inequality will persist at pretty much their present level. Intervention in market processes, for example, means restricting the "right" of individuals to use their natural advantages for private gain. Economic equality requires social and legal sanctions—analogous to those that now exist against capricious firing of employees—against inequality within work settings. It also requires that wage rates, which Americans have traditionally viewed as a "private" question to be adjudicated by negotiation between (unequal) individuals or groups, must become a "public" question subject to political control and solution.

In America, as elsewhere, the long-term drift over the past 200 years has been toward equality. In America, however, the contribution of public policy to this drift has been slight. As long as egalitarians assume that public policy cannot contribute to equality directly but must proceed by ingenious manipulations of marginal institutions like the schools, this pattern will continue. If we want to move beyond this tradition, we must establish political control over the economic institutions that shape our society. What we will need, in short, is what other countries call socialism. Anything less will end in the same disappointment as the reforms of the 1960s.

Human Rights, Equality, and Education
WILLIAM T. BLACKSTONE

In this selection, William T. Blackstone, Professor of Philosophy at the University of Georgia, begins with a brief discussion of the general concepts of "human rights" and "equality of treatment." He then extends his analysis to equal educational opportunity as a human right. Professor Blackstone offers several normative arguments and recommendations based on recent findings, particularly those of the Coleman Report.

Like Komisar and Coombs, Blackstone argues that equal educational opportunity is fundamentally a moral issue. Similarly, he finds the "equal as same" concept (what he calls "purely descriptive criteria") inadequate for arriving at a meaningful interpretation of equal educational opportunity. Blackstone assumes that education is a human right. Accordingly, he contends that equal educational opportunity must first be interpreted as calling for the distribution of educational goods and services in terms of the needs of persons as human beings rather than

SOURCE: William T. Blackstone, "Human Rights, Equality, and Education," *Educational Theory*, Vol. 19 (Summer, 1969), pp. 288–298. Reprinted by permission of the publisher and author.

on the basis of merit. He argues, in short, that if equal educational opportunity is a human right, then criteria of merit—social and economic class, native abilities, etc.,—are irrelevant in regard to the possession of this human right. He notes, however, that "such capacities and conditions are certainly relevant . . . in how education as a right is to be *accorded*." The reader may find it interesting to compare Blackstone's thinking here to Professor Green's analysis of the criteria of merit and need in Chapter 4.

Blackstone stresses that equality of educational opportunity can be attained only through fundamental social and economic changes in our society. He suggests that the stability of our entire democratic system is threatened unless the schools begin soon to serve all socioeconomic classes in terms of their fundamental human rights and, accordingly, their needs. He also believes that achievement of equal educational opportunity depends, in part, upon giving preferential treatment to poor and disadvantaged persons.

In the United States there is very little debate or disagreement over whether the right to an education is a human right or over whether all persons should receive equality of educational opportunity. Education is seen not only as a right but as a necessity made compulsory. True, Senator Goldwater and others remind us that the Constitution of the United States says nothing about education; but as Senator Eugene McCarthy points out, it does say a lot about human dignity, happiness, and inalienable rights.[1] Quite plainly the right to an education or equality of educational opportunity has been taken to be entailed by these fundamental principles. However, there has been and continues to be considerable disagreement over what is meant by the human right to an education or equality of educational opportunity, and consequently, over what conditions the fulfillment of which would assure that right or equality.

In this paper I will consider these issues. My procedure will be both analytic or conceptual and normative. First, I will present a brief analysis of the general concepts, "human rights" and "equality of treatment." Then I will extend this analysis more specifically to education as a human right and equal educational opportunity. I will also offer several normative arguments and recommendations, which themselves involve reference to recently documented empirical facts,

[1] See Eugene McCarthy, "My Hope for the Democrats," *Saturday Review,* November 3, 1966, p. 50.

and conclude by giving a brief summary of what I consider to be the limits of the rational adjudication of moral issues of this type.

The analysis offered, I believe, *is* a morally neutral explication. My normative conclusions, though, are the result of two elements: (1) certain value commitments, which I think are *essential* for anyone who subscribes to the ethic of democracy, but which go in a certain direction *within* that ethic (what I mean by "within" I will make clear as I proceed) and (2) the acceptance of certain empirical states of affairs.

I do not think that the concepts, equality and human rights, are identical, though they do cross at important junctures. Historically, equality has been held to be one of several human rights, as by John Locke. Others have held that equality is the only human right. This seems to be what is held by H. L. A. Hart in his thesis that the equal right to be free is the only natural right.[2] My thesis is that equality is used in several different senses, and *one* of those uses is identical to the notion of a *human* right. This is my reason for treating both of these concepts together in this paper. In effect I want to show that the same sort of problems confront the notion of a "human right" as confront the notion of "equality" (that is, a key use of this concept) and, *mutatis mutandis,* the same problems confront the notion of a "human right to education" as confront the notion of "equality of educational opportunity." I turn first to the concept of human rights.

The Concept of Human Rights

Presumably what differentiates human rights from legal rights is that the latter are the permissions, entitlements, and prohibitions embodied in statute law and which are enforceable by reference to that law, whereas the former may or may not be so embodied or recognized by law and in fact hold independently of laws or social conventions. Human rights are those rights which one possesses simply in virtue of the fact that one is human. They also hold independently of special, acquired characteristics, such as wealth, education, moral character, and so on. No acquired characteristics whatever are relevant and hence, human beings are not gradable in

[2] H. L. A. Hart, "Are There Any Natural Rights?," in *Society, Law and Morality,* ed. Frederick Olafson (Englewood Cliffs, N.J., 1961). First published in the *Philosophical Review*, Vol. LXIV (1955).

regard to the *possession* of these rights. All that is required is that one be human.

This entails nothing about what constitutes the fulfillment of a given human right for a given person on a given occasion. Human rights theorists have never insisted on identity of treatment as necessary for the fulfillment of a human right. They have insisted in fact that there are multiple grounds which require and justify differential treatment of persons (in fulfilling their human rights), that identical treatment in many cases is improper and unfair, and that consequently careful attention to the circumstances and capacities of persons and rational *judgment* are required to properly fulfill a human right. The fact that one is human therefore, and *qua* this fact possesses human rights, entails little about how one should be treated on a given occasion. It seems to me to entail only that one should be treated as any other human being who is similar to oneself in all *relevant* respects. And this is vacuous indeed until criteria of relevance for differential treatment are spelled out.

The problem, then, as I see it, with the concept of human rights is twofold: (1) criteria for being human must be laid down so that we know which beings have human rights (and though this seems a simple problem I will show in a moment with an example that it is not) and (2) criteria of relevance which justify differential treatment in according a person his human right must be specified. These problems are related, but let me speak to (1) first.

What are the criteria for being human? Not criteria for being a brilliant, efficient, or productive human but just human? Well, skin pigmentation, the length of nose, and cranium size seem to be accidental features. Are there any essential ones? I am not so sure that human nature has an *essence* which distinguishes it from other animal natures. Perhaps the difference lies in having the capacity or potentiality for a certain range of qualities and activities.[3] Man differs from other animals in that his rational capacities and perceptual apparatus give him this range—the ability to choose, use concepts and reason—which other animals lack. On this analysis the problem of who is human and therefore has human rights boils down to who has these capacities and potentialities.

[3] S. I. Benn and R. S. Peter's discussion of this in *The Principles of Political Thought* (New York, 1964). Originally published in 1959 as *Social Foundations of the Democratic State*.

What about an imbecile or a moron or a madman? Are they human and do they possess human rights? We say that they do—only that they have impaired capacities. However, and this is the point I want to make here, the notion of "human" can be used in a more flagrantly normative way as Friedrich Nietzsche does when he insists that one is *really* human only if one's capacities are at a certain level— the level of the *ubermensch* or superman.[4] The implication of this for the existence and accordance of human rights is tremendous. In Nietzsche's "master-morality" the scope of rights and duties are severely restricted, depending on one's "slave" or "ubermensch" status. Those persons or bodies without "ubermensch" qualities can in fact be used as a scaffolding for the further elevation and use of those with these *really* human qualities. Everything hangs on what is built into the concept "human."

The Nietzschian thesis can perhaps best be formulated as a choice of criteria of relevance for differential treatment in according rights. That is, instead of simply reading certain bodies out of the human race, what is done is the setting of criteria of relevance for differential treatment so that the characteristics of "slaves" and "ubermensch" are constitutive aspects of the criteria. Then the rules justify including or excluding or qualifying the treatment of certain persons.

Most anything *can* be justified. It depends entirely on the criteria chosen. The question is which criteria *ought* to be chosen and used, for the question of what is *relevant* is in large part normative. This is the crucially important problem and I will return to it. But first I want to offer a brief analysis of the concept of equality (as promised) and show that the same problem of justifying criteria of relevance for differential treatment which confronts the notion of human rights also confronts the principle of equality.

Equality of Treatment

I am not here concerned with uses of equality as a descriptive concept but only with prescriptive uses, in particular with the classical principle which has played such a key role in moral and political contexts over the centuries and was formulated by Aristotle in these

---

[4] See especially Nietzsche's *The Geneology of Morals* and *Beyond Good and Evil.*

words, "Equals are to be treated equally: unequals unequally," and by others as "Everyone is to count for one and no more than one" and "all men are equal" (in the sense of being entitled to equal consideration). As with the human rights norm, this principle is vacuous until criteria of relevance for differential treatment are filled in. It prescribes simply that all persons are to be treated alike and that no person is to be given better treatment or special consideration or privileges unless justifying reasons can be given for such differentiation. It prescribes that all human beings, no matter what natural or acquired characteristics they possess, no matter how unequal their endowments and conditions, are entitled to the same relative care and consideration. The principle does not prescribe identical treatment of persons—unless those persons and circumstances are similar in all *relevant* respects. The problem, however, is specifying and *justifying* criteria of relevance for differential treatment. Again, it is plain that everything in the way of the treatment of persons hangs on those criteria. And here is the rub, for these are fundamental differences in the criteria proposed—at least in their order of priority.

Let me spell this out just a little. The claim that certain criteria are relevant involves both descriptive and prescriptive aspects. The descriptive aspect poses no special problem. It amounts roughly to the assertion that certain factors are causally related to given ends, and as such is straightforwardly verifiable. For example, to assert that I.Q. is relevant to educability is to assert such a causal relationship. The prescriptive aspect of judgments of relevance, on the other hand, poses difficult problems. A host of different *general* criteria of relevance has been recommended by Aristotle, Nietzsche, Karl Marx, Franklin Delano Roosevelt, and so on. They include "merit," "need," "worth to society," and so on. Each of these normative criteria can be explicated or unpacked in different ways. Aristotle and Nietzsche do not agree on what constitutes "merit." But let us ignore the ambiguity of these notions for a moment and concentrate simply on the general, contrasting criteria of "merit" and "need." If "merit" is taken as a general and fundamental criterion of relevance for differential treatment, this amounts to the formulation not only of criteria for particular evaluations of how to treat people but also of a general concept of what society should be like. If "need," on the other hand, is given primary emphasis, then we have different guidelines for treating people and a different concept of a desirable society.

I am *not* arguing here that criteria of merit and criteria of need are mutually exclusive. Obviously they are not, and one can accept both—and other criteria. It would be an odd world, indeed, in which merit-criteria did not exist. I am arguing that the *moral priority* or emphasis in one's scale of relevant criteria or reasons for differential treatment entails very important differences in guidelines for treating people—for distributing goods and services—and for one's concept of a desirable society.

Need-Criteria Priority

Now let us ask this question: Can we justify the claim that need-criteria (admittedly the concept of "need" needs analysis but this is not the place to do it) should take moral priority over criteria of merit and other criteria? For the most part we in this country at least subscribe to this moral priority. We say in a host of contexts, involving medical treatment, legal treatment, basic living conditions, and so on that all human beings ought to be accorded a certain mode of treatment *qua* the fact of humanness, *qua* the fact of equality in that sense; and that acquired characteristics, inherited circumstances, rank, wealth, and worth to society are irrelevant in according these modes of treatment. In other words we do, at least on a doctrinal level, espouse the moral priority of need-criteria, and a good case can be made that this priority is fundamental to the democratic ethic. But is there an argument which will justify this priority or must it simply be a fundamental postulate?

There is an argument implicit in Plato's *Republic* which I think is forceful. Plato there holds that differential treatment on the basis of merit is inescapable but that fairness requires that, first, all be given the opportunity to develop those meritorious qualities. For Plato this involves the fulfillment of certain basic human needs and educational opportunities. Frankena recently argued the same point, that merit cannot be the most basic criterion for distributive justice because "a recognition of merit as the basis of distribution is justified only if every individual has an equal chance of achieving all the merit he is capable of . . . ." [5] The point is that giving priority to merit-criteria is like pretending that everyone is eligible for the game of goods-

---

[5] William Frankena, "Some Beliefs About Justice" (The Lindley Lecture, University of Kansas, 1966).

distribution, while knowing that many individuals, through no fault of their own, through circumstances and deficiencies over which they have no control, cannot possibly be in the game.

The Human Right to Education

Now assuming that human rights extend to education or that equality extends to educational opportunity, what is entailed by what we have just argued concerning criteria of merit, need, and so on? First, if education is seen as a human right, then all are entitled to it simply *qua* the fact of being human. Criteria of merit, however conceived, such as I.Q. or wealth or social class are irrelevant in regard to the *possession* of this right. Such capacities and conditions are certainly relevant, however, in how education as a right is to be *accorded*. There is no question that these capacities and conditions are causally related to the educability of persons or to the extent to which any given person can be educated. If the above argument on the moral priority of need and capacity-criteria is accepted, then the *ideal* fulfillment of the human right to education entails providing those conditions, social, economic, and educational, which will enable each person to fulfill his capacities. It may be that such ideal fulfillment is impossible in some circumstances—due to extreme scarcity of goods and services. It may be that it is possible but that, for a variety of reasons, available goods and services are not properly distributed. What constitutes proper distribution in any given case is a complex matter of three premises or components: (1) norms or criteria of relevance for differential treatment *and an order of priority* among those criteria; (2) empirical facts which bear on the needs, abilities, and circumstances of the person or persons involved, and (3) knowledge of the goods and services *available* for distribution.

I will not concentrate on knowledge of available goods and services. This is obviously essential for proper judgment about distribution. Since these goods vary greatly from one country to another, this fact alone results in great variability in distribution. It would be unreasonable in practice, for example, to insist on the fulfillment of the right of everyone to a university education in India, whereas it might well be reasonable in the United States. It is conceivable, in fact, that goods of various types be so limited or scarce that the very notion of a right to certain goods or of equality of treatment loses its significance. The same holds for conditions of extreme abundance, for no occasion for pressing a right would ever arise if everyone's needs could be satisfied simply by reaching out or asking. This, I take it, is Hume's point about the conditions which give talk about "justice," and I assume, "rights," its point and significance. Rights talk, then, and claims for equal treatment, presuppose conflicts of interests and a world in which there is neither a complete abundance of need-fulfilling resources nor a complete lack of such resources.

Normative Criteria and Empirical Facts

Concerning (1) norms, I have suggested that *genuine* democrats are committed to need-criteria priority, and I will indicate what seems to me to be entailed by this. I want to indicate these entailments by briefly focusing on (2) certain empirical facts or issues.

There are a host of factual issues which must be resolved by sociological and educational research before we can come up with the needed factual premises which, together with our normative principles or commitments, will yield a conclusion about what ought to be done to properly accord the human right to an education or equality of educational opportunity. These facts will vary greatly from one country, or region, to another. My focus here will be on some facts in the United States recently dramatized by the Coleman Report, an 800-page document which is the result of the second largest piece of social science research ever conducted.[6]

A serious obstacle to progress in fulfilling the human right to education in America, and elsewhere, is the absence of adequate, tested information on how well our schools are fulfilling the educational needs of our children and where they are failing to do so. I am not a sociologist or an educational researcher so I am not about to presume to tell you what school factors are of central importance in equalizing educational opportunity or fulfilling the human right to education. The variables involved here are exceedingly complex. But the need for reliable information is plain. This is clear from the furor kicked off by the recent Coleman Report on *Equality of Educational Opportunity*. This survey investigated the relationships of pupil achievement with various aspects of pupil background and some forty-five measures that describe the schools attended. This is un-

[6] James S. Coleman *et al., Equality of Educational Opportunity* (Washington, D.C., United States Government Printing Office, 1966).

doubtedly the most elaborate data collection project conducted thus far. One of its conclusions, not entirely surprising to me, is that the differential effects of schools on pupil achievement "appear to arise not principally from factors that the school system controls, but from factors outside the school proper." [7] This report has been criticized for its almost exclusive use of verbal ability as a criterion of academic achievement (a criterion known to be far more a product of a child's home rather than his school). Henry Dyer, Director of the Educational Testing Service argues that it pays little attention "to the kinds of achievement on which the schools have traditionally focused," and that other criteria in other studies (he cites that of Shaycroft [8]), related specifically to the subjects studied in school, show that among schools there are substantial differences in effects, even when socioeconomic differences are accounted for. [9] Dyer concludes that the results of the Coleman Report "have the unfortunate, though perhaps inadvertent, effect of giving school systems the false impression that there is not much they can do to improve the achievement of their pupils." [10]

Now I am not so sure that the Report gives this impression, but the point I want to stress is that we frequently have fundamental disagreements about what can and what cannot be done by schools to insure equal educational opportunity. Much more research needs to be done to provide this essential factual data about the key causal factors in the home, community, and school related to educability. In some cases it may be difficult, if not impossible, to separate the variables centering around home and community from those of the school, but we must press our demand for knowledge here to the limit. We desperately need a truer assessment of the key factors related to equality of educational opportunity.

We have known for years that there is massive inequality in public school education, which cuts along not only racial lines but also socio-economic lines. Achievement tests show that minority group students of the lower socio-economic class score significantly lower on a variety of tests than middle-class whites, and that far

[7] *Ibid.,* p. 312.

[8] Marion F. Shaycroft, *The High School Years: Growth in Cognitive Skills* (Pittsburgh, Pa.: American Institute for Research and School of Education, University of Pittsburgh, 1967).

[9] Henry Dyer, "School Factors and Equal Educational Opportunity," *Harvard Educational Review,* Vol. 38, 1968, p. 46.

[10] *Ibid.*

from providing equal educational opportunity, our schools in many cases are not even equipping students to function well in our society. One significant conclusion of the Coleman Report, as I read it, is that we *cannot expect* the schools alone to provide this opportunity, that although the schools can and do mold and shape a student, the *massive* inequality which confronts us can be overcome only by confronting those variables in the non-school environment. As the report points out, the achievement differences between racial and ethnic groups simply are not lessened with more years of schooling.

Normative Recommendations

The upshot of all this is that we cannot meaningfully confront the problem of educational equality without confronting the problem of social and economic equality. Given a social order in which there are very wide differences in living standards, in which even minimal living conditions are not satisfied for a substantial percentage of the population, and in which the children of low income families must become wage earners in their early teens, the mere formal access to primary and secondary education will never provide equality of educational opportunity. If, *as we profess,* social class and wealth, not to speak of skin pigmentation, are irrelevant in the distribution of education (irrelevant, *not* in the causal sense, but in the sense that they ought not to count as factors in regard to the *possession* of rights), then we must institute the necessary social and economic changes which will ameliorate these conditions inherited by so many of our children. More than compensatory programs of education, decreased student-teacher ratios, better facilities, improved teacher quality, and so on are required. What is also required are certain fundamental social and economic changes in our society, changes which can overcome the impoverishment and socially-hostile-to-education conditions of the home and community.

This is a tall order, and it cannot be done overnight. And we should not make the mistake of seeing the inequality problem as essentially a racial one. There are millions of poor whites and some rich Negroes. What is required is not merely an end to racism but an end to the political powerlessness of poor people, no matter what their color. This will undoubtedly require fundamental changes in the distribution of political power among social and economic classes.

What is at stake is the promise of democracy. Educated and productive citizens constitute the basis of democratic stability, and our public schools have constituted the principal instrument in making such citizens. But whatever success our public school system has had in the past, it is clearly failing today in many instances, especially in many large city ghettos. There is considerable truth in Kenneth Clark's remark that "American public schools have become significant instruments in the blocking of economic mobility and in the intensification of class distinctions rather than fulfilling their historic function of facilitating such mobility. In effect, the public schools have become captives of a middle class who have failed to use them to aid others to move into the middle class." [11]

The cost of changing this in terms of money will be high but we cannot afford not to do it. It will also involve giving preferential treatment to the poor and the deprived; and though this preferential treatment is justified on relevant grounds (given the ethic of democracy), such a policy will result in conflicts of interest, for it will detract from the interest of other classes. It will increase the competition for good jobs, and some who now obtain those jobs almost by default may not like the competition.

It will also cost us in terms of freedom. Any new social or economic strictures decrease the area of free choice for man. The 18th-century debate on the conflict of equality and freedom did have a point. But again the cost here is worth the product, and we must be willing to admit that on occasion, many of our most cherished values do conflict, and choice must be made.

How far are we willing to go in order to remove the causes of inequality? How far should we go? Getting rid of these causes will require a fantastic array of social policies, including birth control, pre-school environment control, housing regulations, and perhaps a guaranteed minimum income. Our society is clearly moving in the direction of these policies. How far we *will* go can be only a rough guess. How far we *ought* to go requires a continuous debate within the framework of our ethical and normative commitments, one which recognizes that equality of treatment, though a basic value within the ethic of democracy, is not the only such value, that there are other basic values such as individual freedom, which may and do conflict with equalitarian considerations and which necessitate a

[11] Kenneth B. Clark, "Alternative Public School Systems," *Harvard Educational Review*, Vol. 38, 1968, p. 101.

choice, and a loss, *to some extent,* of one of these values. I do not believe that ethical choice is a one-principle affair, and, in my opinion, efforts to reduce all morally relevant considerations to one principle, such as that of utility, have failed. This fact leaves us with the possibility of fundamental conflicts of value, not only with opponents *outside* of the democratic ethic, such as Nietzsche, but *within* the democratic ethic itself. The conflict "within" involves differences not only in priority (or degrees of priority) among criteria of relevance for the differential treatment of persons but also on priority choice when such values as equality *and* freedom conflict.

Metaethical Issues

These comments about conflict of values situations lead me to the final points I want to make in this paper. They are conceptual and epistemological points about moral or normative concepts, or what is generally called metaethical issues.

First, neither the notion of a human right nor that of equality of treatment can be reduced to some purely descriptive criterion or set of criteria. To be sure when these concepts are particularized to some context like education, legal treatment, housing, and so on, various sets of descriptive criteria are formulated which we use as tests for having accorded one his rights or equal treatment. But even in particularized contexts these normative concepts cannot be completely reduced to descriptive criteria. This is at least one thesis that G. E. Moore argued in his talk about a "naturalistic fallacy" in ethics and his "open-question" argument.[12] If Moore's argument has any force, and I believe it does (though we need not be led to talk about "nonnatural" properties by it), it applies to the concept of "equal educational opportunity" just as much as to the concept of "good." Suppose, for example, educational equality is explicated or defined in terms of (a) the racial composition of the school, or (b) the community's input to the school, such items as per-pupil expenditure, school plants, library, and so on, or (c) the similarity of the educational results of the school for individuals with similar backgrounds and abilities, or (d) exposure to a common curriculum, and so on. These are some of the senses of equality of educational opportunity discussed by Coleman. The point of the "open-question" argument

---

[12] G. E. Moore, *Principia Ethica* (Cambridge University Press, 1903).

in the educational context and of the naturalistic fallacy accusation is that it makes perfectly good sense to ask whether a person has been accorded equal educational opportunity or his right to an education even if (a) or (b) or (c) or (d) is the case. These criteria may all be valid ones for assessing equality of educational opportunity but no one of them or all of them *constitutes* the meaning of educational equality. Of course, there may be *some uses* of the notion of equality of educational opportunity which are explicable entirely in terms of descriptive criteria—in the same way in which *some uses* of "good" can be explicated descriptively. But in most uses there is a commendatory function or a normative dimension which cannot be so reduced. It is part of what might be called the logic of the concept that it cannot be so reduced, that it cannot be defined for all time in terms of necessary and sufficient conditions. Both the normative ideals in the concept and the material conditions necessary for implementing the ideal change with time and place. There is no escaping the necessity for judgment both in regard to the content of the concept itself and of the application of it in a concrete situation.

Finally, with reference to my comments on value conflicts "inside" and "outside" of the democratic ethic, I want to indicate, all too briefly, and hence dogmatically, the limits which I believe exist in the justification of human rights and equality claims. These limits, I think, apply to moral conflicts in general, and my comments here constitute part of a metaethic not fully developed in this paper. My concern here is with the normative premises in these claims.

First, it is plain that even if a case can be made out that the very concept of equality or human rights as explicated in this paper is *constitutive* of adopting a moral point of view at all (as opposed to prudential, etc.); that is, even if it could be shown that moral discourse is logically impossible without presupposing the equality principle, this does not take us very far. Some philosophers do just this,[13] and I feel sure that non-equalitarians will quickly shout that this is a case of surreptitiously smuggling in a norm under the guise of a neutral philosophical analysis of the notion of a moral point of view. This issue I will not discuss now. Even if the claim is true that equality is constitutive of moral reasoning, all the substantive problems centering around different criteria of relevance for differential treatment remain.

[13] See R. S. Peters, *Ethics and Education* (Glenview: Scott, Foresman and Company, 1967) as an example, especially p. 49.

Secondly, I am convinced that a descriptivist account of human rights and equality claims is false. Equality and human rights are not descriptive properties of humans. Nor are they somehow embedded in the marrow of reality, from which we can somehow read them off. Nor are they directly inferable from properties possessed by humans, such as "reason." For if reason is a descriptive property, we cannot logically infer any rights or norms from it alone. If reason, on the other hand, is a normative concept with the notion of rights built in, so to speak, then no inference is necessary. The problem is either the "is-ought" gap or circularity.

If I am correct that a descriptivist metaethic is mistaken (which I have not here supported by an argument), that human rights and equality are not norms which are somehow *discovered,* then a number of natural law theorists and others who feel the need for metaphysical underpinning for moral norms may be disappointed. Having some of these inclinations myself, I feel at least a twinge or tug. However, these norms and the segment of moral discourse which accompanies them can be given a *kind* of justification in another direction—so we need not be committed to some sort of complete scepticism concerning them. That direction is simply a pragmatic justification. One can point out that these norms are absolutely essential as instruments in effecting a certain type of society, that they can be given up only at the very high cost of precluding that type of society. This is parallel to H. L. A. Hart's argument that the language of special and general rights logically presupposes the equal right of all men to be free, that consequently one can give up this latter principle only at the cost of giving up an entire segment of moral discourse and its concomitant practices.[14]

Some persons, finding undesirable the kind of society made possible by the wholesale endorsement of human rights and equality, would be unconvinced by this type of argument. That is the weakness of any pragmatic argument, but it may well be all that we have.[15]

[14] H. L. A. Hart, *op. cit.*
[15] I emphasize the word "may" here. In a forthcoming article ("Human Rights and Human Dignity," *The Philosophy Forum,* Volume 9, 1970) I explore the possibility of a kind of justification of human rights which amounts to a halfway house between natural law theory and conventionalism.

The Charlotte-Mecklenburg Case:
Its Significance for Northern School Desegregation
OWEN M. FISS

Owen M. Fiss, a professor at The University of Chicago Law School, predicts that the *Swann* case will be the first legal precedent in the elimination of Northern *de facto* segregation. He believes that deliberate segregation by boards of education in the North should be no more difficult to prove than *de jure* segregation in the South has been. In his article he cites construction policies in large cities as examples of deliberate segregation. In general, Professor Fiss is optimistic about eliminating *de facto* segregation.

Not all observers of the Court believe that *Swann* can be interpreted as Fiss has done in this article. Most believe that if *de facto* segregation is struck down, the argument will be based on the Fourteenth Amendment as it is in *Swann,* but the reasoning will emphasize totally different specifics. Fiss himself stresses that past discrimination and geographic proximity may not be relevant in the North. He also points out that political pressure is mounting for the Congress to strike out against Northern *de facto* segregation (see Chapter 3, pp. 47–50).

Brown v. *Board of Education*[1] stands for the proposition that the equal protection clause prohibits the operation of a "dual school system" and requires the conversion of that system into a "unitary nonracial school system." Under a dual system, students are assigned to schools on the basis of their race in order to segregate them. That is clearly impermissible. But what is a permissible basis for assigning students to schools under a "unitary nonracial school system"? This seems to be the central riddle of the law of school desegregation.

There is one easy answer to this question: Under a "unitary nonracial school system" students may be assigned to schools on the basis of any criterion other than race. But there is an understandable

[1] 347 U.S. 483 (1954); 349 U.S. 294 (1955).

SOURCE: Owen M. Fiss, "The Charlotte-Mecklenburg Case: Its Significance for Northern School Desegregation," *The University of Chicago Law Review,* Vol. 38 (Summer, 1971), pp. 697–709. Reprinted with permission of the author and publisher.

reluctance to accept this answer. This stems from the fact that even if some seemingly innocent criterion is substituted for race as the basis for assignment, virtually the same segregated patterns of student attendance that existed under the dual system might result—whites in one set of schools and blacks in another. Moreover, there are reasons to be concerned with this result, even assuming race is not the basis for assignment. The concern might be predicated on a fear of "evasion"—if the school board is allowed to use any criterion other than race, it might be able to accomplish the same thing as it did under the dual school system. The concern with the result might also be based on the view that a segregated student attendance pattern alone —without regard to the basis for assignment—gives rise to an inequality. The segregation might stigmatize the blacks, deprive them of educationally significant contacts with the socially and economically dominant group, and reduce the share of resources allocated to black schools simply because they are attended only by members of the minority group.

But, of course, the picture is not all one-sided. There are several countervailing factors that have the effect of diluting this concern with the mere result—the segregated pattern of student attendance. One is the uncertainty surrounding the central empirical proposition that a segregated pattern of student attendance itself leads to inferior education for blacks. Another is the price of a remedial order eliminating the segregated school pattern. Such an order would probably divert financial resources because of the expense of transportation and frustrate the intense associational desires of large parts of the community. A court aware of these costs is likely to feel a need to justify its action in terms that have the quality of a moral imperative. A justification couched in terms of the wrongness of excluding individuals from a school because of their race—the classic concept of racial discrimination—certainly has that flavor. But one cast primarily in terms of the alleged inferiority of racially homogeneous schools does not.

These conflicting considerations account for the uncertain nature of the law of school desegregation. The controversy has in large part been over two approaches—one that forbids only the use of the racial criterion as the basis of assignment (sometimes referred to as a *de jure* approach), and the other that focuses on the result, the segregated patterns themselves (sometimes referred to as a *de facto* approach).[2] It is the latter approach which presents the greatest challenge to the school segregation of the North, for the assumption is that students in the North are assigned to schools, not on the basis of race, but instead on the basis of a seemingly innocent criterion—geographic proximity. The controversy between these two approaches is far from resolved, but there has been a historical trend. I would like to suggest that the trend of school desegregation doctrine has been one in which the courts have rejected an approach that forbids only the use of race and have moved in the direction of the result-oriented approach.

I

The first significant development in Supreme Court doctrine occurred in 1968 in *Green* v. *New Kent County School Board*.[3] There the criterion for student assignment was individual choice. Under the Board's plan, no student was assigned to a school on the basis of his race. Instead, all students, black and white, were assigned on the basis of their own choice. The result was that some blacks attended the formerly all-white school, most blacks remained in the black school, and no whites attended the black school. The Court declared that in the school system before it, freedom-of-choice was an impermissible basis for assigning students to schools. The freedom-of-choice plan, the Court concluded, had failed to "work." It had failed to produce a "unitary nonracial school system"—a system, so the Court said, in which there are not black schools and white schools, but just schools.

Despite the captivating quality of these phrases, they do not indicate the basis for invalidating the choice plan. The Court said that it was not ruling freedom-of-choice plans unacceptable in all circumstances, but it failed to identify the particular circumstances that rendered the New Kent County plan unacceptable. The Court carefully avoided resting its decision on the view that the result was the product of threats or that procedural irregularities of the plan interfered with the exercise of choice. However, the Court did not say that a student assignment plan would be deemed to "work" only

[2] These issues are surveyed in more detail in an earlier article of mine, *Racial Imbalance in the Public Schools: the Constitutional Concepts*, 78 Harv. L. Rev. 564 (1965).
[3] 391 U.S. 430 (1968).

when it produces an integrated pattern of student attendance—when it eliminates, to the extent possible, the all-black school. The message that emerges from *Green* is a negative one—that a school board does not fulfill its duty to convert to a unitary system by substituting for a racial criterion one that is innocent on its face. In effect, the Court rejected the simple formula that reduced the equal protection clause to a prohibition against the use of race as a basis of assignment and thereby permitted the use of any other criterion. In 1968 this was a considerable achievement.

Further movement in this direction occurred this past term when in *Swann* v. *Charlotte-Mecklenburg Board of Education* [4] the Supreme Court once again considered the adequacy of student assignment plans. The Court reaffirmed *Green's* rejection of the view that only the use of race is forbidden but took four additional steps.

First, the seemingly innocent criterion held inadequate in *Charlotte-Mecklenburg* was not the freedom-of-choice criterion of *Green* but one more common in the North—assigning students to the schools nearest their homes. This holding was not premised on a finding that the proposed geographic zones were "gerrymandered" in the *Gomillion* v. *Lightfoot* [5] sense. Instead, *Charlotte-Mecklenburg* holds that even if geographic proximity, not race, were the basis for the zones and thus for assignments, the Board's duty to convert to a "unitary nonracial school system" would not be satisfied.

Why is the use of this seemingly innocent criterion—geographic proximity—impermissible? The Court did not answer this question merely by pointing to the resulting segregated pattern of student attendance. The existence of this segregation was an important factor in its analysis, but the Court added another ingredient. It sought to show that the Board of Education was to some degree responsible for the segregation, thereby making it "state-imposed segregation." For this purpose, it focused attention on the Board's past wrongdoing. The Court saw a causal connection between the Board's past discrimination and present segregation, and on the basis of this connection attributed responsibility to the Board for the segregation.

Two types of connections are suggested in the opinion: (1) The past discriminatory conduct of a school board might have contributed to the creation and maintenance of segregated residential patterns

---

[4] *Swann* v. *Charlotte-Mecklenburg Bd. of Educ.,* 402 U.S. 1 (1971).
[5] 364 U.S. 339 (1960).

which, when coupled with the present use of geographic proximity as the basis for assignment, produce segregated schools. The assumption is that, under the dual system, schools are racially designated as "white" or "black" and are located in different geographic areas, and that in the past racial groups chose to live near "their" particular schools. That choice might have been motivated by the desire of families to live close to the schools which their children attended, or it might have reflected the belief that the racial designation of a school also racially designated the residential area. (2) Prior decisions by a school board regarding the location and size of schools might in part explain why assigning students to the schools nearest their homes will result in racially homogeneous schools. Under the dual school system, school sites were selected and the student capacity of schools determined with a view toward serving students of only one race. These past policies are important because assignment on the basis of geographic proximity will not result in a racially homogeneous school unless, in addition to the existence of residential segregation, the school is so small that it serves only a racially homogeneous area or so situated that it is the closest school to students of only one race.

The second advance of *Charlotte-Mecklenburg* relates to the fact that these causal connections between past discrimination and present segregation are no more than theoretical possibilities and obviously involve significant elements of conjecture. The Court's response was to announce an evidentiary presumption that in effect resolves all the uncertainties against the school board. The Court quite consciously avoided holding that segregated student attendance patterns are, in themselves, a denial of equal protection, and instead emphasized the role that past discriminatory conduct might have played in causing those patterns. But the Court also said that it was prepared to presume an impermissible cause from the mere existence of segregation:

> Where the school authority's proposed plan for conversion from a dual to a unitary system contemplates the continued existence of some schools that are all or predominantly of one race, they have the burden of showing that such school assignments are genuinely nondiscriminatory. The court should scrutinize such schools, and the burden upon the school authorities will be to satisfy the court that their racial composition is not the result of present or past discriminatory action on their part.[6]

[6] 402 U.S. at 26.

Granted, the school board has the opportunity to show that the consequence—segregated schools—is not caused by its discriminatory action and that it is therefore not responsible for the segregation. In that sense the distinction between cause and consequence is preserved. But the distinction is likely to become blurred because the burden cast on the board is a heavy one. The burden cannot be discharged simply by showing that the school segregation is produced, given the segregated residential patterns, by assigning students on the basis of a criterion other than race, such as geographic proximity. The school board will also have to show that its past discriminatory conduct—involving racial designation of schools, site selection, and determination of school size—is not a link in the causal chain producing the segregation. This will be very difficult to do, and the difficulty of overcoming a presumption will tend to accentuate the fact that gives rise to it, namely, the segregated patterns, and this will be reflected in the board's assignment policies. Greater attention will be paid to the segregated patterns.

The third development relates to what the Court said must be done to eliminate these patterns—everything possible. Prior to *Charlotte-Mecklenburg* it was generally assumed that even if attention were focused on the result and a school board were obliged to eliminate the segregated pattern, the extent of the obligation would be simply "to take integration into consideration." Under this formulation of the remedial obligation, integration would be one value, along with others (such as minimizing the time and expense of transportation and avoiding safety hazards), that must be considered in designing attendance plans. There would be a rough parity among these values. In *Charlotte-Mecklenburg* the Court constructed a hierarchy among these values in which integration assumes a role of paramount importance. The Court declared that "the greatest possible degree of actual desegregation" must be achieved. The practicalities of the situation must, of course, also be taken into account, but the Court made clear that if there is a conflict between integration and other values, integration will generally prevail.

Thus, the remedial plan in *Charlotte-Mecklenburg* requires a massive, long-distance transportation program: Students living closest to inner-city schools are to be assigned to suburban ones and students living closest to suburban schools are to be assigned to inner-city ones. True, this is the plan that had been formulated by the district court, and there is considerable language in the Supreme Court's opinion about the broad discretion that the district court has in fashioning a remedy. But the discretion the Court vests in the district court goes only to the question of how integration shall be achieved—the details of the remedial plan (such as which particular schools shall be paired for the transportation program). The lower court has no discretion to alter or disregard the central remedial obligation—achieving the greatest possible degree of actual desegregation—and the plan it approves will be measured by that stringent standard. That is why in a companion case involving Mobile, Alabama, the Supreme Court rejected a desegregation plan that allowed some all-black schools to remain in operation.[7] The elimination of that residue of segregation required assigning students across a major highway that divided the metropolitan area. For the Fifth Circuit, this factor constituted a sufficient practical barrier to relieve the school board of its obligation to remove all remnants of segregation from the system.[8] Nevertheless, the Supreme Court remanded because "inadequate consideration was given to the possible use of bus transportation and split zoning." [9]

Fourth, *Charlotte-Mecklenburg* is significant because it validates the use of race in student assignments when the goal is integration rather than segregation. In this context there is little room for the pretense of color blindness. In part this was anticipated in 1969 in *United States* v. *Montgomery County Board of Education*,[10] a case involving faculty assignments. There the Court affirmed a desegregation order requiring that teachers be assigned so that the proportion of white and black teachers in the system as a whole would be mirrored in each school. The achievement of that goal, in the face of preexisting segregated patterns, required that in the process of deciding where to assign teachers some weight be given to each faculty member's race. Similarly, in *Charlotte-Mecklenburg,* the Court recognized that the achievement of student integration requires that race play some role in the process of deciding to which school a student will be assigned, and for that reason the Court permitted the use of this criterion.

This aspect of *Charlotte-Mecklenburg* undermines the constitutional basis for one objection that had frequently been voiced against remedial programs—whether court-ordered or voluntarily adopted—

[7] *Davis* v. *Board of School Comm'rs,* 402 U.S. 33 (1971).
[8] *Id.* at 36.
[9] *Id.* at 38.
[10] 395 U.S. 225 (1969).

that were designed to eliminate segregation. More broadly, it indicates a conceptual departure from the approach to school desegregation that focuses exclusively on the racial criterion. In effect, it says that the prohibition of the equal protection clause against the use of race as a basis of assignment cannot be understood independently of the result. The prohibition against the use of race is linked to the result. Race is a forbidden criterion for assignment when it is used to produce segregation, but not when it is used to produce integration.

II

These four doctrinal advances of *Charlotte-Mecklenburg* occurred in response to a situation, not readily found in the North, in which a school board had maintained a "dual school system" in the recent past. The opinion appears to be further limited in its application by its emphasis on *recent,* as opposed to *ancient,* history. It suggests that the rules announced may be only transitional requirements.[11] Moreover, this concern with history has an analytical basis. It is used to attribute responsibility. The Court's insistence that the school board be responsible for the segregation is satisfied in *Charlotte-Mecklenburg* by finding a pattern of past discriminatory conduct. In time, however, the legacy of past discrimination may become so attenuated that it will be unrealistic to presume the existence of any causal connection between it and the present school segregation.

---

[11] The passage, which was obviously tacked onto the end of the opinion, indicating that it may have been exacted at the last moment in exchange for someone's vote, reads:

At some point, these school authorities and others like them should have achieved full compliance with this Court's decision in *Brown I.* The systems will then be "unitary" in the sense required by our decisions in *Green* and *Alexander.*

It does not follow that the communities served by such systems will remain demographically stable, for in a growing, mobile society, few will do so. Neither school authorities nor district courts are constitutionally required to make year-by-year adjustments of the racial composition of student bodies once the affirmative duty to desegregate has been accomplished and racial discrimination through official action is eliminated from the system. This does not mean that federal courts are without power to deal with future problems; but in the absence of a showing that either the school authorities or some other agency of the State has deliberately attempted to fix or alter demographic patterns to affect the racial composition of the schools, further intervention by a district court should not be necessary.

402 U.S. at 32.

Nevertheless, it should be emphasized that this concern with recent past discrimination does not confine *Charlotte-Mecklenburg* to the South. Until a few years ago, Southern school districts openly maintained dual school systems, and therefore the existence of past discriminatory practices can be established by admission. In Northern systems, there is no such admission. But that, of course, does not mean that the past discriminatory practices of the *Charlotte-Mecklenburg* type did not occur. It only means that they are more difficult, though not impossible,[12] to prove. In my judgment, a very close, hard look at the construction policies of Northern school systems would reveal numerous instances in which school boards in the recent past have chosen sites and determined capacity with an eye toward serving racially homogeneous areas—often called "neighborhoods." Instead of formally and openly designating a newly constructed school as the Negro school, a school board may have called it the Lincoln School or the Booker T. Washington School and staffed it only with black teachers.[13] The same message is conveyed.

Thus, there are some situations where, because of their recent past discrimination, Northern school systems can be assimilated to the Southern systems, and where the rules of *Charlotte-Mecklenburg* are therefore clearly applicable. But beyond that, one cannot simply say that *Charlotte-Mecklenburg* "outlaws" the school segregation of

[12] *See, e.g., United States* v. *School Dist. 151,* 286 F. Supp. 786 (N.D. Ill. 1968) (preliminary injunction), *aff'd,* 404 F.2d 1125 (7th Cir. 1968), *on remand,* 301 F. Supp. 201 (N.D. Ill. 1969) (permanent injunction), *aff'd with modification,* 432 F.2d 1147 (7th Cir. 1970). Following the *Charlotte-Mecklenburg* decision, the Supreme Court denied the school board's application for certiorari. 39 U.S.L.W. 3482 (U.S. May 3, 1971).

[13] While *Charlotte-Mecklenburg* dealt primarily with student assignment, in my judgment the most difficult aspect of school desegregation, it also reaffirmed previous doctrine requiring the desegregation plan to liquidate all aspects of the dual system, including faculty segregation. This has considerable significance for the North. The Court wrote:

In *Green,* we pointed out that existing policy and practice with regard to faculty, staff, transportation, extracurricular activities, and facilities were among the most important indicia of a segregated system. 391 U.S., at 435. Independent of student assignment, where it is possible to identify a "white school" or a "Negro school" simply by reference to the racial composition of teachers and staff, the quality of school buildings and equipment, or the organization of sports activities, a *prima facie* case of violation of substantive constitutional rights under the Equal Protection Clause is shown.

402 U.S. at 18.

the North. Because of its focus on past discrimination, the case does not lend itself to a blanket judgment about the North, as it does with respect to the South. The net effect of *Charlotte-Mecklenburg* is to move school desegregation doctrine further along the continuum toward a result-oriented approach, but the progression is not complete. Additional steps are required. It seems to me, however, that over time this move will probably be made and that, in retrospect, *Charlotte-Mecklenburg* will then be viewed, like *Green,* as a way-station to the adoption of a general approach to school segregation which, by focusing on the segregated patterns themselves, is more responsive to the school segregation of the North.

This forecast is based in part on my view that the Court will want to avoid the appearance of picking on the South. This appearance is derived from the fact that segregated patterns of student attendance are no less severe in Northern cities than in Southern ones. Under *Charlotte-Mecklenburg,* Southern school systems are obliged to eliminate those patterns and to achieve the greatest possible degree of integration. But there is no similar blanket judgment about those patterns in the North. A complicated analysis of causation might, under the *Charlotte-Mecklenburg* theory, serve to justify the differential treatment afforded these otherwise identical patterns. But such an analysis is not likely to be understood or even believed by most people. And no national institution can afford to be unresponsive to the popular pressures likely to be engendered by an appearance of differential treatment of certain regions of the country. Even the Supreme Court is not immune from such pressures, particularly when they become identified with the ideal of equal treatment.

The forecast is based also on my view that the predominant concern of the Court in *Charlotte-Mecklenburg* is in fact the segregated pattern of student attendance, rather than the causal role played by past discriminatory practices. I realize that in *Charlotte-Mecklenburg* the Court used past discrimination to attribute responsibility to the Board for the school segregation, but this theory for attributing responsibility seems contrived. Although the existence of past discrimination cannot be denied, the Court made no serious attempt either to determine or even to speculate on the degree to which it contributes to present segregation. Nor did the Court attempt to tailor the remedial order to the correction of that portion of the segregation that might reasonably be attributable to past discrimination. The Court moved from (a) the undisputed existence of past discrimination to (b) the *possibility* or *likelihood* that the past discrimination played *some* causal role in producing segregated patterns to (c) an order requiring the complete elimination of those patterns. The existence of past discrimination was thus used as a "trigger"— and not for a pistol, but for a cannon. Such a role cannot be defended unless the primary concern of the Court is the segregated patterns themselves, rather than the causal relation of past discrimination to them. The attention paid to past discrimination can be viewed as an attempt by the Court to preserve the continuity with *Brown* and to add a moral quality to its decision.

The Court is not likely to abandon its requirement that a school board be responsible for the segregated patterns before it is ordered to eliminate them. This requirement, however, need not foreclose any doctrinal advance. An alternative theory for attributing responsibility exists—one that is equally applicable to North and South and well rooted in other areas of the law, such as torts. This theory would hold the school board responsible for the foreseeable and avoidable consequences of its own action. In this context, the pertinent action of the school board is its choice of a criterion for student assignments. The board decides how students are to be assigned. The result of using a criterion such as geographic proximity in a system with residential segregation is foreseeable; and in most instances there are reasonable measures that the board could adopt, if not to eliminate, then at least to mitigate the result that flows from the use of that criterion.

This theory for attributing responsibility is not without limitations. For example, the causal chain linking the school board's decision to assign on the basis of geographic proximity and the school segregation might be broken if it could be presumed that present residential segregation is truly voluntary. Moreover, the board might be relieved of responsibility if there were no "reasonable" steps it could take to avoid school segregation. For this reason, this theory might be viewed as holding the school board to a lesser standard than that of *Charlotte-Mecklenburg,* which, through the triggering action of past discrimination, requires the board to take every *possible* step to eliminate segregation. However, this difference in standards roughly parallels tort rules which hold a person responsible for *all* the consequences of an intentional wrongdoing but which limit liability to the proximate consequences when the wrongdoing is not intentional. In this area a rule that requires the school board to take reasonable steps—as opposed to all possible steps—to eliminate segregation seems to be the more sensible one and therefore the one that will predominate. It does not rest on the unrealistic assumption that all present segregation is a consequence of past wrongdoing, and it gives a more balanced appraisal to competing values that should be taken into consideration in assigning students to schools. In any event, the general effect of the theory would be to focus attention on the segregated patterns themselves and to bridge the doctrinal gap between *Charlotte-Mecklenburg* and an approach to school desegregation that emphasizes primarily the result.

Admittedly, this theory for attributing responsibility does not require the construction of a causal chain that includes a racially discriminatory act in the past. But, analytically, that should be unnecessary. The equal protection clause requires that some government agency be responsible for the unequal treatment, but it does not require that the responsibility be predicated on a causal chain involving an earlier discrimination. It does not require double discrimination. There is no need to search for a second discrimination if it is determined that the segregated patterns themselves render the education afforded blacks inferior and thus are a form of unequal treatment. Under this approach the central dispute would be over the factual assertion that segregated education is inferior. Indeed, this is what the dispute should be about.

The Court in *Charlotte-Mecklenburg* appears to have avoided this dispute by relying on past discrimination. Arguably, the denial of equal protection in *Charlotte-Mecklenburg* originated in past discriminatory school construction practices and, although the Court was no longer able to stop those practices, the injunction it issued could be viewed as an attempt to undo the effects of the past wrong. Under this interpretation, the school segregation was a present effect of the past denial of equal protection, and not itself a denial of equal protection. But this interpretation of *Charlotte-Mecklenburg* does not seem persuasive. It seems much more plausible that the segregated patterns themselves, and not the past construction practices, are viewed as the denial of equal protection. To regard all school segregation as simply an "effect" of the past denial of equal protection requires the positing of an unproved and unlikely causal connection between the two. Furthermore, there is no reason why the courts should use their remedial powers to correct the effect of a past wrong unless that effect is itself harmful or disadvantageous. Thus, at the very least, there is an implicit judgment in *Charlotte-Mecklenburg* that segregation itself is harmful or disadvantageous. And if the segregation is viewed as particularly harmful or disadvantageous to blacks, then it can be construed as a form of unequal treatment. Under this interpretation, the only question remaining is whether the school board is responsible for it. In *Charlotte-Mecklenburg* the Court attributed responsibility for segregation on the basis of past discrimination. My point is that there is an alternative theory for attributing responsibility for the segregation that is as intellectually satisfying as the *Charlotte-Mecklenburg* theory requiring a search for past discrimination.[14]

III

Thus far the development in school desegregation doctrine has been largely the work of the courts, and my forecast about future direction is based on the view that the courts will—in the face of popular pressure and logic—evolve an approach to school desegregation that is increasingly result-oriented. Within the weeks immediately following *Charlotte-Mecklenburg* that seems to be precisely what has been happening in a few lower courts.[15] It is important to emphasize, however, that other branches of government need not wait for these projected doctrinal advances.

Local agencies are today free to institute the appropriate measures to correct segregated patterns of student attendance. There is no

[14] It should also be pointed out that the very use of geographic criteria may be as responsible for residential segregation as past discriminatory construction policies. By rigidly adhering to geographic criteria over a long period of time, a school board assures the white parent who does not want his children to go to school with blacks that this desire can be fulfilled by moving into a white neighborhood. The use of geographic criteria also assures the white parent that if he moves out of the neighborhood into which blacks are moving, he will be leaving the blacks behind. They will not follow him to the new school—unless they also change residence.

[15] See, e.g., *Davis* v. *School Dist.*, No. 20477 (6th Cir. May 28, 1971); *Johnson* v. *San Francisco Unified School Dist.*, No. C-70 1331 SAW (N.D. Cal. Apr. 28, 1971). *But see Spencer* v. *Kugler,* Civil No. 1123-70 (D.N.J. May 13, 1971) (rejecting constitutional challenge to state law that made boundaries of school districts conform to municipal boundaries).

suggestion in *Charlotte-Mecklenburg* that such voluntary remedial measures need be predicated on the discovery of past discrimination. Indeed, this term the Supreme Court invalidated two statewide "anti-busing" laws, one in New York [16] and the other in North Carolina,[17] that would have impeded the efforts of local school boards to correct racial imbalance. Moreover, Congress need not wait until the Supreme Court declares a practice a violation of the equal protection clause before requiring (or inducing) local authorities to correct it. Cases such as *Katzenbach* v. *Morgan* [18] and *Jones* v. *Alfred H. Mayer Co.*[19] indicate the lengths to which the Court will go to indulge and even to encourage congressional activity on behalf of the cause of racial equality. Under the Civil War amendments, Congress is free to enact a rule of law that would require (or induce) school boards throughout the country to take reasonable steps to eliminate segregated patterns of student attendance—without regard to proof in each instance of past discriminatory practices and their contemporary vestiges. Such legislation can be predicated on a judgment about the inequality that arises from a segregated pattern of student attendance itself. And if the legislature insists, as does the Court in *Charlotte-Mecklenburg,* that the segregation be "state-imposed," then such legislation can be predicated on a conclusion that the South has no monopoly on past discrimination, or that school boards are responsible for the foreseeable and avoidable consequences of their own actions. In any event, there is no question about the authority to enact nationwide school desegregation laws. For the last several years that has been clear. The only question is about the will. Conceivably, *Charlotte-Mecklenburg,* by imposing such a heavy burden on the South and by requiring the greatest possible degree of actual desegregation, might be sufficient inducement for such legislation. That might be the most significant aspect of *Charlotte-Mecklenburg* for the North and for the law of school desegregation.

[16] *Chropowicki* v. *Lee,* 402 U.S. 935 (1971) (summary affirmance of three-judge district court ruling).
[17] *North Carolina Bd. of Educ.* v. *Swann,* 402 U.S. 43 (1971).
[18] 384 U.S. 641 (1966).
[19] 392 U.S. 409 (1968).

Serrano v. Priest:
Implications for Educational Equality
WILLIAM N. GREENBAUM

Prior to the *Rodriguez* decision, William Greenbaum predicted that despite pronouncements that most state finance structures were illegal, school support systems would change very slowly. He reasoned that long delay would be caused by each state having to study its own peculiar circumstances before it could devise a new finance plan. His implicit assumption was that the Supreme Court would uphold an argument such as that presented in the Serrano case, but the justices would not present a general remedy for all states. Nor would they uphold a finance plan developed by a lower court rather than a state legislature. The author, an authority on educational law, was frustrated by this predicament, so he advocated here that Congress create some inducements to bring a more rapid end to the inequities caused by present school support structures.

Now that the Supreme Court has acted on the *Rodriguez* case and has struck down the "fundamental interest" argument of *Serrano,* the reader may wish to draw his own conclusions about the implications of these two celebrated decisions and their effects on finance reform. In formulating predictions it may be helpful to review the school finance controversy in Chapter 3 and to study the following article by Thomas Shannon.

In the decision of the Supreme Court of the State of California—*Serrano* v. *Priest*—the Court found that the school financing system in California is unconstitutional because it does not provide children with equal protection as guaranteed by the Fourteenth Amendment of the United States Constitution. The decision was based on the fact that children in wealthy communities receive greater educational offerings than children growing up in poor communities.

The Court's conclusion that education is a "fundamental interest" requiring equal protection is so strongly argued that it seems to

SOURCE: William N. Greenbaum, *"Serrano* v. *Priest:* Implications for Educational Equality," *Current* (March, 1972), pp. 3–6. Reprinted by permission of the publisher and the author.

demand either substantial equalization of per pupil spending or perhaps even substantial equalization of the *quality* of educational programs. The mass media have taken the decision to mean just this—
that serious equalization of educational opportunities will soon be
underway. But in reality, the Court's remedy falls far short of its
analysis of the problem. . . .

The Court's extended finding that education is a fundamental
interest in American society—"the lifeline of both the individual and
the society"—is eloquently and persuasively stated. The voting
analogy seems particularly apt—an individual's life is surely affected
more by his or her education than by his or her individual vote.
Explicit in the analogy is the conclusion that if place of residence is
not allowed to reduce any citizen's vote, neither can it be allowed to
reduce any citizen's educational opportunities.

Three times after its discussion of education as a fundamental
interest, the Court implies quite directly that it is *quality* that must
be equalized. The first deals directly with the voting analogy: "If a
voter's address may not determine the weight to which his ballot is
entitled, surely it should not determine the quality of his child's education." Second, the Court declares that the financing system is invalid because it makes the "quality of a child's education depend
upon the resources of his school district and ultimately upon the
pocketbook of his parents." Finally, in its closing paragraph, the
Court states: "By our holding today we further the cherished idea of
American education that in a democratic society free public schools
shall make available to all children equally the abundant gifts of
learning.". . .

There would seem to be only one or two possible endings to the
line of argument developed in the case. It is abundantly clear that
poor school districts tend to end up with substantially less money
per pupil and lower quality educational programs. If the Court is
convinced of its own conclusion that education is a "fundamental
interest" from both individual and societal points of view, the only
possible remedies would seem to be, at the very least, the substantial
equalization of actual per pupil expenditures, and, more significantly,
the substantial equalization of the quality of educational opportunities.

But in fact the decision in *Serrano* v. *Priest* will not lead
immediately, or even necessarily, to either phase of substantial
equalization. The only significant hint of the actual outcome of the

case is contained in one sentence ". . . we are satisfied that plaintiff children have alleged facts showing that the public school financing system denies them equal protection of the laws because it produces substantial disparities among school districts in the amount of revenue *available* for education." [Emphasis added]

Although the distinction implicit in this language is subtle, its implications are significant. Notice that the Court is here referring to disparities in the amount of revenue *available* to school districts, rather than to disparities in the actual amounts of money spent for education or to disparities in the actual quality of educational programs. In other words, in its most limited sense, the standard for remedy provided by the *Serrano* decision does not declare that each state has an obligation to provide equality of educational opportunity for all of its children. Rather, *Serrano* requires that the state must develop a policy of fiscal neutrality—that is, no state school financing policies will be permitted insofar as they create or exacerbate inequities among school districts. In theoretical terms, the states could provide no school financing whatsoever and meet this standard of fiscal neutrality. But in reality what this means is that the state legislatures will have to develop more equitable financing programs that provide each school district with relatively equal financial capacity, regardless of whether substantially equal spending patterns or educational programs are then developed. It is likely that the system ultimately adopted will be a variation of the "district power equalizing" plan proposed by Coons, Clune, and Sugarman (*Private Wealth and Public Education* [Cambridge: Harvard University Press, 1970], pp. 200–244). In other words, poor school districts that are willing to tax themselves proportionately harder would receive increasing amounts of state aid to more or less equalize their spending capacity with that of wealthier districts. Whether or not spending would actually be more or less equalized would depend on the specific political financing formula emerging from the debates in the state legislature and on the willingness of residents of poor communities to tax themselves relatively heavily for educational purposes. Thus the decision does not provide that either per pupil expenditures or the quality of educational offerings be substantially equalized.

This interpretation of the decision is based not only on the subtler aspects of this and other related cases, but also on the opinions of lawyers supporting the arguments of the plaintiffs. Indeed, Coons *et al.* have asked the Court to clarify (and modify) its point that full equality of educational opportunity is required just as each citizen is entitled to a full vote.

But the relative meekness of the remedy asked by the plaintiffs and utlimately implied by the Court is less surprising than it is disappointing and indicative of deeper problems facing American society. First, it is not surprising because both the plaintiffs and the Court are so well versed in both the complexities of equal educational opportunity and the relevant legal precedents that they realize that any substantially more specific remedy would almost surely be denied by the United States Supreme Court. As in desegregation cases, the Supreme Court is not likely to accept any single detailed plan for redressing inequities, impose it on each of the states, and then attempt to enforce it. Rather, the Court is likely to do as it has done in these other cases—issue a "negative decision" that says present arrangements are unconstitutional, indicating that the matter must revert to the political and legal institutions of each state. Viewed from this very important perspective, *Serrano* v. *Priest* is a brilliantly conceived case, not only for its arguments against wealth classifications and in favor of equal educational opportunity, but also for its landmark negative decision that the California financing system is unconstitutional, and its provision for a moderate, but nonetheless measurable, standard for remedies.

Second, however, the implications of the decision are disappointing and symptomatic of deeper problems in that both morality and the nation's own enlightened self-interest demand a much more dramatic solution to the problems so well documented by both the plaintiffs and the Court. To continue to neglect and even destroy the talents of thousands of children on the basis of their residential or class backgrounds is clearly indefensible. The state legislatures that produced the financing systems supporting the current inequities are not likely to develop serious equalization plans without heavy-handed inducements by either the Congress or the Courts.

It is certainly easy to grant that implementing substantial equality of educational opportunity will be very difficult, just as arriving at a suitable definition of the concept is highly complex. At the very least, precautions will have to be taken to see that excellence is protected and fostered; that home rule is maintained insofar as it is functional to the operation of equality educational systems; that experimentation is not stopped by the illusion that money alone will solve all educational problems; that working class districts are not simply aided in providing vocational programs without developing academically-oriented programs as well; and, perhaps, that gross interstate disparities in educational spending are reduced or substantially eliminated. But even given all of these precautions, it remains apparent that for the nation's sake either the Congress or the Courts must develop stronger standards—similar to the "one-man, one-vote" standard underlying the reapportionment cases—that will accelerate a solution to this grave problem. At the very least, in striking down state financing systems, the Courts might mandate a "maximum-possible-variance," providing that after allowing for the inevitable cost differences mentioned earlier no state plan shall permit interdistrict disparities in actual expenditures to vary by more than 1.2 or 1.5 to 1. (See Arthur E. Wise, *Rich Schools, Poor Schools* [Chicago: University of Chicago Press, 1968], pp. 143–158.) Such a standard would not only be measurable; it would also eliminate the grossest inequities as they exist today, and speed intrastate development of new financial aid systems so that other important problems blocking equality of educational opportunity can be given long overdue attention.

Rodriguez: A Dream Shattered or a Call for Finance Reform?

THOMAS A. SHANNON

Thomas Shannon, attorney for the San Diego city schools, raises several questions of immediate concern to practicing school administrators and taxpayers alike. Following a brief summary of the Supreme Court decision in the *Rodriguez* case, Shannon speculates about the future of the school finance cases now awaiting court action in more than 50 percent of the states. He predicts that the basic concept of *Serrano* has not been put to rest. The general tone of this provocative article is that

SOURCE: Thomas A. Shannon, *"Rodriguez:* A Dream Shattered or a Call for Finance Reform?," *Phi Delta Kappan* (May, 1973), pp. 587, 588, 640.

school finance reformers should continue to fight vigorously to correct what Shannon believes are inequities in state financial structures.

In August, 1971, American public educators were startled into virtual euphoria by the eloquent decision of the California Supreme Court in *Serrano* v. *Priest.* In *Serrano,* the highest court of our nation's most populous state declared that no longer may the financing of a child's education in the public schools depend upon the wealth of the school district where he lives. Instead, the California court said, public schools may be funded only upon the basis of the wealth of the state as a whole. In short, assessed valuation based on the real property of a district was significant in public school finance only in the sense that it was part of the total state's assessed valuation and not any more because it qualified a district to be designated either "rich" or "poor." Under *Serrano* there would be no more "rich districts" or "poor districts"; there would only be "districts," entitled to fund an educational program at the same level, with the same local tax effort, as any other district.

About four months later, the *Serrano* theory, which was generally acclaimed either as the complete fruition of years of hope by school finance people or as a giant step toward equalizing public school money resources *among* the states on the broad federal level, was applied by the U.S. District Court in San Antonio in a lawsuit filed by Demetrio P. Rodriguez challenging the constitutional validity of the Texas public school financing laws. The Texas public school financing system, the San Antonio federal court said, violates the Equal Protection Clause of the Fourteenth Amendment to the U.S. Constitution and is a "tax more, spend less system." To correct this invalid unequal treatment of poor school districts, the state must observe the "principle of fiscal neutrality." That is, the court declared that "the state may adopt the financial scheme desired so long as the variations in wealth among the governmentally chosen units do not affect spending for the education of any child."

On March 21, 1973, when the *Serrano* case was in the midst of trial in the Los Angeles Superior Court pursuant to the August, 1971, judgment of the California Supreme Court, the U.S. Supreme Court handed down its landmark 5–4 decision reversing the San Antonio federal court and rejecting Mr. Rodriguez's complaint. In the *Rodriguez* case the nation's High Court identified its fundamental task thus:

We must decide, first, whether the Texas system of financing public education operates to the disadvantage of some suspect class or impinges upon a fundamental right explicitly or implicitly protected by the Constitution, thereby requiring strict judicial scrutiny. If so, the judgment of the district court should be affirmed. If not, the Texas scheme must still be examined to determine whether it rationally furthers some legitimate, articulated state purpose and therefore does not constitute an invidious discrimination in violation of the Equal Protection Clause of the Fourteenth Amendment.

In determining that the Texas public school finance system did *not* "operate to the disadvantage of some suspect class," the Supreme Court observed that: (1) the poorest families are not necessarily residents of the poorest school districts; (2) the lack of personal financial resources of the persons living in the poorer school districts has not resulted in an absolute deprivation of their education at public expense; and (3) even if individual income characteristics of school district residents were ignored, discrimination based on school district wealth (i.e., assessed valuation differences among school districts) would point to a disadvantaged class of persons too large, diverse, and amorphous for identification, as it would be composed of either (a) every child in every school district except the district that has the most assessable wealth and spends most on education, or (b) every child in districts with assessable property that falls below the statewide average, or median, or below some other artificially defined level.

Accordingly, the High Court said:

The system of alleged discrimination and the class it defines . . . is not saddled with such disabilities; or subjected to such a history of purposeful unequal treatment, or relegated to such a position of political powerlessness as to command extraordinary protection from the majoritarian political process. We thus conclude that the Texas system does not operate to the peculiar disadvantage of any suspect class.

The Court then turned to the question of whether education is a "fundamental right," in the sense that it is among the rights and liberties protected by the Constitution. The Court commenced its discussion of this issue by saying:

Nothing this Court holds today in any way detracts from our historic dedication to public education. We are in complete agreement that . . . the grave significance of education both to the individual and to our society cannot be doubted. But the importance of a service performed by the state does not determine whether it must be regarded as fundamental for the purposes of examination under the Equal Protection Clause.

The Court said that the key to deciding whether education is a "fundamental right" is not found in the societal importance of education but in assessing whether there is a right to education explicitly or implicitly guaranteed by the Constitution. Finding that education is not among the rights afforded explicit protection, the Court refused to conclude that education was implicitly protected because:

1. While the Court has afforded zealous protection against unjustified governmental interference with First Amendment free speech rights, for example, it never presumed either the ability or the authority to guarantee to the citizenry the most *effective* speech or the most *informed* electoral choice. By analogy, it could not tell states how best to finance the public schools.

2. There is no indication that the present levels of educational expenditure in Texas provide an education that is inadequate. Instead, only relative differences in spending are involved.

3. There is virtually no logical end to the "fundamental right" argument, in that education could not be differentiated, for example, from the significant personal interests in the basics of decent food and shelter.

4. Finally, every step in the development of the Texas system was implemented in an effort to *extend* public education and improve its quality, and such steps could fairly be described as "affirmative and reformatory."

Therefore, the Court held that education is not a "fundamental right" entitled to constitutional protection.

In light of the High Court's conclusion (1) that there is no "suspect class" which validly can be identified as being disadvantaged by the Texas public school finance law and (2) that education is not a "fundamental right" entitled to constitutional protection, the Court held that the *Rodriguez* case would *not* be judged on the basis of the difficult "strict scrutiny test" of constitutional analysis.

Other good reasons for not applying the "strict scrutiny test" to the *Rodriguez* case, the Court remarked, are:

1. The *Rodriguez* case involves a direct attack on the way in which Texas raises and disburses state and local tax revenues, and

this is an area in which the courts have traditionally deferred to state legislatures, because the courts lack both the expertise and the familiarity with local problems so necessary to making wise decisions with respect to the raising and disposition of public revenues.

2. The controversy over basic issues in education among educational experts, including (a) the extent to which there is a correlation between educational expenditures and the quality of education, (b) the proper goals of a system of public education, and (c) the most effective relationship between state and local school boards, indicates that the judiciary is well advised to refrain from imposing upon the states "inflexible constitutional restraints that could circumscribe or handicap the continued research and experimentation so vital to finding even partial solutions to educational problems and to keeping abreast of everchanging conditions."

3. The basic issue of federalism is involved. Because of the immense impact of the Court's decision, support of the district court in *Rodriguez* could ultimately have resulted in the abrogation of systems of financing public education presently existing in virtually every state.

Instead of the "strict scrutiny test," the Court said that the "traditional standard" of review by the judiciary would be used. Under this standard Texas need only show that its state system of public school finance bears some rational relationship to legitimate state purposes.

The Court held that the Texas statutory plan for funding the public schools is valid because it bears a rational relationship to legitimate state purposes. Ten arguments supporting this contention were offered.

In conclusion, the Court declared:

> The consideration and initiation of fundamental reforms with respect to state taxation and education are matters reserved for the legislative processes of the various states. . . . We hardly need add that this Court's action today is not to be viewed as placing its judicial imprimatur on the status quo. The need is apparent for reform in tax systems which may well have relied too long and too heavily on the local property tax. And certainly innovative new thinking as to public education, its methods, and its funding is necessary to assure both a higher level of quality and greater uniformity of opportunity. . . . But the ultimate solutions must come from the lawmakers and from the democratic pressures of those who elect them.

As a result of the High Court's decision in *Rodriguez,* several practical questions could be posed by school people. These questions, and answers, are:

1. *What will be the final disposition of* Serrano *and the other* Serrano-*type cases already decided by state and federal courts throughout America, in light of the U.S. Supreme Court decision in* Rodriguez?

The answer depends upon the extent to which state court decisions are keyed to the U.S. Constitution. The U.S. Supreme Court is the final authority on the federal Constitution but, generally, state supreme courts are the ultimate interpreter of state constitutions. If the state court's decision is pegged mainly to the state constitution, as in the New Jersey *Serrano*-type case of *Robinson* v. *Cahill,* then the state high court would not be bound by the U.S. Supreme Court's decision in *Rodriguez.* As the New Jersey Supreme Court said in its *Robinson* decision, New Jersey's state constitution "could be more demanding" than the federal constitution. The California Supreme Court may take that same position when *Serrano* again reaches it on appeal as a result of the Los Angeles Superior Court's decision after trial of the merits of the case.

2. *From a federal constitutional viewpoint, is the* Serrano *concept dead at law?*

Not necessarily. The U.S. Supreme Court's decision in *Rodriguez* was riddled with references to holes in the factual record compiled during the lower court hearings. It may be that, using the factual analysis of the U.S. Supreme Court in *Rodriguez* as a guide, a new case could be built which would provide critical facts. Finally, the fact that the decision in *Rodriguez* was split 5–4 would indicate that, while the door of the Court was shut in the face of the case, the door was neither slammed nor necessarily locked forever.

3. *Does the* Rodriguez *decision prohibit states or the Congress from taking action to embody the* Serrano *concept in state or federal public school finance statutes?*

No. At the end of its lengthy opinion in *Rodriguez,* the Supreme Court unequivocally states that it had not placed its "judicial imprimatur" on the status quo of public school finance. In fact, the Court gave eloquent expression to the need for fundamental and far-reaching reform of the system of funding the public schools based largely on the property tax. The Court found no fault with the *Serrano* concept as a matter of *legislative* policy. The Congress, acting to

equalize school district financing among the states, and each individual
state legislature, acting to equalize school district financing within its
state, have no legal hobbles placed upon them by the U.S. Supreme
Court's decision in *Rodriguez.*

4. *Does the* Rodriguez *decision mean that the U.S. Supreme
Court has changed its attitude about the importance of education in
today's world?*

No. The Court took pains in *Rodriguez* to emphasize that
education is crucial to the successful functioning of American society.
As a matter of law, however, the societal importance of education is
not germane to the determination that it is a federal constitutional
right, the Court said. But the determination that education is not
among those few "fundamental rights" guaranteed by the U.S. Constitution does not detract from its critical importance, the Court
concluded.

5. *Does the* Rodriguez *decision imply that the U.S. Supreme
Court will alter its approach in public school desegregation cases?*

No. The decision of the Court in *de jure* segregation cases since
Brown v. *Board of Education* in 1954 will abide unaltered. It is
difficult to say, however, which direction the High Court will take in
de facto segregation cases. On the same day the Court heard oral
arguments in Washington, D.C., on *Rodriguez* (October 12, 1972),
the Court also heard oral arguments in the Denver City Schools case,
which is generally considered to be the first *de facto* segregation case
to be squarely faced by the U.S. Supreme Court. Many of the
principles enunciated in *Rodriguez* would seem to apply in the Denver
City Schools case. The decision in that case should be issued
momentarily by the High Court.

6. *Is the U.S. Supreme Court's decision in* Rodriguez *a reason
for despair among public school people who are advocates for fair
and adequate financing of U.S. public schools?*

Regardless of how the courts finally decide *Serrano,* there is
really no reason for persons interested in the fair and adequate
funding of public education to despair. The eloquent logic of the
California Supreme Court in the *Serrano* case has focused public
attention squarely on the plight of public school funding in California
and other areas throughout America. In that sense local public education has won a great moral victory, and with it a strong, broadly based
movement for public school finance reform. In fact, the Court's final
decision in *Serrano,* even if it ultimately means the death of the legal

concept of *Serrano,* must be taken by school people as only a bugle call signaling the need for a regrouping and as the first step in a revitalized campaign with state legislators and congressmen. Research must be intensified and sound proposals must be developed to convince the state legislature and the Congress of the real merits of fair and adequate public school funding such as that contemplated in *Serrano.* While school people may not be able to wave court decrees, the moral tide is with them. And in the political arena today, to which the U.S. Supreme Court in *Rodriguez* apparently has shifted the issue, this counts.

School Segregation: Its True Nature
CONGRESS ON RACIAL EQUALITY

The Congress on Racial Equality (CORE) has taken the position that desegregation of one-race schools may not be in the best interests of black children. In this article, CORE develops its arguments in detail, including its own alternative plan, which is assumed to be within the legal limits of the various court decrees handed down since *Brown.* In effect, CORE's alternative is a form of community control of the schools whereby governance of the local schools would be delegated by the state to school districts which correspond to "natural community" lines. The idea is to place school decision making in the hands of those who choose freely to accept it—whether or not district boundaries result in one-race schools. The basic assumption of the entire document is that isolation of the races does not necessarily result in inferior schools.

CORE's point of view differs considerably from many of the principles underlying the desegregation cases. When reading this CORE document it might be helpful to compare CORE's philosophy with the ideas presented by Fiss, Bowles, Coleman, and Bernasek. Of particular significance are the implications of the CORE position for overall Northern school desegregation.

School segregation is a system designed and structured to serve the needs of Whites at the expense of Black pupils. When normal standards of educational excellence are applied to Black schools

SOURCE: "School Segregation: Its True Nature," a brief filed by the Congress on Racial Equality in the *Swann* case (in Appendix to *Swann* v. *Charlotte-Mecklenburg Board of Education,* 91 S. Ct. 1267, 1971), pp. 1–15.

under segregation, it becomes clear that they are inferior to White schools. This is a fact with which no one can argue. Unfortunately, it has caused those who did not in the past and do not now understand the true nature of segregation to arrive at the faulty conclusion that all-Black schools are inherently inferior under any set of circumstances. A simple extension of logic prompts the following questions:

If racial exclusivity means inferior schools, then why are the schools—White *and* Black—not equally inferior? If the racial composition of a school *in and by itself* causes that school to be inferior, where then are our inferior all-White schools?

Let us take the "isolation equals inferior schools" theory to its farthest logical extension: President John Kennedy and many of his socioeconomic class attended schools that were not just isolated from Blacks, but from Whites belonging to different socioeconomic classes as well. Needless to say, one would not even consider looking for the kind of inferiority in Mr. Kennedy's schools that so often characterizes Black schools.

The "inherently inferior" theory is not only spurious on its face but insidiously racist in its implication that Black children alone among the different races and groups of the world must mix in order to be equal. Blacks who subscribe to this theory are suffering from self-hatred, the legacy of generations of brainwashing. They have been told—and they believe—that it is exposure to Whites *in and by itself* that makes Blacks equal citizens.

Years of heavy propaganda from liberal well-wishers on one side, and ugly declarations from racists on the other have further confused the issue. This confusion must be cleared up now if we are to proceed in an orderly fashion toward the achievement of true equality in education.

Whether or not a given school is inferior or superior has nothing, *as such,* to do with whether or not it has an admixture of racial and/or ethnic groups, but it has everything to do with who CONTROLS that school and in whose best interest it is CONTROLLED.

Many social scientists who have issued papers and written books on education have missed this very salient point. They have shown too much concern with spatial relationships, and not enough or none at all with the relationship between those who govern a school and those who are served by that school.

No, the problem is not *simply* that Blacks and Whites attend different schools. A look at segregated school systems, whether *de jure* or *de facto,* will show that they generally have, aside from attendance of White and Black pupils at different schools, three common characteristics which make segregation the obnoxious system that it is.

The first of these is that Whites set Blacks apart, by law or in fact, without their choice or consent. This constitutes the arbitrary imposition of authority from without. The act of Whites telling Blacks what schools they can or cannot attend stigmatizes Blacks and is a slap at their dignity.

The second characteristic of a segregated system is that the local school board, usually all White or predominantly White, exercises control over both White and Black schools and favors the White schools. The school board enjoys a more intimate relationship with the White community and White parents than it does with the Black community and Black parents. It is more sensitive to their problems, their needs and aspirations than it is to those of Blacks. This deprives Black educators and pupils of much-needed support from the policy makers and managers of the schools and literally guarantees the failure of the Black school to achieve excellence in education. A positive relationship between parents and those who govern the school is one of the most important factors affecting the quality of schools. Under segregation, Black parents have not enjoyed that kind of relationship.

Finally, the local school board systematically deprives Black schools of resources. The money allotted by law to each and every school district when received by the local board is directed as the local board sees fit. Traditionally, part of the money intended for Black schools has been directed by the local board to White schools. This is true of Southern schools as well as Northern schools.

In short, it is the local school board, the dispenser *and* regulator of money, rewards, good will, and other benefits, which makes Black schools inferior. Under segregation, Blacks have been locked into a system over which they exercise no control, for which they have no responsibility, and for which they are powerless to effect meaningful change.

When segregation is placed in its proper context and defined in terms of who manages and controls the schools, it becomes apparent that the chief characteristic of a segregated school system—the imposition of oppressive outside authority—makes school systems in the North no different from those in the South.

The surest measure of how much Blacks can trust any school system to educate their children is how much actual—not illusionary—control they have over that system. Therefore, whatever is proposed to replace segregation must be measured strictly in terms of how much control is held by the Black community itself. This is the surest possible guide to determining the potential success of any proposed new system.

School Integration: Is It a Good Assumption?

Having learned from bitter experience that White schools are favored by White school boards and having become tired of the stigma attached to being told where their children could go to school, it was natural that Black people considered sending their children to White schools. Since 1954 at least, the assumption has been that the segregated and unequal treatment of Black children could be rectified by integrating them into White schools. What is basically wrong with this assumption?

1. There is a failure to recognize Black people as a valid special interest group with needs that are unique to Black people.
2. There are a number of agreed upon components of a good education. It has not been established that integration guarantees these components.
3. Equal education implies more than just equal physical space in the same classroom, the same teacher, or the same principal. It implies equal right in the curriculum, equal access to all available resources, and equal access to school policy makers and managers. The question is: Does integration guarantee Black parents these additional rights?
4. An integrated setting is as potentially damaging psychologically as a segregated setting. The assumption that integration cures all the evils of segregation does not take into consideration what the National Advisory Commission on Civil Disorders affirmed—that is, the essentially racist character of American society. Since there is no indication that racism will disappear overnight, Blacks must approach all institutional settings with extreme caution.

Where integration is mandated and there is unwillingness on the part of Whites to integrate schools, Black people lose much more than they gain in such a merger. One such community was studied by the National Education Association. The following is an excerpt from their report:

> The desegregation of East Texas schools is proceeding at a faster pace than in most southern states. School officials of most districts studied can report that they are in compliance either with federal desegregation guidelines or with court orders. But, as the study made abundantly clear, it is only a paper compliance. As desegregation continues, the grievances of the black community become more wide-spread and more severe. There is every evidence of racial discrimination in the continuing displacement and demotion of black educators; there is every evidence of racial discrimination in the increasing employment of white teachers in preference to blacks; there is every evidence of racial discrimination in the frequent exclusion of black students from participation and leadership positions in the student organizations of desegregated schools; and there is every evidence of racial discrimination in the treatment that black students commonly receive from white classmates and, in some instances, from their white teachers and principals as well.
>
> These grievances have long remained unresolved; they continue to be unrecognized by school officials. And finally, now that the Supreme Court has ordered the immediate elimination of dualism in all southern districts the prospect is that the situation will become worse—in East Texas and throughout the South. The frequency of teacher displacement and student mistreatment that accompanied desegregation "with all deliberate speed" is likely to accelerate as the rate of desegregation accelerates. The laws, including desegregation laws, have never worked well for black people. Unless present trends are halted, the new Supreme Court ruling will serve them no better than did the *Brown* decisions of 1954–1955.

The fact is that the court can offer Black children, teachers, and administrators very little protection from the crippling abuses which arise daily in an *integrated* setting where Whites don't favor the union. Some of the stories of injustices and psychological abuse emerging from integrated settings in the South are difficult to fight with litigation, but that does not make them any less damaging to the psyches of Black children, parents, teachers, and administrators:

> Item: White teachers have been known to absolutely refuse to look at Black children when addressing them in the classroom.

Item: The principal of an all-Black school became the assistant principal of an elementary school under integration in one Southern town.

Item: The principal of a Black high school was replaced by a younger White man with less experience and fewer formal credentials. The principal became an assistant principal under the new White principal.

Item: Examinations are geared to favor the White child. In fights, Black children are always assumed to be in the wrong.

The sad fact of the matter is that in most cases where integration has been tried, the same White board of education that once ran the dual school system—one White, one Black—is the same board that runs the integrated system. The superintendent of education under the old system becomes the superintendent of education in the new system. The policy makers and managers are therefore the same. Since their negative attitudes toward Blacks and favoritism toward Whites remain the same, Black parents can hardly expect that any attempt will be made to change the curriculum to reflect the needs of Black pupils, or that they will have any say in the running of the school. In other words, even where integration has come about, the schools remain White-controlled.

It must not be assumed that things will get better with time. The dynamics of *forced* school integration are very different from those of *forced* desegregation of hotels, restaurants, buses, and other public facilities and services. These are what might be called transient settings of Blacks and Whites sharing or functioning in the same approximate space. Integrated schools, on the other hand, constitute an ongoing situation that is seen as far more threatening. This is underscored by the fact that the relatively mild and short-lived resistance to the desegregation of public facilities and services was nothing compared to the massive resistance that has been mounted and that will be continually mounted against integration of the schools. Moreover, when integration does occur in the schools, the few strengths Blacks did have are rapidly eroded so that with time they operate less and less from a position of strength.

Blacks who have gone along with integration have done so in search of dignity, but have found humiliation at the end of the rainbow. They integrate for equality but find they are *together but still unequal*. They have less control and less influence, if that is possible, than ever before. In short, the integration that Blacks are likely to get in most instances, North or South, has proven to be token equality, mere show and pure sham.

What about those areas where White resistance is not so high as to frustrate the integration effort? Even then we should keep in mind that effective integration is more than mere physical proximity of White and Black students. We should seriously consider whether the dispersal of Black pupils would help or hinder the chances of meeting their unique needs.

Integration, as it is designed, places the Black child in the position of implied inferiority. Not only is he asked to give up much of his culture and identity, but with the dispersal of Blacks he loses many of the communal ties which have traditionally been the cornerstone of the Black community. Moreover, there can never be true integration between groups until there is a real parity relationship existing between them.

It is an established fact that children learn best in a supportive environment—one in which they can develop an appreciation and acceptance of self. Self-appreciation must come before one can truly appreciate others.

White schools at this time do not constitute the kind of environment which can foster the healthy development of Black children. White school boards make it difficult for even Black schools to respond to the special needs of Black children. In this respect, however, many Black teachers and administrators have tried, within the narrow limits allowed them, to satisfy these needs.

With the guarantee of equal resources and with the freedom to proceed as is expedient, Black schools would be a superior learning environment and could graduate students who can succeed in an interracial world.

What about the stigma attached to going to an all-Black school? That stigma was half destroyed when Blacks succeeded in smashing the laws which restricted their freedom to choose. Inasmuch as the stigma arises in part from the established inferiority of Black schools, the remaining stigma would be destroyed completely once the Black community has a board of education which could be called theirs and which would guarantee a truly equal, truly democratic education for its children.

Furthermore, Black people today have a very healthy attitude toward themselves as a people. They are not ashamed of being Black and see nothing wrong in being together and doing things together. They see strength in unity, not guaranteed failure. More than ever, Blacks place a premium on working together for progress. They are beginning to feel that it is through their strength as a group that they will win human dignity and power. If reality is taken into account when Blacks chart their course, it will become abundantly clear that in some situations school integration may not be the most effective means to equality.

From a financial, legal, economic, political, social, psychological, and most important, educational standpoint, the integrated school emerges wanting. This set of parameters must be consistently used when examining integration, segregation, and any proposed alternative to the two.

The Need for a New Alternative

Desegregation is now the law of the land. Because the road is rocky and treacherous, Blacks need to chart a careful course if they are to land on their feet. The next section will offer a desegregation approach applicable primarily to urban areas, North and South. In these areas we generally find natural definable communities made up of persons with common interests and special problems.

Within Mobile County, Alabama, for example, there is a natural community comprising the Davis Avenue, Toulminville, Bullshead area. This community alone has more students than do many existing school districts throughout the state. The citizens and students in this community happen to be Black Americans. The schools attended by the youth from this community have been badly run by the Mobile County School Board. For years, the talent and energies of the best citizens of the community have been expended in fighting the school board—but without significant results. This community has many special needs different from those of the general population of Mobile County. A healthy pride and sense of purpose is evident and growing in this community. The educational hopes of the residents, however, are continually frustrated by a school board which has shown no sensitivity to their problems. The residents of this community have lost irretrievably all faith in the school board's capability of being responsive to their needs.

The tragedy is that the human input needed to solve the major eductional problems which have plagued this community are within the reach of this community. The talent and energy displayed over years of struggle for relief prove that. The material now needed to solve this area's school problems lies in the public money the law presently allows if the money were to arrive directly from the source to a truly local school board. The rising aspirations, the dashed hopes, and the displaced energy will result in a steadily rising level of hostilities which will inevitably spill over into the surrounding communities.

We contend that it is possible to bring dignity and true equality of opportunity to this community without severing the human and constitutional rights of any other community. Only good sense and meaningful alteration of a faulty structure can avert this. It is in the spirit of attempting to avert chaos and establishing harmony that this proposal is presented.

The Solution: Natural Community School Districts

The people of the above-mentioned community are seeking to exercise their basic human and constitutional right to form an institution that is accountable to them. They are seeking to be delegated by the State of Alabama to exercise its exclusive competence to determine its own educationtional needs and set its own educational policy, as do other peoples in America, by becoming a duly constituted state school district under the state law.

This move is not without considerable precedent in American history. One such precedent occurred early in the history of this country and culminated in a document which begins with the words, "We hold these truths to be self-evident," and includes the statement, "That whenever any form of government becomes destructive of these ends"—these ends being the securing of certain inalienable rights and "governments being instituted deriving their just powers from the consent of the governed. . . . It is the Right of the People to alter or abolish it, and to institute new government, laying its foundations on such principles and organizing its powers in such form as to them shall seem most likely to effect their safety and happiness."

> *The Plan:* To desegregate public schools by creating state school districts which correspond to natural com-

munity lines, where the parties affected are in agreement.

The School Board: Within each school district so formed, the residents would elect a school board. Each school board would be a legal entity *enjoying all the rights, privileges, and obligations as provided for by the State Education Law.* Each school board would run a unitary school system within its district.

The community school board would, pursuant to state law and as every other school district in the United States does, seek out persons with educational expertise—a superintendent who meets state qualifications as chief executive officer of the board of education, and a staff of professionals to administer and execute the policy established by the board. The board would seek the best man possible to fill the position of superintendent by selecting from a special screening committee and would solicit advice on candidates from the leading universities and professional associations as well as other organizations and individuals. Once employed, the superintendent would submit names to fill the other top-level administrative positions to the screening committee of the board and the board would choose from among the resultant list of candidates.

For the position of superintendent, the board would seek a man of unquestioned executive ability who indicates an openness to new solutions to the desperate educational problems of the community's children, and a willingness to employ newly available educational innovations such as the reading program developed by the Institute for Behavioral Science for the Washington, D.C., public schools; programmed instruction with audio-visual teaching machines; and use of media techniques. Most important of all, the board would seek a superintendent who is community-oriented.

The Community school district would hope to attract the best minds as consultants to the staff to help design the program. This would be a truly pioneering effort in the field of education.

The Teaching Staff: The community school district would welcome all teachers presently in their schools, who are excited by the prospect of being a part of this pioneering effort. Every attempt will be made to recruit to the teaching staff the best teachers regardless of race, creed, or national origin. The community school district will offer in-service training programs, for up-grading, if necessary, so that all teachers in the district will have the security of having skills and training that are relevant to the unique needs of the children of the community.

The community school board would adopt fair practices with respect to teachers employed in that it is in the interest of the district to satisfy the most essential ingredient of a school system—the class room teacher.

The community school board would seek to allow for maximum participation in the school program by encouraging strong parent associations and establishing people from the community as teacher aides and teacher apprentices so that every child will have in-depth contact with a caring adult, and the teacher will be freed to teach.

Financing: The community school district will receive public funds directly from the presently existing sources of education money—the state, the federal government and the local government unit.

State: The community school district would receive state moneys according to the existing provisions in the state law prescribing state money to school districts.

Federal: Federal moneys would come to the school districts according to the existing provisions described in the Federal Elementary and Secondary Education Act.

Local: A legal and formal agreement will be made whereby the local educational dollar will be directed to each school district on a per student basis.

Is This Plan Legal?

It is of extreme importance that the Supreme Court's ruling on school desegregation be clearly understood. Confusion on this point has abounded, aided and abetted by those who have fallen into the trap of viewing desegregation as synonymous with integration. Integration is only one possible way—not necessarily the best or most pragmatic way—of desegregating and creating a unitary school system. The plan herein described is another way of desegregating and creating a unitary school system in a school district. It would destroy segregation, and it clearly provides for equal protection under the law. Moreover, unlike integration, this plan makes it easier to *guarantee* equal protection under the law.

A careful and unprejudiced reading of the decisions of the Supreme Court on school desegregation shows that this plan does not violate the letter or the spirit of the law.

The Supreme Court has ruled that each school board must run a unitary school system in a school district. That is, if there are White and Black children in a school district, the school board may not set them apart.

Each district proposed in this plan would be run as a unitary system. Moreover, the process of redistricting proposed here can only be done with the consent of the persons affected and with the legal agreement of the state. This is equivalent to the parties to an action arriving at a settlement out of court, without violating any law.

Conclusion

Schools are the transmitters of values, the molders of self-image, the instrument for providing youngsters with the technical and psychological equipment necessary to function properly in this highly competitive society. The schools in most Black communities have failed dismally on all three counts. They have not and will not, under the present school system, perform their proper function.

Integration as the means of addressing the educational problems of Black people, even if attainable, is of questionable worth. Where integration has occurred, the results suggest that it causes more problems than it solves.

Black people have tried everything there is to try under the

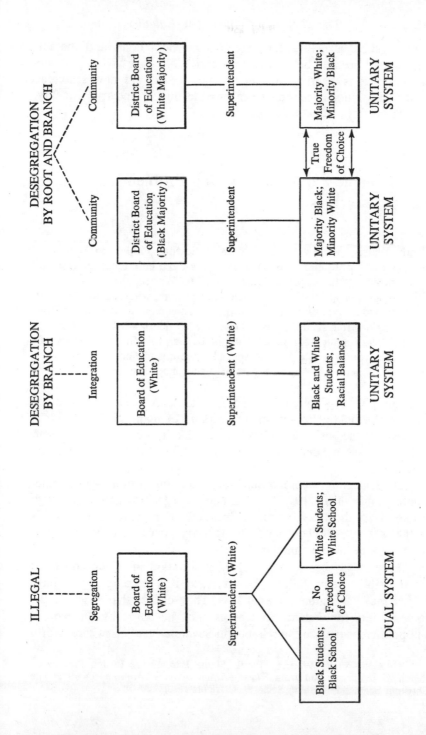

present school structure. The escalating school crisis and the unprecedented hostility between Blacks and Whites are vivid reminders that patience is wearing thin all around. Blacks are now searching for a real solution, one which can provide dignity and true equality. We submit this plan as that solution.

Pupils Blame Parents for Busing Problems
WENDY WATRISS

Wendy Watriss, writing for the Christian Science Publishing Society, suggests that busing per se is not the cause of the emotionalism created when school systems begin to desegregate. Ms. Watriss attributes much of the racial unrest in schools to meddling parents whose ignorance and fear have led to explosive situations in numerous communities throughout the country. After reading this article, one wonders whether massive educational programs for parents might be helpful. In the opinion of the author, young people need no special programs to help them adjust. They simply accept busing as a part of their school life.

Savannah, Ga.—Communities across the United States are being torn by the politics of school integration. In many cities, the emotionalism of the busing issue has been carried into the classroom itself, and politicians condemn court-ordered busing for the racial unrest in schools.

In Savannah, where busing for racial integration was a nine-month reality in the 1971–1972 school year, junior and senior high schools were disturbed by racial disorders. For many of Savannah's 18,000 secondary-school students, security guards and federal marshals have become a familiar sight.

Parents say busing has created a situation in which education is impossible. Many students, however, say it is the parents who have helped make the situation what it is. They charge that much of the responsibility for violence in schools must be borne by the parents and politicians outside the schools [in Savannah and elsewhere, North and South], because they have not allowed busing or integration to operate in a climate of calm and reason.

"How can you say busing is the issue when busing has been going on for so many years? It's not busing. It's integration," says Pat Washington, a black senior-class president. "And everyone worries whether the kids are ready for integration. It's the parents and administrators who aren't ready."

"I don't think busing will work. We've been thrown together too fast," says Eric Williams, a white football player at one of the city's most troubled high schools. "But I'll tell you one thing: if we didn't have the parents bugging us, it wouldn't be so bad."

"Parents are the problem. They should leave the kids alone and let us go to school together in peace," says Sandra Mitchell, a black sophomore.

But for some Savannah citizens—those who have been most vocal—there can be no peace until busing for racial integration is stopped.

"You want to know what's happening in Savannah?" asked one of a group of mothers picketing a recent conference of federal judges in the city. "Busing. We had to integrate schools on a 60–40 ratio, white–black, last September. Since then, a number of high schools have been closed and any number of children hospitalized. Racial unrest! My kid is not even graduating this year, and she's a senior. I've got nothing against the black race. I just don't want them touching my child."

In this old cotton-port town of less than 20,000 people, where economic power is concentrated in the hands of a few, change comes slowly.

"How can you change, or improve, a city which excludes almost half its people—the 45 percent that's black?" asked a black high-school student in Savannah.

It took 15 years and a handful of determined people to make the city realize it had something of value in the oak-shaded squares and colonial architecture of the original downtown area. Now, the area is a national historic landmark—bounded on three sides by clapboard slums.

It took Ralph Nader to show Savannah how its air and water were being affected by the city's major industry. Now, two years later, with the smell of industrial waste still in the air, people shrug their shoulders and say: "I guess we're just used to it."

To many students in Savannah, these things reflect the kind of attitudes that have made the school crisis what it is today.

"Savannah is a city which likes to hide its head in the sand. If there's a problem, we try to ignore it. We think if we don't talk about it, it will go away," said Holly Deal, a graduating senior and one of the city's outstanding white students. "Take education . . . What most people want is an eight-hour babysitting service.

"For the first 11 years I was in public schools, I never heard a word from the community about quality education—until busing. Now that white parents see the conditions of black schools, they scream about quality education."

Eight years of legal action by the National Association for the Advancement of Colored People preceded the 1970 U.S. District Court ruling against freedom-of-choice and neighborhood zoning in Savannah–Chatham County schools. When a newly elected school board presented its plan for "total integration" of the secondary schools last May, only one of the city's 17 junior and senior high schools had more than token integration. The plan, which called for a 15 percent increase in secondary-school busing, was denounced for being "discriminatory to all."

When schools opened last fall, most were ill-prepared to meet the needs of a new student body where whites, blacks, suburbs, and slums were coming together for the first time.

"The whole attitude of the community seemed to be: 'Well, we won't let it happen,'" said Holly Deal. "So nothing was done. There were no orientation programs for students over the summer."

The school year began amid the noise of marches, motorcades, and mass meetings to protest busing. Mothers burned the school-board president in effigy, shouted at city officials, and blocked elementary school entrances. A 10-day boycott kept thousands of students home. The mayor appealed to Chief Justice Warren E. Burger for "antibusing aid."

A freedom-of-choice bill was pushed through the Georgia legislature.

Before the last major boycott in February this year, widespread publicity was given the local school superintendent's statement attributing the district's poor showing in statewide scholastic tests to the "transfer of 5,000 upper-income white students to private schools in the last two years." Less notice was given a school board statement that boycotts were helping an already struggling school system lose nearly $1.9 million in state funds. [The funds are budgeted according to daily attendance records.]

The antibusing boycott on February 28 kept 17,500 students out of class. Five days later, fighting broke out between white and black students at a prestigious local high school. Racial strife caused the temporary closing of two junior high schools the following week. Minutes after President Nixon's call for a moratorium on busing, Savannah's Mayor John P. Rousakis made a televised plea for peace in the city's public school system.

When Mr. Nixon blamed busing for the "anger, fear, and turmoil" in many local communities, many Savannah students questioned his understanding of the situation.

"What the President said really bothered me. If we go back the other way now, it will upset things more," said Kim Paddison, a white student in her junior year at one of the city's troubled high schools. "Kids are talking now; they're getting along. I've been to school every day, and I don't feel threatened. Kids who want an education can get one."

"Nixon listens to the older people. They're the prejudiced ones. They don't want blacks in their schools," said Eric Odum, a black student being bused to a formerly "lily-white" high school. "I look at it this way: The President should be working for both whites and blacks. There's a new generation growing up, and a lot of men have laid down their lives so we can get a good education. A black man has to have an education to get any place today. We don't want to be white. We want to have what the whites have—an equal opportunity."

"I laugh at Nixon. He's playing cheap politics," said Blanton Black, a thoughtful black senior who says he has been bused to five different schools in the last six years. "He talks about busing. Where was he when we were being bused to segregated schools? What about the white parents who walk the hallways at school and interrupt classes to take their children home? What about the fact we've had less extracurricular activities this year because the government won't pay busing costs?"

Unable to get federal or state funds for the extra busing in 1971–1972, the school board had to take funds from music, art, and physical-education programs to pay regular transportation costs. In September, the U.S. Department of Health, Education, and Welfare rejected the board's request for $74,000 to help pay transportation for after-school activities. The lack of extracurricular activities in many of the city's schools has been a major source of student discontent.

Students also complain about the loss of senior positions in former school clubs and councils, the failure of principals to discipline troublemakers, and the racial prejudices of many classroom teachers. The most common complaint of all, however, relates to parents. Of 297 secondary school students recently interviewed in Savannah, almost all—white, black, militant, and moderate—say parental attitudes are behind much of the trouble in schools this year.

"A lot of rumors start with parents. They tell us the blacks are going to gang the whites. One father told his kid the blacks were out to get him with knives," said a blonde girl who is going to private school next year.

"Parents get all worked up when there's a little trouble, and they egg a lot of kids on. They get pretty nasty sometimes," said Debra Schneider, a senior who in 1971–1972 met black students for the first time. "I had to stay home during the boycotts."

"The minute there's a fight, the parents are lined up in front of school with their popcorn and Coke to watch the fun. One father came over with a pistol in his belt," remarked a white boy who said his parents told him the courts were putting "integration ahead of education."

"How do you think it feels to come to school, a long way from home, and listen to people shouting: 'Nigger go home'?" asked Darrell Ancrum, a black high school student who said he had done some fighting himself. "We didn't come to fight. We came to go to school. But we already had a chip on our shoulder, and we didn't want to be taken advantage of. We've had to grow up scuffling. All we need is a little more pushing around. We aren't going to leave. If we go back, it'll be a moral victory for the whites."

Parental interference together with public protests, boycotts, and 200 years of enforced segregation have made for an explosive situation.

"You can watch the tension rise after a public protest. Community prejudice is carried right into school. Kids start walking down the halls like monsters. Bombs, ready to explode. If you hit one by accident, a fight breaks out. And suddenly there are black and white students going after each other," said Larry Drago, a white student in his junior year at one of the city's newest schools.

"A lot can depend on how your parents make you feel about school: Do you think a kid whose mother is down yelling at the board of education is going to care about getting along at school?" asked Scott Center, a white student who was transferred to a black neighborhood school this year.

Chapter 6

Epilogue

To say there is a crisis in American public education is to comment upon the commonplace. There are numerous decisive issues whose possible consequences could spell dramatic, revolutionary changes in public education. Even those persons for whom public education is the most remote of concerns cannot escape the stormy debates over busing, teacher strikes, increased taxes, financially bankrupt school systems, student protest, sex education, court decisions over school financing—and many more issues which testify to the pervasive crises.

Few Americans, then, are unaware that the public school is in trouble. Most recognize that the public school system has failed to serve a substantial portion of the population adequately. Indeed, what were long regarded as sacred truths about the success of the public school are coming to be recognized as myths. And those myths are crumbling. Educators realize, and the public at large is beginning to sense, that we have overexaggerated the "commonness" of the public school.[1] We have mythologized its function as a vehicle for upward social mobility for the lower socioeconomic classes. We have painted an inaccurately rosy portrait of its value for many white ethnic groups. Moreover, there is the haunting possibility, implied by the Coleman survey, that the school has little to offer to the middle and upper social economic classes. Educators are facing the distressing possibility that the public school has little influence upon academic achievement that is independent of the social and cultural background that pupils bring to school.

Failures and limitations of these sorts extend far back into the history of the public school. Nevertheless, most Americans were

[1] Lawrence Cremin, *The Genius of American Education* (New York: Vintage Books, 1966).

unaware of them until racial minorities and lower class whites loudly demanded a fair share of political, economic, and eductional opportunity. Only recently have Americans recognized their poverty amidst plenty—in the nation's school system as well as in its economy.

One major ingredient in the current controversy over education is the dispute over who is responsible for the school's current shortcomings. Some people contend that any pupil's failure to profit from public schooling should be explained in terms of that youngster. The student is somehow culpable in this regard; not directly, necessarily, but the student carries with him those handicaps—whether physical, social, cultural, or economic—which cause his failure. In short, his skills, intellectual and otherwise, are not those necessary to academic success.

At the other end of the continuum are those people who claim that when pupils fail, the school system itself is a major, if not *the* major, culprit; hence, the schools themselves need basic overhaul. Whereas the former analysis calls, essentially, for therapeutic social action "out there," this one calls upon the school to diagnose the learner's needs, concerns, and cognitive and affective style—and it demands the *school* to adjust accordingly.[2]

Like many educational problems, the answer to who is responsible probably lies somewhere between the two views cited above. Recent research suggests that both assertions have merit. Indeed, as analyzed and discussed in preceding chapters, equal opportunity to profit from public schooling is a function of a number of variables—many of them interdependent, and not all of them centered in the school. For example, we have discussed how equality of educational opportunity is related to such variables as social class, race, school facilities, curriculum, place of residence, ethnicity, teacher background, property taxes, subcultural values, and nutrition. These variables illustrate, as do others examined in preceding chapters, that equal educational opportunity and failures within schools are not merely school or social problems. Our analysis of equal educational opportunity makes two points abundantly clear: inequalities in equal educational opportunity are social as well as school problems; furthermore, the achievement of equality of educational opportunity will

---

[2] Mario D. Fantini, "Discussion on Implementing Equal Educational Opportunity," *Harvard Educational Review,* Vol. 38, No. 1 (Winter, 1968), pp. 160–175.

require major changes in the economic and political sectors of American society as well as in education.

Suppose, however, that we knew precisely what constitutes true equality of educational opportunity. Would all the important actors agree on which social, economic, legal, political, and educational reforms would lead to equality in education? Probably not; witness the controversies over those practices and programs through which educators are now trying to achieve equal educational opportunity. Some of these practices, along with the elements of the debate over them, are outlined in the following paragraphs.[3]

Compensatory Education. The goal of compensatory education is to overcome presumed handicaps in the learner—handicaps whose origins are seen to be principally in the learner's social, cultural, and economic environment. Some compensatory practices are, for example, Title I programs of the Elementary and Secondary Education Act, Project Head Start, and the Higher Horizons Program in New York City. Compensatory efforts are designed to overcome short-comings which hinder the learner's profiting from public schooling. Some compensatory practices are *preventive;* these provide experiences early in life which eliminate or limit the influence of disadvantageous environments. Others are essentially *curative,* providing "enriching" experiences designed to dwarf a backlog of "handicapping" experiences.

A great deal of money, effort, and intelligence has gone into developing compensatory programs. Nevertheless, recent research indicates that "even the best efforts . . . are having little significant impact on the problem of low achievement among disadvantaged children." [4] Those who advocate such practices argue that not enough resources have been made available to indicate the true value of these efforts. On the other hand, many people are growing increasingly disdainful of compensatory education, particularly because it presumes that failure lies in the students.[5]

Integration. Nearly all the research on school integration indicates that low-achieving black pupils improve their acdemic skills in integrated schools. Coleman's survey suggests that such improvement should be attributed more to social class variables than racial factors.

<hr>

[3] Some of the practices identified here are based upon those mentioned in Fantini, *ibid.*
[4] Fantini, *ibid.,* p. 164.
[5] *Ibid.*

In any case, school integration not only brings us closer to equality of educational opportunity, but also is considered a social good. It is clear, nevertheless, that many persons from all races are shifting away from stressing school integration as the key factor in attaining higher academic achievement among poor black pupils. The CORE paper in Chapter 5 presents one interesting alternative to school integration.

Community School. The redistribution of political power relative to control of education is another controversial approach in the quest for equal educational opportunity. The debate over community schools has many ramifications, one of which is often considered a separate approach to providing quality education—accountability.

Accountability. The defining characteristics of this issue are so amorphous as to make precise description difficult, if not impossible. At base, however, *accountability* is the attempt to make schools responsible to their consumers: parents and students. The nature of such responsibility takes many forms. There is discord not only over how such responsibility can be achieved, or what counts as evidence of it, but also over whether or not schools can indeed be accountable for a youngster's schooling success, given the many variables outside the school which influence the pupil's ability to learn.

Alternative Models. One approach to quality education is that which allows students who are either unhappy, not achieving, or both, to drop out of the public school system and enter an alternative school outside the public school, or to enter experimental alternative schooling programs within the public school itself. This approach assumes that those who are not happy, not achieving, or both, in the typical public school curriculum should have options available to them.

The alternative school movement, which takes many forms, is growing rapidly and, as might be expected, attracting criticism in proportion to its growth. Emerging alternative modes are legion. They range from the highly touted voucher plan, at present being tried on an experimental basis in selected school systems in California, to the now pervasive "free school."

Total System Overhaul. All the above approaches possess such weaknesses or are the object of such discord that many people concerned with public schooling are demanding a total reconstruction of the present public school system.[6]

6 *Ibid.,* p. 169.

There are several approaches to the concept of total overhaul, which are discussed in the Fantini paper cited above. Perhaps the one element which contains within it the seed for the most dramatic upheaval, however, is the restructuring of the school finance system. This approach, of course, finds its origins and sustenance in recent state court decisions which have declared the property tax base of financial support unconstitutional. These decisions raise numerous and difficult questions. What should state legislators do about the high per-pupil expenditure in some districts and the low expenditure in others? Should the high spending district be leveled down to the lower or *vice versa?* Should there be some appropriate, standardized middle ground? How should financing be divided among the federal, state, and local governments?

These are just a few of the questions posed by the finance controversy, and they are not likely to be answered in the immediate future. But court decisions like those discussed in Chapter 3, and elsewhere, give impetus to, and provide a major target for, total reform of the system.

The controversy surrounding these crucial issues makes it clear that the struggle for equality of educational opportunity is going to be around for a long time. Some educational issues are like forgotten loves: once "out of love" with them we wonder what made us so excited. Equal educational opportunity is not like that. Indeed, the controversy over equality of educational opportunity grows in passion and in complexity as we learn more about it. The very instability of the principle, its change in meaning over the years, can be attributed in large measure to increased knowledge about education, opportunity, and the many, many variables which play upon one's ability to profit from schooling. Moreover, the principle of equality in education has always been affected by issues seemingly unrelated to it. These issues owe their existence to increased knowledge, or, in some cases, to an increased sensitivity of the collective American conscience concerning equal opportunity and human and civil rights. In the not too distant future we can expect the principle to grow both more important and more complex in meaning as women's liberation, bi-lingual education, open door admissions, behavior modification, gay liberation, ethnicity, and accountability, to cite only a few current issues, emerge more fully developed in relation to institutions, social policies, and practices.

Bibliography

This list of references has been chosen selectively. It is not intended to be an exhaustive listing on the topic of equal educational opportunity.

BOOKS

BAGDIKIAN, BEN H. *In the Midst of Plenty: The Poor in America*. Boston: Beacon Press, 1964.

BLAUSTEIN, ALBERT P. and CLARENCE CLYDE FERGUSON. *Desegregation and the Law*. New Brunswick, N.J.: Rutgers University Press, 1957.

BLOOM, BENJAMIN, A. DAVIS and ROBERT HESS. *Compensatory Education for Cultural Deprivation*. New York: Holt, Rinehart and Winston, 1965.

BUCHHEIMER, ARNOLD and NAOMI BUCHHEIMER. *Equality Through Integration*. New York: Anti-Defamation League, 1965.

CLARK, KENNETH B. *Dark Ghetto: Dilemmas of Social Power*. New York: Harper and Row, 1965.

COLEMAN, JAMES S., *et al. Equality of Educational Opportunity*. Washington, D.C.: U.S. Office of Education, 1966.

COONS, JOHN, WILLIAM CLUNE, III, and STEPHEN SUGARMAN. *Private Wealth and Public Education*. Cambridge, Mass.: Belknap Press of Harvard University Press, 1970.

CREMIN, LAWRENCE. *The Genius of American Education*. New York: Vintage Books, 1966.

DONOVAN, JOHN C. *The Politics of Poverty*. New York: Pegasus, 1967.

DUNNE, GEORGE H. (Editor). *Poverty In Plenty*. New York: P. J. Kennedy, 1965.

GARDNER, JOHN W. *Excellence: Can We Be Equal and Excellent Too?* New York: Harper and Row, 1961.

GLAZER, NATHAN, and DANIEL MOYNIHAN. *Beyond the Melting Pot*. Cambridge: The M.I.T. Press, 1963.

GREENBERG, JACK. *Race Relations and American Law*. New York: Columbia University Press, 1959.

GREER, COLLIN. *Cobweb Attitudes: Essays on Educational and Cultural Mythology*. New York: Teachers College Press, Columbia University, 1970.

————. *The Great School Legend: A Revisionist Interpretation of American Public Education.* New York: Basic Books, 1972.

GRIER, GEORGE, and EUNICE GRIER. *Equality and Beyond.* Chicago: Quadrangle Books, 1966.

GUTHRIE, JAMES W., *et al. Schools and Inequality.* Cambridge, Mass.: M.I.T. Press, 1969

HARRINGTON, MICHAEL. *The Other America: Poverty in the United States.* New York: Macmillan, 1962.

HENTOFF, NAT. *The New Equality.* New York: Viking Press, 1966.

HERRIOTT, ROBERT E., and NANCY HOYT ST. JOHN. *Social Class and the Urban School.* New York: John Wiley, 1966.

KARDINER, A., and ROBERT OVESEY. *The Mark of Oppression.* New York: Norton, 1951.

MOYNIHAN, DANIEL P. (Editor). *On Understanding Poverty.* New York: Basic Books, 1969.

PASSOW, A. HARRY (Editor). *Education in Depressed Areas.* New York: Teachers College Press, Columbia University, 1963.

PENNOCK, J. R., and A. W. CHAPMAN (Editors). *Equality.* New York: Atherton Press, 1967.

ROSENTHAL, R., and L. JACOBSEN. *Pygmalion in the Classroom.* New York: Harcourt, Brace and World, 1968.

SEXTON, PATRICIA CAYO. *Education and Income: Inequalities of Opportunity in Our Public Schools.* New York: Viking Press, 1964.

SILBERMAN, CHARLES. *Crisis in Black and White.* New York: Random House, 1964.

————. *Crises in the Classroom: The Remaking of American Education.* New York: Random House, 1970.

TEN BROEK, JACOBUS. *Equal Under Law.* New York: Collier Books, 1965.

THERNSTROM, STEPHAN. *Poverty and Progress.* Cambridge: Harvard University Press, 1964.

U.S. Department of Health, Education, and Welfare. *Do Teachers Make a Difference?* Washington, D.C.: U.S. Government Printing Office, 1970.

ARTICLES AND JOURNALS

AIKEN, HENRY DAVID. "Rationalism, Education, and the Good Society," *Studies In Philosophy and Education,* Vol. VI, No. 3 (Summer, 1968), pp. 249–281.

ALLPORT, FLOYD, *et al.* "The Effects of Segregation and the Consequences of Desegregation: A Social Science Statement," *Minnesota Law Review,* Vol. 37 (1953), pp. 427–439.

ANDERSON, C. ARNOLD, and PHILIP J. FOSTER. "Discrimination and Inequality in Education," *Sociology of Education,* Vol. 38 (Fall, 1964), pp. 1–18.

ASKEW, REUBIN. "Temporary Hardship or Continuing Injustice?," *Integrated Education* (January–February, 1972), pp. 3–6.

ASUSBEL, D. P. "Ego Development Among Segregated Negro Children," *Mental Hygiene,* Vol. 42 (1958), pp. 362–369.

BECKER, HOWARD S. "Social Class Variations in the Teacher-Pupil Relationship," *Journal of Educational Sociology,* Vol. 35 (1952), pp. 451–465.

BELLAMY, L. G. "Looking Backward: The Impact of Supreme Court Decisions on the American Educational System, 1969–1980," *Phi Delta Kappan* (February, 1970), pp. 313–315.

BERKE, JOEL S. "The Current Crisis in School Finance: Inadequacy and Inequity," *Phi Delta Kappan,* Vol. 53 (September, 1971), pp. 2–7.

BERKE, JOEL S., ROBERT J. GOETTEL, and RALPH ANDREW. "Equality in Financing New York City's Schools: The Impact on Local, State, and Federal Policy," *Education and Urban Society,* Vol. IV, No. 3 (May, 1972), pp. 261–291.

BERLIN, SIR ISAIAH, and RICHARD WOLHEIM. "Equality," *Proceedings of the Aristotelian Society,* Vol. 56 (1955–1956), pp. 307ff.

BOWLES, SAMUEL, and HENRY M. LEVIN. "The Determinants of Scholastic Achievement—An Appraisal of Some Recent Evidence," *Journal of Human Resources,* Vol. II (Winter, 1968), pp. 35–48.

BRONFENBRENNER, URIE. "The Psychological Costs of Quality and Equality in Education," *Child Development,* Vol. 38, No. 4 (December, 1967), pp. 909–925.

BROOKOVER, W. B., and DAVID GOTTLIEB. "Social Class and Education," in W. W. Charters, Jr., and N. L. Gage (Editors). *Readings in the Social Psychology of Education.* Boston: Allyn and Bacon, 1963, pp. 3–11.

CASSIDY, JOSEPH. "Property Tax Decision (California)," *Compact,* Vol. V (December, 1971), pp. 38–41.

CHACHKIN, NORMAN J. "Metropolitan School Desegregation: Evolving Law," *Integrated Education* (March–April, 1972), pp. 13–25.

"Chaos over School Busing: Tale of Two Cities," *U.S. News and World Report* (March 16, 1970), pp. 29–33.

COHEN, DAVID K. "School Resources and Racial Equality," *Education and Urban Society,* Vol. I, No. 2 (February, 1969), pp. 121–137.

———. "The Economics of Inequality," *Saturday Review* (April 19, 1969), pp. 64–65, 76–80.

COLEMAN, JAMES S. "Equal Schools or Equal Students," *The Public Interest* (Summer, 1966), pp. 70–75.

———. "Towards Open Schools," *The Public Interest* (Fall, 1967), pp. 20–27.

CONANT, JAMES B. "Financing the Public Schools," *School and Society,* Vol. 100 (April, 1972), pp. 219–222.

"Constitutional Law: Florida Limitation on Local Property Tax Rate for Education Violates Equal Protection," *Duke Law Journal* (October, 1970), pp. 1033–1039.

COONS, JOHN E., WILLIAM H. CLUNE, III, and STEPHEN D. SUGARMAN. "Educational Opportunity: A Workable Constitutional Test for State

Financial Structures," *California Law Review*, Vol. 5, No. 2 (April, 1969), pp. 305–421.

COONS, JOHN, and STEPHEN SUGARMAN. "Family Choice in Education: A Model State System for Vouchers," *California Law Review*, Vol. 59 (March, 1971), pp. 321–348.

CRESSWELL, ANTHONY M. "Unequal Educational Opportunity and State Politics: The New York City Schools and the New York State Legislature," New York: Teachers College, Columbia University, 1970 (mimeographed).

CRONBACH, LEE J. "Heredity, Environment, and Educational Policy," *Harvard Educational Review*, Vol. 39, No. 2 (Spring, 1969), pp. 273–356.

DAVIS, KINGSLEY, and WILBERT E. MOORE. "Some Principles of Stratification," *The American Sociological Review*, Vol. 10, No. 2 (1945), pp. 242–249.

DENTLER, ROBERT A. "Equality of Educational Opportunity: A Special Review," *The Urban Review* (December, 1966), pp. 14–31.

DEUTSCH, M. "Minority Group and Class Status as Related to Social and Personality Factors in Scholastic Achievement," *Monograph of the Society for Applied Anthropology*, No. 2 (1960), pp. 1–32.

DEUTSCH, M., and B. BROWN. "Social Influences in Negro–White Intelligence Differences," *Journal of Social Issues*, Vol. 20 (1964), pp. 24–35.

DOCHTERMAN, CLIFFORD, *et al. Understanding Education's Financial Dilemma*. Denver, Col.: Education Commission of the States, April, 1972.

FISS, OWEN M. "Racial Imbalance in the Public Schools: The Constitutional Concepts," *Harvard Law Review*, Vol. 78 (January, 1965), pp. 564–617.

————. "The Charlotte-Mecklenburg Case—Its Significance for Northern School Desegregation," *The University of Chicago Law Review*, Vol. 38 (Summer, 1971), pp. 697–709.

GANS, HERBERT J. "The New Egalitarianism," *Saturday Review* (May 6, 1972), pp. 43–46.

GARRETT, H. E. "The Equalitarian Dogma," *Mankind Quarterly*, Vol. 1 (1961), pp. 253–257.

GREENBAUM, WILLIAM N. *"Serrano v. Priest:* Implications for Educational Equality," *Harvard Educational Review* (November, 1971). Also in *Current* (March, 1972), pp. 3–6.

GREENE, LEROY. "School Financing (California)," *Compact*, Vol. 5 (December, 1971), pp. 35–37.

GUTHRIE, JAMES W., *et al.* "Dollars for Schools: The Reinforcement of Inequality," *Educational Administration Quarterly*, Vol. 6 (Autumn, 1970), pp. 32–45.

HAMILTON, CHARLES V. "Politics of Educational Policy." Lecture delivered at the University of Kentucky, Lexington, Kentucky, October 13, 1969 (mimeographed).

HARRINGTON, MICHAEL. "The Politics of Poverty," *Dissent,* Vol. 12 (Autumn, 1965), pp. 412–430.
Harvard Educational Review, Vol. 38, No. 1 (Winter, 1968). Special issue on equal educational opportunity.
HAVIGHURST, ROBERT J. "Who Are the Socially Disadvantaged?," *Journal of Negro Education,* Vol. 38 (1964), pp. 210–217.
HESS, ROBERT D., *et al.* "Some New Dimensions in Providing Equal Educational Opportunity," *The Journal of Negro Education* (March, 1968), pp. 220–230.
HOWE, HAROLD, II. "Anatomy of a Revolution," *Saturday Review* (November 20, 1971), pp. 84–88, 95.
JERREMS, RAYMOND. "Racism: Vector of Ghetto Education," *Integrated Education* (July–August, 1970), pp. 40–47.
JOHNS, ROE L., and KERN ALEXANDER. *Alternative Programs for Financing Education.* Gainsville, Florida: National Educational Finance Project, 1971.
————. *Future Directions for School Financing.* Gainsville, Florida: National Educational Finance Project, 1971.
KAPLAN, ERIC F. "Constitutional Law: Financing Public Education Under the Equal Protection Clause," *University of Florida Law Review,* Vol. XXIII (1971), pp. 590–597.
KAPLAN, JOHN. "Part II: The General Northern Problem," *Northwestern Law Review* (May–June, 1963), pp. 157–167.
KATZ, I. "Review of Evidence Relating to Effects of Desegregation on the Intellectual Performance of Negroes," *American Psychologist,* Vol. 19 (1964), pp. 381–399.
KENT, JAMES K. "The Coleman Report: Opening Pandora's Box," *Phi Delta Kappan* (January, 1968), pp. 242–245.
KIRP, DAVID L. "Community Control, Public Policy, and the Limits of Law," *Michigan Law Review,* Vol. 68 (June, 1970), pp. 1355–1388.
————. "The Poor, the Schools and Equal Protection," *Harvard Educational Review,* Vol. 38, No. 4 (Fall, 1968), pp. 635–668.
————. "The Role of Law in Educational Policy," *Social Policy* (September–October, 1971), pp. 42–47.
KURLAND, PHILIP B. "The Supreme Court, 1963 Term Forward: Equal in Origin and Equal in Title to the Legislative and Executive Branches of the Government," *Harvard Law Review,* Vol. 77 (November, 1964), pp. 143–176.
LEFLAR, ROBERT A., and WYLIE H. DAVIS. "Public School Segregation," *Harvard Law Review,* Vol. 67 (1954), p. 392.
LEVIN, HENRY M. "What Difference Do Schools Make?," *Saturday Review* (January 20, 1968), pp. 57–58, 66–67.
————. "Why Ghetto Schools Fail," *Saturday Review* (March 21, 1970), pp. 68–69, 81–85.
LEVINE, DANIEL U. "Unequal Opportunities in the Large Inner-City High School," *National Association of Secondary School Principals Bulletin,* Vol. 52 (November, 1968), pp. 46–55.

LIEBERMAN, MYRON. "Equality of Educational Opportunity," in *Language and Concepts in Education*. B. O. Smith and Robert Ennis (Editors). Chicago: Rand, McNally, Inc., 1961, pp. 127–143.

MAY, HENRY STRATFORD, JR. "Busing, *Swann* v. *Charlotte-Mecklenburg*, and the Future of Desegregation in the Fifth Circuit," *Texas Law Review*, Vol. 49 (May, 1971), pp. 884–911.

MEHRIGE, ROBERT R. "The Richmond School Decision," *Integrated Education* (March–April, 1972), pp. 51–53.

MONTAGUE, ASHLEY. "Just What is 'Equal Opportunity'?," *VISTA* (November, 1970), pp. 23–25, 56.

MORTIMORE, G. W. "An Ideal of Equality," *Mind* (April, 1968), pp. 222–242.

MYLES, NAOMI. "North Carolina Over the Hump," *The Nation* (February 14, 1972), pp. 206–209.

"Nixon and Desegregation: It Is Time to Strip Away Hypocrisy and Prejudice," *U.S. News and World Report* (April 6, 1970), pp. 80–87.

PETTIGREW, THOMAS P. "Race and Equal Educational Opportunity," Paper presented at the Annual Meeting of the American Psychological Association, Washington, D.C., September 3, 1967 (mimeographed).

"Richmond Decision," *National Review* (February 4, 1972), pp. 82–83.

RILES, WILSON. "California and the *Serrano* Decision," *Planning and Changing—A Journal for School Administrators*, Vol. 2 (January, 1972), pp. 169–173.

ROSEN, B. C. "Race, Ethnicity, and the Achievement Syndrome," *American Sociological Review*, Vol. 24 (1959), pp. 47–60.

SCHRAG, PETER. "End of the Impossible Dream," *Saturday Review* (September 19, 1970), pp. 68–70, 92.

SCHUCK, PETER H. "Discrimination as Public Policy," *Saturday Review* (June 24, 1972), pp. 16–48.

SHANKS, HERSHEL. "Equal Education and the Law," *The American Scholar* (Spring, 1970), pp. 255–269.

SHANNON, THOMAS A. "Has the Fourteenth Done It Again?," *Phi Delta Kappan*, Vol. 53 (April, 1972), pp. 466–471.

———. "*Rodriguez:* A Dream Shattered or a Call for Finance Reform?," *Phi Delta Kappan* (May, 1973), pp. 587, 588, 640.

TENENBAUM, SAMUEL, "The Teacher, the Middle Class, the Lower Class," *Phi Delta Kappan* (November, 1963), pp. 82–86.

"Turn Around on Integration," *Time*, Vol. 95, No. 10 (March 9, 1970), pp. 9–16.

TURNER, RALPH H. "Modes of Social Ascent through Education," *American Sociological Review*, Vol. 25 (1960), pp. 121–139.

WILLIAMS, BERNARD. "The Idea of Equality," in *Philosophy, Politics and Society*, Peter Laslett and W. G. Runciman (Editors). Oxford: Basil and Blockwell, 1964, Chapter 6.

WISE, ARTHUR E. "The California Doctrine," *Saturday Review* (November 24, 1971), pp. 78–79.

————. "Is Denial of Equal Educational Opportunity Constitutional?," *Administrator's Notebook*, Vol. 13 (February, 1965), pp. 1–4.

————. "The Constitutional Challenge to Inequities in School Finance," *Phi Delta Kappan* (November, 1969), pp. 145–148.

WISE, ARTHUR, and HAROLD HOWE, II. "Financing Schools: Property Tax Is Obsolete," *Saturday Review* (November, 1971), pp. 78–81.

WRIGHT, J. SKELLY. "Public School Desegregation: Legal Remedies for *De Facto* Segregation," *Western Reserve Law Review*, Vol. 16 (May, 1965), pp. 478–501.

YUDOF, MARK G., JOHN E. COONS, and SARAH C. CAREY. *"Serrano* and Segregation," *Integrated Education*, Vol. 50 (March–April, 1972), pp. 71–74.

COURT CASES AND RELATED MATERIALS

Brown v. *Board of Education of Topeka, Kansas.* United States Supreme Court. 347 U.S. 483 (1954).

CHAMBERS, JULIUS L., *et al.* Brief of Counsel in *Swann* v. *Charlotte Mecklenburg Board of Education.* 28 L. ed. 2d 554 (1971).

Hargrave v. *Kirk,* United States District Court for the Middle District of Florida, 313 Federal Supplement 944 (M.D. Fla., 1970).

Marshall, Thurgood, *et al.* Briefs of Counsel in *Brown* v. *Board of Education of Topeka, Kansas.* 99 L. ed. 1083 (1954).

McInnis v. *Shapiro,* United States District Court for the Northern District of Illinois, *Federal Supplement,* Vol. 293 (1968), pp. 327–337.

"Schools and Colleges," *The United States Law Week,* Vol. 40 (January 4, 1972), pp. 2398–2399. (*Rodriguez* v. *San Antonio Independent School District,* USDC West Texas, December 23, 1971).

SELF, WILLIAM C., *et al.* Testimony in *Swann* v. *Charlotte Mecklenburg Board of Education.* United States Supreme Court. 91 S. Ct. 1267 (1971). Appendix, Vol. 1.

Serrano v. *Priest,* California Supreme Court. *California Reporter,* Vol. 96, pp. 601–626.

Swann v. *Charlotte-Mecklenburg Board of Education.* United States Supreme Court. 91 S. Ct. 1267 (1971).

United States v. *School District 151 of Cook County of Illinois,* U.S. District Court for the Northern District of Illinois. *Federal Supplement,* Vol. 286 (1968), p. 786.

REPORTS

BAILEY, STEPHEN K. *et al. Achieving Equality of Educational Opportunity.* A report for the Ohio Foundations, May, 1966.

BURKHEAD, JESSE, and THOMAS O. FOX. *Input and Output in Large-City High Schools.* Syracuse, N.Y.: Syracuse University Press, 1967.

Chamber of Commerce of the United States. *The Concept of Poverty.* A report prepared by the Task Force on Economic Growth and

Opportunity. Washington, D.C.: Chamber of Commerce of the United States, 1965.

DALY, C. A. (Editor). *The Quality of Inequality.* Chicago: University of Chicago Policy Center, 1968.

Racial Isolation in the Public Schools. A Report of the United States Commission on Civil Rights. Washington, D.C.: U.S. Government Printing Office, 1967.

WEINBERG, MEYER. *Research on School Desegregation: Review and Prospect.* Chicago: Integrated Education Associates, 1965.

WILSON, ALAN B. *Educational Consequences of Segregation in a California Community.* Berkeley: University of California, Survey Research Center, 1966.

Youth in the Ghetto: *A Study of the Consequences of Powerlessness and a Blueprint for Change.* New York: Harlem Youth Opportunities Unlimited, 1964.